Rethinking the Origins of the Eucharist

SCM STUDIES IN WORSHIP
AND LITURGY

Rethinking the Origins of the Eucharist

Martin D. Stringer

scm press

© Martin Stringer 2011

Published in 2011 by SCM Press
Editorial office
13–17 Long Lane,
London, EC1A 9PN, UK

SCM Press is an imprint of Hymns Ancient and Modern Ltd
(a registered charity)
13A Hellesdon Park Road
Norwich NR6 5DR, UK

www.scm-canterburypress.co.uk

British Library Cataloguing in Publication data

A catalogue record for this book is available
from the British Library

978-0-334-04214-3

Originated by The Manila Typesetting Company
Printed and bound by Lightning Source UK

Contents

Acknowledgements

When I sat down to write my book on the *Sociological History of Christian Worship* (Stringer 2005), I fully expected the first chapter, on the first
300 years of Christian worship, to be the easiest to write. Many other
scholars had explored this field, the texts were clear and well known,
there was I thought a general consensus on what the text meant and
therefore the writing should have been easy. I ended up, however, spend-
ing months, if not years, on the first 150 years and probably had to give
less time to the following 1850 years than I would have liked. The more
I looked at the texts, at what other scholars had written and at the possible interpretations of the material, the more convinced I became that
our understanding of this period is severely limited and that much more
work still needed to be done. I knew at that time that if I was ever to do
it justice I needed to produce a whole book on this material not just 20
pages. Whether I do manage to achieve that within this text is, however,
for others to decide.

Having recognized that much more work needed to be done I was fortu-
nate enough to have the opportunity to present elements of the main argument of this book as papers for the Oxford Liturgy Group, the Society for
Liturgical Study and the Instituut Voor Liturgische en Rituele at Utrecht
University. The discussions and arguments that followed these presentations proved very formative for the final text. I am also very grateful to
many colleagues with whom I shared elements of the work and whose
questions and critiques proved invaluable. In particular, I would like to
thank Juliette Day, Charlotte Hempel, David Parker, David Taylor, Phillip
Tovey and Markus Vinzent. I also want to thank Natalie Watson and all
her colleagues at SCM Press who have been extremely helpful in the production of this text. Finally, I have to thank David whose gentle pressure
and prodding has ensured that the text did eventually get written despite
so many other calls on my time.

Introduction

'The Lord Jesus, on the night that he was betrayed, took bread and when he had given thanks, he broke it and said . . .' (1 Cor. 11.24). And so, for almost two thousand years the Church has followed the instruction of Jesus at his Last Supper and has taken bread, blessed it and broken it saying . . . That, at least, is what many of those sitting in our churches Sunday by Sunday, and often day by day, of whatever theological position, still believe to be the case. Whether Catholic or Evangelical, Orthodox or Pentecostal, what Christians do when they come together to share bread and wine (and whatever theological position they take on the significance of that bread and wine) the overwhelming understanding is that this is something that Jesus did, this is something that Jesus commanded his disciples to continue doing, this is something that the followers of Jesus began to do immediately following the resurrection and the coming of the Spirit at Pentecost, and this is something that Christians have continued to do for two thousand years. We only need to look at the hymn to eucharistic practice as presented by Gregory Dix in his classic book, *Shape of the Liturgy*, to get a feel for the scope and spread of this practice throughout the Church (1945, p. 744), and yet many churchgoers sitting in the pews Sunday by Sunday still believe it all started in that upper room on the night before Jesus was betrayed.

Perhaps it was. The reality is that we do not know, and for just over a hundred years scholars from different churches, different disciplines and different theological persuasions have been arguing among themselves about a wide range of different possibilities. The fact that they have never reached a consensus on what they believed did happen, and probably never will, does not mean that scholars should ignore the question. If historians are going to write a history of Christian worship, then one of the first questions that will inevitably confront them is what happened at that Last Supper, and how does what may, or may not, have occurred at that moment relate to the central act of Christian worship for much of the following two thousand years?

I

There is no question that historical scholarship informed the liturgical revisions that occurred in practically all the churches in the latter half of the twentieth century. It is also clear, however, that the historical period that was most influential at that time was focused on the third and fourth centuries. This period preceded many of the debates that have caused subsequent divisions within the Church, but it was also late enough to provide a significant body of evidence about what actually happened, whether that is the Eucharistic Prayer of Hippolytus (ignoring the debates about its authorship and whether it was in fact ever used) (Bradshaw et al. 2002) or the baptismal practices of fourth-century Jerusalem (Yarnold 1994). The earlier period, the first 150 years of Christian development, was conveniently overlooked, although the informality of Justin Martyr is often quoted as a model to be followed.

In current thinking the role of historical precedent in contemporary liturgical practice and innovation has declined. Many commentators believe that contemporary worship ought to reflect contemporary issues, whether that is in terms of language, culture or technology (Burns et al. 2008; Ward 2005). Alternatively there are large sections of the Church that see a direct link between the words of scripture and contemporary practice without the need for any kind of historical mediation (Peterson 1992). Meanwhile, in the scholarly community, there is a strong sense that because there is so little evidence, and so little can be said with any kind of certainty about what might or might not have happened, then perhaps nothing should be said at all (Bradshaw 2004). I have considerable sympathy for all three of these positions and my own aim in researching this area was not to influence contemporary liturgical practice. I strongly believe that the exploration of the history of Christian worship is a worthwhile activity in its own right without the need to find an alternative justification from within the Church.

I come to this research because, like others who have studied this history before, I became curious about the questions that I have already mentioned. Why was it that the sharing of bread and wine, with all the imagery and theological reflection that surrounded it, became so central to Christian practice? How did it originate? What were the precedents, and how can the limited, and quite disparate, range of evidence that is available be interpreted?

It could be argued that after a hundred or more years of study, with very few new sources of evidence, there is nothing more to say. That if liturgists have not found the solutions to these problems by now, then, short of finding a new text or providing a radical reinterpretation of a known text that will convince other scholars, there is nothing more to say and scholars should simply accept that they do not know, and probably will never know, what actually happened. This may be true. There is very limited data: just a few texts – none of which are really about the subject in hand – which are scattered in time and space. This is unlikely to change. But this, in itself, throws down a challenge. Lack of data, and the disparate nature of the evidence, does not stop historians of the classical world from speculating about possible practices and understandings. As I will show in Chapter 4 these historians do not have all that much more data than the historian of Christian worship, and yet they tend to be much more confident in their use of that data and, what is more, liturgical scholars tend to assume that what they are presenting is authoritative (Smith 2003; Alikin 2009).

Historians of the classical world, like all historians, are constantly looking again at the evidence before them. They are asking new questions, bringing it together with other evidence in new juxtapositions, drawing on new theoretical insights in order to see it from a new angle, and so on. There is no reason why the historian of Christian worship should not be doing the same. My aim in this text, therefore, is to ask different questions, from a different perspective, and to see what kind of understandings and insights might emerge from that process. It is for my colleagues to assess these questions, and the answers that I have explored, and to see which may be of lasting value, which need rethinking and which remain mere curiosities. Between us, over time, it is hoped that the discipline as a whole will move forward.

In this first chapter, therefore, I wish to begin by looking at the kinds of questions scholars in the past have asked of these first few decades of the Christian community and the role of rituals involving meals and the sharing of bread and wine within this period. I will end the chapter by outlining a few of the principles by which I am working within the rest of the text.

Two types of Eucharist

Up to the end of the nineteenth century the prevailing view of the vast majority of liturgical scholars was, either implicitly or explicitly, that Jesus used a form of the worship at the Last Supper that would have been familiar to the scholars themselves. They argued that Jesus passed this liturgy on to his disciples who, in their turn, passed it on to subsequent generations, who either embellished it or corrupted it depending on the particular churchmanship of the scholar concerned. It was rarely questioned whether the format of the Last Supper was anything other than a formal liturgical event, albeit with a meal included, or that Jesus would have needed to provide fixed words for the blessing of the bread and wine and perhaps for other elements of the rite. The merest impression of that original rite is seen in the accounts that are offered in the Gospels and in Paul's first letter to the Corinthians, and some biblical scholars would argue among themselves as to which of these was the most likely to be the original wording. Other elements of the rite could also be seen in other texts from the New Testament, although by the time the writings of the 'church fathers' are written then things were probably too corrupted to be entirely retrievable. What remained, however, was the idea of a direct and single line of transmission from Jesus to his disciples and on to the earliest Christian communities.

The earliest critical questions concerning the origins of the Eucharist, therefore, came from those scholars who began to explore, and to a certain extent to rethink, what has become known as the 'historical Jesus' (Hagner 2001). In 1835–36 Strauss produced a book in which he set out to trace exactly what could be discovered about the real Jesus of history from the evidence that was available. This led him to ask critical questions about the nature of the Gospel texts, which are the primary source for the life of Jesus, and to seek to question whether the Jesus presented by these texts was plausible in any historic sense. Much of this work consists of questioning the historicity of the miracles and other elements of the traditional gospel narrative. Within this wider critical analysis, however, the tradition of the Last Supper was also investigated and Strauss comes to the conclusion that Jesus was expecting that 'within a year's time the pre-messianic dispensation will have come to an end and the messianic age will have come', although he did suggest that this might have been a pious hope on the part of the writers of the Gospels (Schweitzer 2000, p. 88).

The historical Jesus controversy was one that raged in academic circles throughout the second half of the nineteenth century and much of it revolved around questions of miracles and the message that scholars believed Jesus was preaching (Schweitzer 2000). The question of the Last Supper, and its role within the wider narrative of Jesus' life, was touched upon but never explored in depth by any of these authors. It was when scholars began to apply similar critical historical techniques to the early Church, especially as that was portrayed in the book of Acts and the writings of Paul, that the role of a cultic meal became more relevant.

Two authors in particular came to very similar conclusions from this kind of study. Spitta, writing in 1893, distinguishes between the *agape*, or love feast, derived from the meal accounts in Acts, and the Pauline version of the Eucharist with its focus on the death of Jesus and the Last Supper (Higgins 1952, p. 57). Weiss develops a similar view in his *History of Primitive Christianity* (1959), first published shortly after his death in 1914. Weiss argues that the 'breaking of bread' in Acts reflects a specifically Christian way of designating a meal and is the first step in the development of the Eucharist. A joyful eschatological atmosphere accompanied the breaking and sharing of bread linking the celebration of the community with the practice of Jesus and his disciples. Paul's linking of this joyful celebration with the death of Jesus and the tradition of the Last Supper is a later development, encouraged, according to Weiss, by reflection on the sharing of wine at the meal. As he comments, 'the moment when someone, as the red wine was being poured from the skin into the cup, first thought of the out-poured blood of Christ, was one of the greatest importance in every respect' (Weiss 1959, p. 61).

Much of this early scholarship was brought together in one of the most detailed and most often quoted texts that focused specifically on the origin of the Eucharist, Lietzmann's *Mass and Lord's Supper* (1979), first published in 1926. Lietzmann argues backwards from the principal families of the liturgical tradition to what he identifies as two distinct forms of the Eucharist in the later second century, the Hippolytan-Roman, or that found in the *Apostolic Tradition*, and the Egyptian, which is essentially that of Serapion, Bishop of Thmuis in Egypt (1979, p. 142). Lietzmann aims to demonstrate that all the material found in the Eucharistic Prayer attributed to Hippolytus can be traced back to the writings of Paul, including its sacrificial elements. The understanding of sacrifice in the anaphora of Serapion, however, is not seen in relation to the death of Jesus but rather in terms of 'the laying of the elements on the Lord's table and in their consecration by prayer' (1979, p. 159).

This is followed by a discussion of the *agape*, especially as that is seen in the *Apostolic Tradition*, and by a detailed discussion of the Last Supper. Lietzmann is keen to demonstrate that the Last Supper could not have been a Passover meal, as it does not contain any of the elements that would be expected in such a meal. Rather he sees the Last Supper as a *haburah* meal or 'a Jewish festal meal in a narrow circle of friends' (1979, p. 185), which takes the form of 'the blessing of bread at the beginning, the blessing of wine at the conclusion, [and] the actual meal between the two' (1979, p. 185). The text of the *Didache* is then investigated to show that this contains a 'type of the Lord's Supper with

5

no reference to the tradition extant in Mark and Paul' (1979, p. 193), but with language and content that is similar to that of Serapion. 'This confirms us in assuming', Lietzmann suggests, 'a connection between the ancient Egyptian liturgy and that of Didache' (1979, p. 194).

It is only having dealt with all this material that Lietzmann can begin to present his own ideas about the primitive form of the Lord's Supper. Here he draws on material from the apocryphal *Acts of John, Thomas* and *Peter* to illustrate a form of the Lord's Supper that included bread and water instead of bread and wine and so suggests that this was the earliest form of the supper, relating to the breaking of bread in the Acts of the Apostles. This was also a *haburah* meal, following the practice of Jesus and his disciples, but with no reference to the death of Jesus, and with the idea of sacrifice contained in the offering of the bread and the saying of a blessing or thanksgiving over it. Lietzmann refers to this as the 'Jerusalem type' (1979, p. 205). It is Paul, Lietzmann suggests, who creates a 'second type' (1979, p. 205) by combining the Jerusalem type with ideas derived from the Hellenistic meals held as memorials for the dead to create a supper that focuses on the death of Jesus and links the ideas of sacrifice specifically with the words over the bread and wine. These two types are then developed through the *Didache* (and on into the Egyptian tradition) and through Hippolytus.

Through the whole of his analysis Lietzmann pays particular attention to the forms of words used in worship, with most of the first two-thirds of his text being a detailed analysis of elements of the Eucharistic Prayer. It is by taking these ideas back, through the application of Baumstark's comparative method (1958), that he is justified in arguing behind the extant manuscripts to the origins of the texts that they contain, and then behind the texts to the reconstruction of ideas that predate the written material. It is where this backward movement of archaeological analysis meets the forward development of Spitta and Weiss that the construction of the theory of origins is developed. It is also in the speculative and controversial nature of much of this backwards analysis that the work of Lietzmann ultimately fails, and has been critiqued by many scholars over the years (Richardson 1979). Unfortunately by criticizing those elements that cannot stand up to scrutiny, the whole theory has been dismissed, along with the idea of the two types of the Eucharist that forms the core of its central thesis.

Other authors in the early part of the twentieth century, however, did follow up on Lietzmann's work and developed it in different ways. Cullmann, for example, provides one of the most convincing developments in a short essay originally published in 1936 (1958). This focused particularly on the meal tradition that Lietzmann associates with Jerusalem and, like Weiss before him, Cullmann linked this to the traditions surrounding the resurrection appearances, many of which are associated with meals and have a joyful eschatological feel (1958, pp. 8–12). Cullmann argues that it is the meal that keeps the resurrection memories alive within the community and he links this to thoughts about the second coming. He identifies the '*maranatha*' used both by Paul and by the compiler of the *Didache* as a link to this eschatological tradition (1958, pp. 13–16). Even Cullmann's analysis, however, could not save the two Eucharists theory and this was eventually swamped by another more substantial line of enquiry, that which related the earliest Eucharists to contemporary Jewish models.

Discovering Jewish roots

Lietzmann linked the 'Jerusalem type' of the Eucharist and the Last Supper with the *haburah* meal from Jewish tradition. He also looked for Jewish roots to many of the texts that became part of both types of Eucharist and their subsequent developments. In particular he identifies the texts of the *Didache* and the Hippolytan *agape* with Jewish meal blessings (1979, pp. 161–71), and sees the development of the preface in the Eucharistic Prayer of the *Apostolic Constitutions*, concluding with the Sanctus, as deriving from the morning service of the synagogue (1979, pp. 100–11). In doing this Lietzmann is part of a much wider tradition within the literature that has looked for Jewish origins to the Eucharist and its associated texts.

Duchesne, for example, in his classic work on the origin and evolution of Christian worship, simply states 'the Christian Liturgy to a great extent took its rise from the Jewish Liturgy, and was, in fact, merely its continuation' (1904, p. 46). He goes on to clarify that this is only true for synagogue worship, temple worship having no influence on Christian worship at all, and that the Eucharist is an exception to this general statement as this derives directly from the Last Supper which constitutes 'the principle elements of the Mass in its entirely Christian and original aspect' (1904, p. 49). Others, however, have also sought Jewish antecedents for the Eucharist. The most detailed of the early studies in this area is Oesterley's work, *The Jewish Background of the Christian Liturgy* (1925).

Oesterley begins his study by asking about the reliability of the Jewish documents. He claims to be drawing primarily on the *Mishnah* and other related texts, and while he acknowledges that these were compiled in the early years of the third century he notes that 'what it records is prior to this date' and could perhaps go back as far as 250 BCE (1925, p. 32). He also notes the importance of the Old Testament, intertestamental literature and the development of the oral tradition. From this Oesterley develops what he calls the pre-Christian elements of the Jewish liturgy and then looks at the general view of early Christian worship and notes in particular the paucity of data that is available. However, he does identify a number of examples to show that Jewish liturgical influence is a reality (1925, p. 154). When looking specifically at the Eucharist, Oesterley notes that the institution of the rite took place at the end of a meal. The real question, therefore, for Oesterley is to determine what kind of meal this was.

Oesterley focuses on the Last Supper, which he argues was a festal meal on the eve of Passover (transferred from Friday to Thursday because of the date of the feast in that particular year) that ended with a *kiddush* or sanctification ceremony. 'This consisted', according to Oesterley 'of the commemoration and institution of the Sabbath, the blessing over the cup and its partaking by all; then the memorial of redemption from the Egyptian bondage, followed by the blessing over the bread and its distribution' (1925, p. 171). Oesterley links the supposed text of the Passover *kiddush* to the language of the *Didache* and to other early Christian texts. Finally, Oesterley sees the *agape* as a continuation, within a Christian context, of the Jewish Sabbath meal with the term *agape* being 'a Greek equivalent to the neo-Hebrew *Chaburah*' or fellowship (1925, p. 204).

Undoubtedly the most famous author in this tradition is Gregory Dix who, in the *Shape of the Liturgy*, follows Oesterley in arguing that the Last Supper was probably a *haburah* supper, one that had a special religious status among a group of pious friends (1945). It is not the link with the *haburah* meal, however, that particularly distinguishes Dix's approach. More significant is his emphasis on the sequence or 'shape' of the meal rather than the content of any of the words used. It is the shape of the liturgy, Dix argues, that could be 'genuinely apostolic tradition' while the words demonstrate considerable differences (1945, p. 5). In doing this Dix prefigures some of the more sociological approaches that became more common towards the end of the twentieth century. He emphasizes that the Eucharist was something that was done, that it is a communal act within the assembly, and he stresses the possible structure and spatial context of that assembly (1945, pp. 12–35).

Dix sees the liturgy as having two elements, a *synaxis* or service of readings, preaching and prayer and the Eucharist proper. These two elements, he stresses, have different origins. For Dix the *synaxis* is 'simply a continuation of the Jewish synagogue service of our Lord's time' (1945, p. 36). The origin of the Eucharist is a little more complex. The problem Dix outlines is that the accounts of the Last Supper present a seven-action scheme (the taking, blessing, breaking and distributing of bread followed by the taking, blessing and distributing of wine), while 'with absolute unanimity the liturgical tradition reproduces these seven actions as four' (taking bread and wine, blessing bread and wine, breaking bread, and sharing bread and wine) (1945, p. 48). One point that Dix draws from this is that 'liturgical practice was not understood by the primitive church to be in any way subject to the control of N. T. documents' and so 'this liturgical tradition must have originated in independence of the literary tradition in all its forms' (1945, p. 49).

Dix follows Oesterley in designating the Last Supper as a meal held by a *haburah*, or Jewish religious society, on the eve of the Passover itself (1945, p. 50) and then uses material from the *Mishnah* to fill in the details. In stressing the importance of the *haburah* meal, Dix is able to argue against Lietzmann that if the emphasis had been entirely on the bread then the rite that followed would have been a private, individual activity. However, by emphasizing the wine, an essential part of a *haburah* supper, Jesus was able to accentuate the communal nature of the new rite (1945, p. 59). The rite itself must, in Dix's view, go back to Jesus' command at the Last Supper because pious Jews would not normally associate a *haburah* supper with death or with the Last Supper itself, and, most importantly, how otherwise would they have thought of the idea of drinking human blood as a sign of a new covenant (1945, p. 69)? Dix then looks at a range of texts and traditions associated with the *agape*, which he also sees as originating in the *haburah* meal, but being those elements that remained once the Eucharist itself had been removed (1945, p. 95). He is, however, very tentative in his suggestions for when the meal and the Eucharist are separated except to say that it must have been in apostolic times and must have been undertaken by those who had a real and deep knowledge of Jewish customs (1945, pp. 101–2). From here Dix goes on to develop his understanding of the history of the shape of the liturgy through the subsequent centuries.

In a paper published in 1965, Dugmore divided previous studies on the origins of the Eucharist between those that treated the Last Supper as a Passover meal and those that did not (Dugmore 1965). Practically all the texts that have been looked at so far fall into the second category and this became something of a consensus among serious scholars in the field. In 1935, however, Jeremias published his text on *The Eucharistic*

9

Words of Jesus and made a plea for the Passover theory of eucharistic origins (1955). Jeremias dives straight into his main thesis in Chapter 1 of his book by asking, 'was the Last Supper a Passover Meal?' (1955, p. 1). The first 60 pages then consist of very careful textual analysis of the Pauline and Synoptic accounts of the Last Supper, looking at all the evidence in favour of the Passover theory and all the main objections. It is the little things that suggest that the Last Supper must be a Passover: the time of the meal (only a Passover was held at night), the reclining at table, breaking the bread during the meal (rather than at its start), the use of red wine, the hymns at the end of the meal, and the fact that Jesus did not go back out to Bethany but rather stayed within the confines of a larger Jerusalem. This is detailed analysis and it is the cumulative effect of each new item of evidence that builds into a plausible and authoritative argument.

When looking at the account of the Last Supper within the framework of the Passion story, however, some of Jeremias's other assumptions begin to emerge. In order to address the lack of eucharistic words in John's Gospel, Jeremias resorts to two distinct tactics. First he emphasizes the commonality in structure between Mark and John, focusing once again on the smaller details, which leads Jeremias to reconstruct a history of the wider Passion narrative itself. Then, when he comes to ask about the words of institution, he argues that the silence of John's Gospel is due to an already existing *disciplina arcani* (1955, pp. 72–3), a practice that he also uses to explain the form of the eucharistic narrative in the *Didache* and other troubling texts. Jeremias traces the eucharistic words at the heart of the Last Supper to a cultic formula that he claims existed in a pre-Pauline form at Antioch where Paul had settled in the early 40s (1955, p. 131) and, previous to that, in a pre-Markan Aramaic form that originated in Palestine. He states 'that in the remaining space of at most a decade after the death of Jesus the Eucharistic rite should have been freely created, and the account of the Lord's Supper invented as an aetiological legend, is as much incapable of proof as it is improbable' (1955, p. 132). The origin of the rite, therefore, is the Passover meal that Jesus shared with his disciples on the night before he was betrayed.

Jeremias takes it entirely for granted that the earliest Christian community would have celebrated some kind of Eucharist from the earliest days after the resurrection on a weekly, or even daily, basis and that in doing so they would have used some kind of institution narrative. This assumption is never in doubt for Jeremias and the whole purpose of the book is to show how the accounts of the Last Supper that exist in Paul and the Gospels preserve this ancient tradition. Jeremias ends, therefore, with a chapter speculating on the possible meaning of the words of interpretation as used by Jesus at the Last Supper, a meaning that shows Jesus equating himself with the sacrificial lamb of the Passover.

Through very careful textual analysis Jeremias was able to restate the official church position and counter many of the alternative views. His work is based on highly technical textual and linguistic analysis and this, in itself, has given the book a level of authority that is difficult to refute by anybody who does not share Jeremias' own technical skills. Many Church-based authors, therefore, who wish to find support for the view that the Eucharist originated in the Last Supper, and was passed on to the earliest Christian community almost complete in its conception, have turned to Jeremias to support their position and have quoted his work with little or no critical engagement (Martin 1974, pp. 110–19). A text such as La Verdiere's *The Eucharist in the New Testament and the Church* (1996) has no difficulty in assuming a weekly rite very similar to contemporary Catholic practice from the days following the resurrection, and he draws on many different and disparate New Testament passages with the unquestioning assumption that the author's shared his own Catholic theology. The root and support for this position is founded primarily through references to Jeremias.

The sociological turn

During the 1970s and 1980s a new approach to biblical scholarship developed that became known as 'social-scientific criticism' (Elliott 1995). In this work scholars began to use ideas and theories from the sociological literature to explore issues raised within the biblical texts. Two of the most prominent figures within this tradition were Gerd Theissen and Wayne Meeks, both of whom undertook detailed sociological analysis of Paul's first letter to the Corinthians (Theissen 1982; Meeks 1983). In their work both scholars explored the social context of the meal described in chapter 11 of the letter and both developed theories about the nature and form of the community and the meal itself. Neither, however, went so far as to speculate as to the origins of the meal within the early Christian communities. I will come back to look at their work in more detail in Chapter 1. Their approach, however, and the tradition of social-scientific criticism that developed out of it, did inspire a number of authors who have asked more direct questions about the origin of the Eucharist, what Rouwhorst describes as the new paradigm in origins studies (Rouwhorst 2007). In this section I want to focus on just three of those who have been particularly influential, Andrew McGowan (1999a), Dennis Smith (2003) and Paul Bradshaw (2004).

In some ways McGowan's book *Ascetic Eucharists* (1999a) does not belong in this survey, as he is not strictly speaking aiming to provide a theory of origins. In fact he makes clear on a number of occasions that he is not going to discuss the question of the origins of the Eucharist at all. However, he is exploring what he calls 'eucharistic meals' in the first few centuries of the Christian community and he establishes two basic principles that are central to all the texts that follow him. First, McGowan begins with an exploration of food and society. He stresses that any investigation of meals within the Christian communities of the first three or four centuries have to be set within the food culture of the period, most specifically that of the Graeco-Roman world. Second, he stresses that it is important to look at all the texts as they stand rather than try to link them all together, and takes the possibility of diversity within Christian practice as a starting point. His interest is primarily in those eucharistic meals that appear in the literature to involve bread and water rather than bread and wine. Others, including Lietzmann, have discussed these texts in passing but have either seen them as anomalous or as heretical and therefore have not focused on them as a specific eucharistic tradition. For McGowan the bread and water tradition is as important and as interesting as the bread and wine tradition, and this forms the focus of his work.

McGowan starts with a theoretical chapter focusing on the cultures of food, drawing primarily on the work of Mary Douglas (1966, 1970, 1972), and the idea of diversity. He then moves on to look more closely at the food culture of the Graeco-Roman world. He focuses specifically on the eating of meat and the drinking of wine and associates this with what he calls the 'cuisine of sacrifice' (1999a, pp. 60–7). In identifying a code of food practices that are associated with sacrifice McGowan can then look at those who reject this code, both in relation to Jewish meals and to what he calls 'ascetic meals' (1999a, p. 67) among certain philosophical schools within the Graeco-Roman world. Asceticism, he stresses, is not just about the rejection of all food, it has to be constructed within the wider food culture and can only be understood in terms of what is rejected from that culture. In the Graeco-Roman world McGowan sees asceticism as primarily a rejection of the cuisine of sacrifice and therefore as a rejection of meat and wine. It is in this context that he moves on to look at Christian meals.

An important central chapter provides a survey of foodstuffs mentioned by Christian texts in the first three or four centuries and he identifies the sharing of bread, wine, oil, cheese, vegetables and other foodstuffs among specific communities and sometimes more generally within communal meals. Out of this he identifies a specifically bread and water tradition of eucharistic meals that is associated with a number of texts, primarily the Apocryphal *Acts* of the Apostles but also other related texts from the eastern empire and beyond. What McGowan identifies through a close analysis of these texts is a similar rejection of the cuisine of sacrifice that he had already identified among Cynics and other groups within the wider Graeco-Roman culture. What he argues, therefore, is that this ascetic tradition, developing in Palestine or Syria from a very early date within the Christian community, can be traced through a series of examples and probably forms the base for later monastic asceticism in the same part of the world.

It is only in the last two chapters that McGowan traces this tradition back into the New Testament texts, where he sees a number of instances in which the authors appear to be arguing against this tradition, but little evidence for the tradition itself, and then, in the final chapter, to ask about the sources of the bread and water tradition. It is possible, he argues, that there might have been Jewish precedents, but there is in fact very little evidence for this. There is nothing specifically within the Christian tradition that can form the basis for these practices and so he has to argue that it is the wider prevalence of the cuisine of sacrifice and the recognized rejection of this by a number of different groups that forms the discursive context for the development of this tradition. What is important, therefore, is not that the bread and water tradition should be seen as an 'origin' of the Eucharist, or even a second strand of eucharistic development as Lietzmann appears to suggest, but that it is a distinct tradition within the eucharistic meals of the early Christian community and probably one of a number of such traditions within a much more diverse range of practices than previous scholars were sometimes willing to accept.

Smith's book, *From Symposium to Eucharist* (2003), builds on many of the ideas in McGowan's text and is probably the most overtly sociological of the three works that I am looking at in this section. Along with Matthias Klinghardt, Smith initiated a seminar within the Society for Biblical Literature to explore Graeco-Roman meals and their associations with early Christian practices (Alikin 2009, p. 3). Smith's own work builds on that of Klinghardt who had published a similar theory in German in 1996 (Klinghardt 1996). In his own book Smith sets out to argue that 'although there were many minor differences in the meal customs as practiced in different regions and social groups, the evidence suggests that meals took similar forms and shared similar meanings and interpretations across a broad range of the ancient world' (2003, p. 2). This includes Jewish and early Christian meals as well as those of the wider Graeco-Roman world. Smith argues that earlier writers on the origins of the Eucharist, particularly Lietzmann and Jeremias, despite their differences, all 'construct a model for analysing the ancient data based on the form of the Eucharist in the later church' (2003, p. 4). Alternatively, Smith proposes that the Eucharist developed out of a range of early Christian meals that were themselves part of the common banqueting tradition of the ancient world.

Smith then goes on to explore this common banqueting tradition through an exploration of Graeco-Roman banquets, Jewish banquets and finally banquets in the writings of Paul and in the Gospel traditions. He is specifically working within a sociological tradition that, like McGowan, he associates with the work of Douglas. This leads Smith to identify idealized models which he claims are presupposed by the ancient literature and which, using Douglas' terminology, can be linked to the 'social codes' that they represent (Smith 2003, pp. 8–9; Douglas 1970). The two specific idealized models that he chooses to explore are the symposium and the messianic banquet. These come together within the meal tradition of the early Christian communities and, according to Smith, do not simply determine the structure of the meal but also, through the codes contained within them, determine much of early Christian theology.

Smith argues that the earliest references to Christian meals come from the writings of Paul and refer specifically to meal traditions at Antioch, Corinth and Rome. All of these must, Smith argues, predate Paul's own writing and yet it is the ideology of the meal, or to use Douglas's term their 'social code', that informs Paul's own theology. The emphasis on boundaries, for example, is seen in the discussion of the meal at Antioch in Paul's letter to the Galatians, community identity, ethics and social equality are developed in relation to the meal at Corinth, and ideas of hospitality and fellowship are developed with reference to the meal in Rome (2003, pp. 216–17). It is not only the wider social code of the Graeco-Roman banquet that informs the meals within the Pauline churches, however. Smith also claims that the shape of the meal, as outlined in 1 Corinthians, is also modelled on the wider social norms. The meal begins with 'a benediction over the food, represented by the bread' and ends with 'a benediction over the wine marking the transition from *deipnon* to symposium' (2003, p. 188). It is the symposium that is seen in chapter 14 of Paul's letter.

The following chapter, on the 'Banquet in the Gospels', takes Smith back into more conventional biblical criticism as he looks at the narrative traditions and their underlying codes in relation to the wider narrative traditions of banquets and table fellowship within the Graeco-Roman world. He shows that these wider cultural narratives have clearly influenced the Gospel writers, or their sources, and have been adapted by each author for their own theological purposes. 'The table of Jesus', Smith argues, 'is a literary phenomenon' (2003, p. 276) and one should not 'read the Gospel narrative as an exact model for the Gospel community', but rather 'the story told in the Gospel narrative, would have functioned to provide an idealized model for the life of the community as it should be' (2003, pp. 276–7). In conclusion Smith asks, 'what kind of meal did the early Christians celebrate?' and he provides a simple answer: 'Early Christians celebrated a meal based on the banquet model found commonly in their world' (2003, p. 279). While this model clearly provided the early Christian community with the basis for their social ethics and much of their theology, 'no further explanation for the origin of early Christian meals is needed' (2003, p. 279).

It is impossible to complete a history of histories of the origin of the Eucharist without mention of Paul Bradshaw. While his is not the most recent text to be published on the subject (see Alikin 2009), Bradshaw's scholarship and his radical approach does probably make it the most definitive of the most recent group of writings. Bradshaw's work on *Eucharistic Origins* (2004) builds on the two editions of his more general text on the origins of Christian worship (1992, 2002). In these earlier books Bradshaw is keen to point out just how little evidence there is for the origins of Christian worship of any kind and, by implication, how little can be said in any definitive sense. It is the scarcity of the evidence, and its very wide distribution across time and space, that makes any attempt to provide a single narrative for the origins of Christian worship impossible. Bradshaw goes further than this, however, to suggest not only that a single common narrative is impossible to construct, but also that this is not the best way of thinking about origins at all. For Bradshaw, what evidence there is points to a variety of different practices within the early Christian communities and hence to the possibility of a variety of different origins.

If there is one theme, therefore, in his work on *Eucharistic Origins* (2004) it is that liturgists must never assume that there is one narrative, one origin, and that they must always be alert to the great diversity of practice and hence the potential for a great diversity of origins. In this he follows very closely on the work of McGowan, but takes McGowan's conclusions, such as they are, much further. Apart from the radical nature of the conclusions, however, the structure of the book is far more conventional and tends to disguise the radical use of the sociological material that it contains. Bradshaw begins by looking at the Last Supper and the institution narratives and moves on from there to look in turn at the *Didache*, other early Christian meals, and Justin, taking a textually based starting point for each chapter.

The first chapter in particular, on the Last Supper and the institution narrative, follows through the very limited evidence for the use of the institution narrative in either forming the ritual of the Eucharist or having a role within that ritual. In relation to the first question, Bradshaw can say, 'we do not possess one scrap of direct testimony that the earliest Christian Eucharist ever conformed itself to the model of the Last Supper, with a bread ritual before the meal and a cup ritual afterwards' (2004, p. 13). Even the example from 1 Corinthians is dismissed in this assessment as Paul does not say, or even suggest, that the meal he is critiquing follows the model of the tradition that he recounts. While many other authors quote from, or use traditions related to, the institution narrative when discussing the Eucharist it is not until the *Sacramentary* of Serapion that the narrative actually appears within a Eucharistic Prayer. The other point that Bradshaw makes is that very few of those who do refer to an institution narrative actually quote directly from any of those found in the Gospels or in Paul.

Bradshaw then provides a very detailed discussion of the various scholarly treatments of the *Didache*, emphasizing the Jewish roots but refusing to draw any conclusions from the text for the origin or development of the Eucharist as such:

> If the meal in the Didache were thought of simply as one of a number of different patterns that existed side-by-side in early Christianity, each being the practice belonging to a particular community or group of communities, then there would be no pressure to slot it into an especially early time frame. (2004, p. 32)

It is this same principle that is picked up in the following chapter on other early Christian ritual meals. Each of these – Paul's account of the meal at Corinth, wineless Eucharists, the 'breaking of bread', etc. – exist, for Bradshaw, as alternative forms with no obvious or necessary connection between them. What is more, he concludes by suggesting that 'a number of different combinations' of bread, wine, water and other foodstuffs 'might have existed in the first 250 years of Christianity's history' and not just the few examples that are represented within the remaining literature (2004, p. 60).

This takes Bradshaw to a discussion of Justin Martyr, which has often been seen as the traditional end point of whatever development the Eucharist may have undertaken in the first hundred years or so of its development. In Justin there is a rite with bread and wine, held in the morning and linked with the reading of scripture, a sermon and prayers of intercession. Bradshaw, therefore, uses a discussion of Justin's accounts of the Eucharist to challenge accepted notions of the separation of the bread and wine from the rest of the meal, the issue of timing, the move from a sevenfold to a fourfold shape and the proposed link with a synagogue-type liturgy of the word. In much of this Bradshaw is actually challenging Dix's theories rather than engaging with a wider range of possibilities, but he draws on a selection of authors and a significant amount of sociological style analysis to make his own points. In the following chapters, however, he tends to move back towards a more text-based and theological understanding of the development of the rite in the second, third and fourth centuries.

What can be seen in all these different approaches, therefore, along with many others that have not been mentioned in this survey but will find a place at the appropriate point in the following text, is that there are almost as many ways of understanding the origins of the Eucharist as there are scholars who write about it. There will never be a definitive answer to this question, but that does not mean that there are not new things to say, alternative ways of looking at the evidence, and new questions that can be asked from slightly different perspectives.

Principles underlying the current text

Anton Baumstark, in his study of *Comparative Liturgy*, sets out six laws for the development of liturgy (1958). Richardson in his further enquiry into Lietzmann's *Mass and the Lord's Supper* sets out six principles and probabilities for any satisfactory account of eucharistic origins (1979, p. 220). Paul Bradshaw, in the first edition of his work *Search for the Origins of Christian Worship* outlines ten principles for interpreting early Christian liturgical evidence (1992, pp. 63–78), although these were reduced to three warnings in the second edition (2002, pp. 17–20). Many of these principles or rules I happen to agree with, others I find extremely problematic. It would be very tempting, therefore, for me to lay out my own seven, eight or twelve principles on which the following text is based. In their place I want to set three parameters. These are not rules or principles that all those who study eucharistic origins should be expected to follow, they are self-imposed limits to my own work that enable me to make the following text more manageable and to provide a clearer perspective on what it is that I am doing and, perhaps more importantly, what it is that I am not doing.

The first parameter that I want to set is in relation to the kind of activity that I wish to discuss. Most, if not all, of the studies that have been discussed in this chapter talk throughout of the 'Eucharist', even when they are dealing with a series of meal practices that may not have been given that title by those who practised them. The more sophisticated do distinguish between that which they consider to be truly 'eucharistic' – that is, those activities that involved bread and wine, and/or a reference to the body and blood of Jesus – from other kinds of meals. As McGowan (2004) has clearly shown, however, such a distinction does not really work for much of the evidence that is available. When does a sharing of bread (with or without any further accompaniment) cease to be 'eucharistic'? Others are very clear to distinguish between Eucharists proper and what has generally been termed the *agape*. Again the question of boundaries remains problematic. A significant number of the more recent accounts blur these boundaries completely and simply refer to all meals held within the early Christian communities as Eucharists, so following a standard position among biblical scholars to see any reference to eating or drinking in the New Testament as 'eucharistic'. What interests me within the following study, however, is any activity that involves shared eating and drinking among early Christian communities. So far I would position myself with McGowan and those who follow him. Where I would want to differ, however, is that I do not want to presuppose that the communities concerned saw all these activities, or even the majority of them, as 'eucharistic', even if they did have such a concept to work with. Throughout the text, therefore, I will be careful to refrain from using the term 'Eucharist' in any way, unless it is clearly used by the evidence that I am considering – and then I will want to be very careful about how the word is interpreted – or by modern authors that I am engaging with. I will also do all that I can to prevent myself, and the reader of this text, from assuming that we know what 'eucharistic' means.

The second parameter is related to this, and focuses on the difference between action and meaning. Almost all the studies that have been discussed, even the most sociological, have been primarily concerned with the meaning that communal meals had for the early Christian community. Even Smith, who is interested in seeing the roots of the early Christian meals in the wider Graeco-Roman symposia, is using Douglas to develop what she describes as the 'social code' of the meal and hence bringing the discussion back round to one of meaning and even theology (Smith 2003). Meanings are, of course, important and a study of the development of imagery and ideas surrounding eating and drinking in the first 150 years of Christian existence could be very interesting. That, however, is not what this study is about. Having said that, I must also note that it is not going to be possible to discuss activity – what people did – without asking some questions about meaning – what people thought about their activities – as the two are intimately linked. It is the action, however, what can be discovered about who did what, and perhaps from my point of view most importantly, when they did it, that is going to form the core of this study.

Third, therefore, I want to set a parameter in relation to the material that I am using: the evidence that is available. It is true that the number of relevant texts for the period up to 160 CE is very limited. All of them have been studied extensively and there may not be much more to find out from them. However, it is also the case that the archaeological evidence for the same period is almost non-existent, particularly that related to specifically 'Christian' evidence. It is this that has led many scholars, especially in recent years, to look beyond the Christian evidence at what is available within Jewish literature, or at evidence from the wider Graeco-Roman context. It has also encouraged those with a sociological concern to look for theoretical material that will help them to interpret the evidence they have. The parameter I am setting myself, however, is to begin with the Christian evidence that is available and to ask what this does suggest, and also, and just as importantly, what it does not indicate about what people were doing. I am not, therefore, going to begin with wider discussions and theories. I am going to begin with the earliest documentary evidence that is available, that is, Paul's first letter to the Corinthians. I will then build from this through the various texts, and, where relevant, with reference to other kinds of data (Stringer 2005, pp. 26–9). In my final chapter I will return to the wider theoretical consideration.

Taking these three parameters into account – to focus on all kinds of eating and drinking; to focus on the practice of the early Christian communities rather than on meanings; and to focus on the evidence in roughly chronological order – it might be thought that very little that is new could ever be said. In the strictest of terms this is entirely true. Very little is known, and there is probably very little else to know. There is, therefore, one other element of my methodology that I need to explain at this point before I move on to the evidence itself.

I am going to work on the assumption that it is possible, and appropriate, for the scholar to make some wild guesses about what was going on within, or behind, the various texts under scrutiny (Stringer 2009). Without some level of imaginative engagement with the texts the study becomes very dry and uninformative. Scholarship moves forward by trial and error on the part of those who make informed guesses when the evidence does not provide the answers. I am going to be making a series of informed guesses, therefore, throughout this work, and I will be very explicit about what these are. In each case it is my contention that the guess provides the best explanation of the gaps within the literature. I do not expect every reader to agree with me. I do, however, expect other scholars to look at the evidence and to argue against me in relation to that evidence and to suggest that other guesses may provide a better fit. What I arrive at, in Chapter 8, as my own narrative of the origins of the Eucharist may or may not be historically accurate. The reality will never be known. What I do contend, however, is that it will provide a reasonable narrative based on the evidence available, and a narrative that has to be taken seriously as a possible contender for the origins of the Eucharist among all the other possibilities that have been looked at within this Introduction.

In what follows, therefore, I will begin with the biblical material and through Chapters 1–3 I will look in turn at Paul's first letter to the Corinthians, the Passion narratives in the Synoptic Gospels (particularly Mark) and the range of other evidence of meals in the rest of the New Testament. In Chapter 4 I will look at the evidence from the wider Graeco-Roman context and the Jewish material from this period. In both cases I will argue that there is very little relevant evidence of any kind that can inform our view of Christian practice. In Chapters 5–7 I will look at the second and third generation of Christian authors focusing on Antioch, Asia Minor and Rome respectively. This will give me the opportunity to look at the *Didache*, the letters of Ignatius, and the work of Justin Martyr among others, and to try and track the development of meals and the sharing of bread, wine, water and other foodstuffs through the first half of the second century. In the final chapter I will bring all this together and outline my own speculative narrative of the origins of the Eucharist based on the evidence that I have presented in the previous seven chapters.

I

Paul's first letter to the Corinthians

In this study I am breaking with much of the tradition in the search for the origins of the Eucharist by beginning, not with the accounts of the Last Supper in the Gospels, but with the account of the Lord's Supper in Paul's first letter to the Corinthians. This is partly because this account is the first literary record of a 'Christian' meal that still survives and partly because I am convinced that if it is possible to rethink what this meal may or may not have been then all the other accounts of meals in the early Christian literature will have to be rethought in the light of this re-analysis. There is no indication within the text of how often the Lord's Supper was held. The only reference to any regular activity comes in the recommendation by Paul to put some money aside each week for the collection he is due to take to Jerusalem (16.2). It is only the subsequent history of the Eucharist, and particularly the accounts in the *Didache* and in the writings of Justin Martyr, that has led to the assumption that because the Lord's Supper has some elements in common with what was to become the Eucharist, it must have been held on a weekly basis. If that subsequent history did not exist then what kind of assumptions might be drawn from the account given in the letter?

Any solution to this question must be suspect on two grounds. First, it is clear that the subsequent history does exist and therefore it is not possible to look at the account without some pre-formed ideas. Second, as the account does not provide information on the frequency of the supper then any proposal has to be speculative and one guess might well be as good as another. Let me, therefore, rephrase the question that I want to address in this chapter: is it plausible to suggest that the Lord's Supper represented in chapter 11 of 1 Corinthians was an annual event? If it is, then, I would suggest, it might make scholars look again at the rest of the texts that are available in a very different light.

This Chapter, therefore, will have four parts. I will begin by setting the account of the Lord's Supper within the wider context of the letter as a whole. Second, I will look at what this text can say about the meal that is being described. Third, I will relate this to other references to meals and to eating within the rest of the letter. Finally, I will look to the rest of Paul's writing, and writing attributed to Paul, to see how this account relates to other elements in the wider corpus.

The Lord's Supper in the context of 1 Corinthians

As with all of Paul's writings there has been considerable debate about the purpose and structure of the first letter to the Corinthians (Mitchell 1992; Thistleton 2000; Hall 2003). Much of this is not directly relevant to this discussion, but there are a number of questions that need to be addressed if the account of the meal in chapter 11 is to make sense. The first asks whether the text presented in the New Testament is the letter as Paul originally wrote it, or whether a subsequent editor has put it together in its current form (Hall 2003, pp. 30–50). Or, to rephrase the question, does 1 Corinthians represent a single letter or should it be divided into two or more texts? There have been various attempts to show that the letter is made up of different elements, led largely by apparent contradictions in the author's position on the eating of meat offered to idols and the role of women in worship. De Boer for example, would want to divide the letter between chapters 1—4 and chapters 5—16 (de Boer 1994). He says, 'there are considerable points of continuity between the two sections of the epistle . . . But points of continuity are to be expected . . . They are not worthy of special notice and certainly need no explanation. The discontinuities, or discrepancies, however, do' (de Boer 1994, p. 242). While this appears to be eminently reasonable, if this were to be taken to the extreme then every chapter, or subsection of each chapter, would have to be considered as a different letter (Hall 2003, pp. 44–5).

In practice few, if any, of the attempts to discern a division in the letter would affect the interpretation of chapter 11, and so the simplest and safest solution at this stage in the discussion is to follow the current scholarly consensus and assume that the letter is one text, and that the letter as it exists today is pretty much the letter as Paul originally wrote it (Hall 2003). The next question, therefore, is to ask when Paul might have written the letter. While there is considerable debate about the place of the letter within various reconstructions of Paul's life and travels (Hurd 1965, pp. 3–42), the dating of 1 Corinthians appears to be uncontroversial. It is dated at about 53–55 CE, following Paul's first visit to Corinth, where he founded a Christian community, and before any second visit that may have taken place (Fee 1987, p. 15).

The next series of questions relate to the reasons why Paul might have written this letter, and the kind of issues that he is addressing within it. Any reading of the letter will show that it ranges over a series of essentially random concerns that appear to have no common thread. Scholars have attempted to discover a thread, or to demonstrate one or more underlying themes to the letter as a whole. Mitchell, for example, argues that the central theme is reconciliation and that Paul's dominant purpose in writing the letter was to persuade the community to become united (Mitchell 1992). Despite Mitchell's attempts to match the letter to the features of classical rhetoric this analysis does not provide an adequate explanation for the structure of the text. More profitable are those analyses that begin with the hints offered within the letter that it was written as a response to a series of questions that have come to Paul from the Corinthian community.

One of the most interesting of these is still Hurd's 1965 study, *The Origin of 1 Corinthians*. Hurd aims to reconstruct the dialogue that occurred between Paul and the Corinthian community from Paul's first visit through to the writing of the letter. Hurd sees 1 Corinthians as being constructed out of Paul's responses to three different kinds of communication from the Corinthians (Hurd 1965, pp. 48–9). First, there is a letter that is mentioned in 7.1. Second, it is clear that Paul has had some personal communication from people associated with Chloe (1.11). Finally, towards the end of the letter, there is mention of Stephanas, Forunatus and Achaicus who had recently arrived from Corinth (16.17). From this Hurd demonstrates that there are two types of material within the letter: that which is written in response to the letter from Corinth, and that which is written in response to personal communications. He goes on to note that this distinction is reflected in Paul's level of emotional response to the issues covered, with Paul being more detached in his discussion of the material from the letter and more forthright and emotional in his response to material from personal communication (Hurd 1965, pp. 62–3). Finally, this enables Hurd to identify those passages that begin with the words 'now concerning (περί δέ)' (7.1; 7.25; 8.1; 12.1; 16.1; 16.12) as responses to the letter (Hurd 1965, p. 63). If this is followed through, then the first section of the letter (chapters 1—6) is largely a response to verbal communication (with the possible exception of 5.9–13a), and the second section (chapters 7—16) is largely a response to issues raised in the letter, with the notable exception of 11.17–34 (Hurd 1965, p. 93).

It is precisely 11.17–34 that is of concern. The discussion of the meal derives, according to the text (11.18), from what Paul has heard from personal communication. Hurd argues that the section is placed here because, like the rest of chapters 11—14, it deals with the issue of worship (Hurd 1965, p. 182). Unlike chapters 1—6, however, 11.18 does not say who is the source of the information. Hurd simply assumes that it is the same 'Chloe's people' who informed Paul of other difficulties and disputes within the Corinthian community (Hurd 1965, p. 82). Dunn assumes that it was Stephanas and his companions (Dunn 1995, p. 19). Neither author, however, has much to say about what they think were the intentions and purposes of Chloe's people or Stephanas, and where these might fit within the relationship between Paul and the Corinthians. Hurd concentrates too much on the reconstruction of the letter to Paul from the Corinthians, and does not really consider the content and motivation of the verbal communication. Dunn simply does not raise the question.

1 Corinthians 11.17–34

Turning to the text itself, the first point to note is that it opens with a condemnation of divisions within the community (11.18). There are a number of points within the letter that deal with divisions and a considerable amount of debate within the scholarly literature discusses what the nature of these divisions might be. Hall, for example, argues that the opposition faced by Paul in 1 Corinthians was inspired by teachers from elsewhere (Hall 2003, pp. 3–18). Hurd and Fee see the opposition as coming from within the Corinthian community itself (Hurd 1965, pp. 95–113; Fee 1987, pp. 4–15). Goulder (2001) is explicit in seeing the opposition as between Pauline and Petrine factions. Dunn (1995) simply sees the community as being prone to factionalism. The literature spends many pages debating the nature and identity of the various 'parties' that are mentioned in the opening of the letter (1.12), and there are numerous theories about who these might be. If it is assumed that the account of the meal was given to Paul by the same person, or people, who provided the account of the internal divisions at the beginning of the letter, whether this was Chloe's people or some other informant, then it might be assumed that there is a relationship between the divisions of chapter 1 and those of chapter 11. However, the text of chapter 11 makes it very clear that the division that is being highlighted at this point is not one between 'parties' as such. It appears to be between those who come to eat their own meal and those who have nothing, and the text does not indicate that it represents any kind of ideological or theological difference among the people involved.

Some scholars have assumed that the division being alluded to is one between the rich and the poor within the community (Meeks 1983, pp. 67–8), but this is not stated explicitly in the text. Unfortunately, the text itself is not very clear. The issue appears to revolve around the translation of the word προλαμβάνει in verse 21. The compound 'pro' might normally indicate a sense of time associated with the word, in the sense of 'before', and so would suggest that some of those present go ahead with their meals before the others arrive (Fee 1987, pp. 540–5). However, other scholars say that this element of waiting is not necessarily implied by the word, and that there is no other context in which the word is used in this way in the New Testament. What Paul might be indicating, therefore, is merely a distinction between those who eat their own meals and those who get nothing to eat at all (Winter 2001, pp. 144–8; Lampe 1994). Either way, the text does not suggest that the division between those who eat and those who do not eat is an easy distinction between rich and poor. Further sociological analysis is needed in order to draw out that conclusion and I will come on to look at that in the following section.

Before moving on, therefore, I need to discuss briefly the issues related to the name, the 'Lord's Supper' (χυριακὸν δεῖπνον, 11.20). This is the only point within the New Testament where the phrase 'Lord's Supper' is used and there is no internal evidence to suggest what Paul might mean by this. The term was never taken up in any consistent way in other early Christian literature, and where it does occur, in the *Apostolic Tradition* and in the writings of Tertullian, there is no direct reference to Paul and the letter to the Corinthians, and so this does not help to determine its meaning (Bradshaw 2004, p. 44).

Next comes Paul's statement of the 'tradition' that was handed on to him concerning the Last Supper (11.23–24). A number of commentators note that the structure that Paul uses at this point is similar to that used in some Jewish traditions for the passing on of teaching: 'I delivered to you . . . what I also received' (Donfried 2002, p. 302; Alexander 2001, pp. 116–21). This is also one of a number of places within the letter where Paul makes specific reference to what has been passed on to him (Furnish 1999, pp. 21–2; Ellis 1986). Throughout the letter it appears that Paul is very particular about making a distinction between what is being presented on his own authority and what he has received from 'the Lord' or 'the Lord Jesus'. Hurd notes that references to authority, whether of Jesus, scripture, common sense, custom or his own apostolic authority is a feature of those passages that are responding to the Corinthians' letter (1965, p. 74). However, this section is dealing with an oral communication. The distinction Hurd makes is that 'it is noticeable that Paul's rehearsal of the Lord's teaching here does not seem intended to give the Corinthians new information to settle a new problem, but seems intended rather to recall them to earlier behaviour from which they had strayed' (1965, p. 79). Here another distinction between responses to the letter and responses to oral communication is highlighted, that is, instruction about the future as opposed to correction of past errors. In this reference to the tradition Paul is clearly referring to the past. What, however, is the nature and source of this tradition?

It is possible to suggest, and some scholars clearly argue, that when Paul talks about receiving a ruling or phrase from the Lord, or from Jesus, this was granted in a vision, whether that on the road to Damascus or some other subsequent experience. If this were the case then these sections would relate to direct communication between Jesus and Paul. The vast majority of commentators, however, argue that this is not what Paul means in these contexts, and that the phrase, or ruling, has been passed on to Paul as being authentically from Jesus by his immediate disciples, whether directly or indirectly (Bornkamm 1966, pp. 130–2; Fee 1987, pp. 547–9). What then are the distinctions that Paul wishes to make between rulings or phrases that come from Jesus and those given on his own authority?

In an earlier passage, in chapter 7, Paul states that 'to the married I give this command (not I, but the Lord): A wife must not separate from her husband' (7.10). Here Fee and others have argued that the reference is to an actual statement of Jesus, whether one that is preserved in the gospel tradition or another along similar lines, but this does not suggest how this command came to Paul (Fee 1987, pp. 291–4). The usual, and generally unquestioned, assumption is that Paul must have learnt about it in Antioch during his stay there following his conversion, or directly from the disciples in Jerusalem during one of his visits. The same has generally been assumed of the tradition of the Last Supper (Dix 1945, p. 64). This is certainly possible, but also raises more interesting questions about what role this text had within the community at Antioch or Jerusalem. That, however, is an issue I want to come back to in Chapter 5. For now all that is relevant is that the text is constructed to suggest that the account of the Last Supper is not something that Paul has made up for himself; it forms a tradition that he has heard before and passed on to the Corinthian community, either in exactly the same form that he received it or with his own additions and modifications.

What is important to note is that this is not the first time that Paul has told the Corinthian community about this tradition (11.23). He is

reminding them of something that he has previously shared with them. ✓
In Hurd's reconstruction of the relationship between Paul and the Corinthians, it seems most probable that the teaching on the Lord's Supper would have been given while Paul was in Corinth during his initial
founding of the community (Hurd 1965, pp. 213–39). The real question, however, is whether Paul expected the community to repeat, or
otherwise remember, the text every time they met for a meal, or whether
this was something he taught them when he first instructed them to celebrate the meal, and that they have subsequently forgotten. This question cannot be answered from the limited information provided in the
text, but the question is central to the discussion of how often the meal
was held within the Corinthian community and it is an issue I will be
returning to in the following sections.

The next few phrases are probably the most difficult element of the
whole text. This is the eschatological reference in verse 26 and the
comments on judgement at the end of the chapter (11.27–34). One
difficulty is that it is not at all clear whether verse 26 is a new interpretation that Paul is passing on to the Corinthians in this letter or
whether it has always been a part of Paul's understanding of the meal
and was something that was passed on to the community at the same
time as the tradition. Most scholars tend to assume that this eschatological reference is part of Paul's own gloss on the meal, something
that fits in well with his way of thinking and the particular stage in
his developing thoughts about the death and imminent return of Jesus
(Fee 1987, pp. 556–8).

The section on judgement, however, is even more difficult to situate. At one level it reads like a general statement about the worthy
reception of the bread and the cup. However, the context that is set
up by the issues raised at the beginning and end of the account of the
meal (11.20–22 and 11.33–34) suggests that the particular 'sin' that
the Corinthians are committing relates to their failure to share the meal
as a community. It is judgement on this sin that is being called down,
because this lack of respect for others in some way fails to recognize
the presence of the body of the Lord (11.29), and this in turn has led
to sickness and death in the community (11.30). Is the reference to the
'body' in verse 29, however, drawing our attention back to the association of the bread as the body of the Lord (11.24) or is it, as most recent
commentators suggest, looking forward to the idea of the community
as the body of Christ (12.27) (Fee 1987, pp. 562–4)? Both are possible
and it may be that Paul himself is establishing a double meaning. It
must be stressed, however, that it is the division within the community

that is being judged and not any failure to understand a nascent doctrine of the real presence.

Finally, therefore, does the end of the chapter mark a natural break, and does this material form a clear and coherent section within the letter? Given that the next section opens with the 'now concerning . . .' (12.1) that Hurd defines as a reference to the letter Paul received from the Corinthians (1965, p. 63), then it is fair to see this as the end of the discussion of the meal. The subsequent discussion of spiritual gifts and the meeting at which each member brings a hymn or a testimony (14.26) relates to different issues. This is important only in relation to those who argue that the order of Paul's letter, with a discussion of the meal in chapter 11 followed by a discussion of the meeting for prayer and singing in chapter 14, might represent a primitive order of service based, perhaps, on the model of the Graeco-Roman symposium or Philo's account of the meal among spiritual Jews in Alexandria, where the meal is followed by discussion/teaching and/or ecstatic prayer (Alikin 2009, p. 28; Smith 2003, pp. 200–1). It is fairly clear, however, that Paul is simply moving through the series of issues raised by the Corinthians, either in their letter or by personal communication. These two sections clearly belong to different answers to different issues, and are not connected in any formal way within Paul's text.

The structure of the Corinthian community

Having looked in detail at the text itself, and explored a number of the issues raised by biblical scholars in relation to the text, it is necessary to move on and ask what, if anything, can be said about the reality behind the text. It is not possible to say that this text describes a particular kind of event with specified people being present and so on. That kind of detail is not available. However, it is possible, from the text, and from sociological thinking about what is actually possible within a small enthusiastic community of recent converts to a new ecstatic cult, to make some statements about what is, and more importantly what is not, likely to have occurred. Before looking at any kind of detailed questions about the meal, however, it is necessary to look more closely at the social and cultural make-up of the Corinthian community itself.

Early in the twentieth century, Deissmann (1957) reinforced a popular view, based on his travels in the Middle East, that the earliest Christian community came from the poorer strata of society. However, by the 1970s Malherbe was able to state that 'a new consensus may be emerging' that the community was made up of a wide range of social strata, probably reflecting the social structure of the surrounding society (1983, p. 31). The most detailed study of the social structure of the Corinthian community as it relates to the Lord's Supper is found in Theissen's article 'Social Integration and Sacramental Activity', which was original published in 1974 (1982, pp. 145–63). This paper builds on a series of related papers that were brought together in an edited volume in the early 1980s (Schütz 1982).

In 'Social Stratification in Corinthian Community' (1982, pp. 69–119) Theissen looks at the passages in Paul's writing that deal with the community as a whole, those that refer to individuals associated with the Corinthian community and those that comment on the various subgroups within the community. All these show the clear presence of some individuals who are of high social status and who act, in part, as patrons to the community, offering their houses for hospitality to Paul and other visiting preachers, and for meetings of the community as a whole (Chow 1992). Assuming that the rest of the community is made up of traders, artisans, and probably slaves and freedmen, Theissen argues that the community has a high level of social stratification, something that is considered by Theissen to be unusual for social gatherings at this time (1982, p. 99). Meeks follows Theissen's basic outline but adds the rider, based on his understanding of the nature of Corinth as a 'new town', that most people within the community had an ambiguous relationship to social status and may have been moving up or down the social ladder (Meeks 1983). Fiorenza also says that the community contained a significant number of women and these played an important role as patrons and perhaps as leaders of the community (1983, pp. 175–84).

In a further paper, 'The Strong and the Weak in Corinth' (1982, pp. 121–43), Theissen suggests that the distinction that Paul makes between 'the strong' and 'the weak' throughout the letter is the same as that which can be made between the few high-status members of the community and the many lower-class members. This is argued primarily through the way in which each group is assumed to react to the question of meat offered to idols, which is discussed in chapters 8 to 10. The 'strong', the richer members of the congregation, would be expected to attend formal meals where such meat is served on a regular basis, while the 'weak', the poorer members, would hardly ever get a chance to eat meat anyway. The distinction, therefore, can be seen to mirror the economic and social profile of the community. Such an analysis, however, fails to take into account the possibility that the categories of the 'strong' and the 'weak' may be part of Paul's rhetorical strategy rather than representing real social groupings within the community (Smith 2003, pp. 193–6). Theissen does not really consider this and goes on to suggest that Paul generally sides with the weak against the strong but that the letter itself is addressed to the strong, to those who can read, or to the wealthier members of the congregation. This distinction, between the poorer majority and the richer few, is also essential to Theissen's analysis of the meal in chapter 11.

Theissen begins his analysis by stressing the divisions mentioned in verse 21 and identifying these as distinctions between the rich and the poor. There are two main reasons why he takes this position. First is the use of the phrase 'those who have nothing' in verse 22 (1982, p. 148). Theissen argues that having nothing must refer to a permanent state rather than to those who have nothing on this particular occasion. Second, he notes the use of the word 'houses' in verse 34 and argues that Paul is clearly addressing the wealthy at this point, as they are the only ones who would have 'houses' to eat their meals in. Both of these assumptions need to be challenged (Smith 2002, pp. 195–8). By emphasizing those who have nothing as a permanent state, Theissen does not acknowledge Paul's rhetorical distinction between those who are hungry and those who get drunk, and it is never suggested that being 'drunk' should be seen as a permanent state (Fee 1987, p. 543; Winter 2001, pp. 147–8). As to the 'houses', this again should not perhaps be taken literally and could be translated as 'homes' (as it is in the NIV and other translations) rather than referring to a particular high-status 'house'. All members of the community would have some kind of home to eat their meals in. It is fair to assume, therefore, that sociologically the community in Corinth was mixed, with both richer and poorer members but that this may not have been the only division in the meal.

The cultural, or religious, make-up of the community is far more difficult to determine, and it is not something that those who are concerned about the sociology of the Pauline communities spend very long discussing (Winter 2001, p. 150; Meeks 2001, p. 135). If, however, the account in Acts is taken at face value, then Paul's first contact in Corinth was a Jew named Aquila (Acts 18.2). Paul also began his teaching in Corinth, as in all cities, within the synagogue (18.4), and when he was thrown out he moved next door, presumably taking some members of the synagogue with him. One leader of the synagogue, Crispus, is mentioned by name (18.7–8). There were, therefore, some Jews among the community. It is also clear, from Theissen's list of named members of the Corinthian community, that other members of the community were Greeks or even Romans (Theissen 1982, pp. 73–96). One common suggestion is that many of the non-Jews could have been so-called 'God fearers', Greeks and Romans who had a great deal of sympathy for, and knowledge of, Jewish beliefs and traditions but were reluctant for whatever reason to convert (Esler 1987). Unfortunately so little is known about synagogue life and organization, especially within the Diaspora, during the first century CE, that it is impossible to make any firm statement on this (Runesson 2001; Lieu 2002). The text of both first and second Corinthians also makes it clear that there are a significant number of Gentiles within the community who probably had no previous association with the Jews. Given all this, it is fair to suggest that the Christian community in Corinth was made up of some Jews, although perhaps not very many, some Greeks or Romans who had knowledge of, and sympathy for, Jewish ideas, although again perhaps not very many, and some who were converted directly without any previous knowledge of Jewish scriptures and traditions. While no firm predictions can be made about the relative proportions of these groups, it is fairly clear that the leaders of the community, including the leaders of worship, would most likely have come from one or other of the first two groups.

Finally, therefore, in this discussion of the community, what can be said about the number of members who might have attended the meal? Like so much else in this area, making any accurate statements is of course impossible. Goulder notes that Luke says twice that many believed at Corinth and paints the picture of the community reaching perhaps 50 members in 50–51 CE and moving from the house of Titus to that of the wealthy convert Gaius. However, he notes that even here 'the house would probably not have rooms with space for fifty people to eat together, and we have to think of the church as meeting in his garden' (Goulder 2001, p. 225). White also notes that 'the assembly was regularly convened in the dining room of the house' but that this might have taken a number of different forms within the cities of the Aegean (1990, p. 107). From all the information that is available, and based on sociological models, it is most likely that the group was relatively small, with a maximum of about 100 members and a minimum of 50. One implication of this is that the members of the community probably sat for the meal rather than reclining as was usual at many Roman banquets (Smith 2003, p. 177). This is going to be significant for anything that might be said about the nature and frequency of the meal below.

The Lord's Supper within the Corinthian community

For all of his analysis of the social make-up of the community and his emphasis on the rich and the poor, or the weak and the strong, the essence of Theissen's reconstruction of the meal itself is not entirely dependent on these assumed divisions (1982, pp. 153–63). Theissen argues that the institution narrative must, in some way, reflect the heart of the 'cultic' meal, the 'Lord's' Supper (χυριακὸν δεῖπνον), which he suggests was probably a limited meal consisting only of bread and wine. This, Theissen argues, is what Paul had instituted within the community. The rich, however, were holding a pre-meal, a 'personal' supper (ἴδιον δεῖπνον), probably containing meat and other foodstuffs, before the Lord's Supper begins and it is this personal supper, Theissen argues, that Paul is objecting to. The Lord's Supper in this view must have followed the personal meals because it begins, according to the text of the tradition, with the blessing of bread. If such a blessing took place at the very beginning of the event then many of those who came late (after others had begun the meal) would have missed an important element of the cultic event. This, in Theissen's view, would have been unthinkable so the meal that people came late to must be a pre-meal. Such a view would certainly fit the text, but has no kind of precedent in the ancient world as a structure and clearly makes too many assumptions to be comfortable.

The crux of Theissen's analysis depends on his assumption that the Lord's Supper itself must reflect the narrative of the Last Supper; that is, the 'sacred, cultic formula' for the meal. This, he argues, would have been followed meticulously because Paul had instituted it with a specific reference to what Jesus had done. Theissen states, 'in my opinion it is unthinkable that Paul would quote a sacred, cultic formula, expressly state that he received it in just this and no other form, and yet at the same time tacitly suppose that its order is not to be followed' (1982, p. 152). If, however, the narrative was not a regular part of the meal, and therefore not seen as a sacred blueprint for the meal, then the whole argument begins to fall apart (Bradshaw 2004, pp. 13, 45).

Mazza suggests that the order cup–bread, as presented in 10.16–17, underlies the structure of the meal, but this is based on comparison with the *Didache* and other texts and cannot be justified from 1 Corinthians itself (Mazza 1995, pp. 76–8). The meal itself could have consisted of any number of foodstuffs, including, of course, bread and wine, and it does not need to be held in any special, sacred or, as Theissen describes it, 'cultic' fashion (Lampe 1994). It could simply be a shared meal, or a meal to which each person brought their own food and which each member of the community started as soon as they arrived, what Lampe (1994) identifies as an '*eranos*' meal. Winter even goes so far as to suggest that apart from bread and wine the meal itself was an entirely individual affair and some brought significant quantities while others went without and had to wait till the rest had finished (2001, pp. 142–63). It is the individual nature of the different meals that Paul is clearly objecting to and the lack of sharing among the community, not to some assumed distinction of social status within the community.

If the leaders of the community are more likely to have been Jews, or perhaps Greeks who had considerable knowledge of Jewish scriptures and practices, then it seems probable that any meal would have had a Jewish structure and shape. This would have included blessings of some kind (although there are no texts of these from this particular period) and the principal blessings would most likely have been said in relation to bread and the cup. Paul clearly chooses to emphasize the bread and the cup in his letter, although it is worth pointing out that throughout the letter wine as such is never mentioned, either in chapter 11 or in other places where the bread and the cup are referenced (McGowan 1999a, pp. 221–6). Essentially, therefore, very little can be said about the nature of the meal.

Finally, there is the question of frequency. The text offers no hint whatsoever of how often the meal may have been held. The only reference to anything that was to happen weekly within the Corinthian community comes, as I have already indicated, towards the end of the letter when Paul advises the Corinthians to put aside some money each week as a kind of savings plan to build up a sum of money that could be sent to the community in Jerusalem (16.2). It is sometimes assumed that this collection would be taken during the weekly worship, but again there is no direct evidence to support this (Bradshaw 2004, p. 39). If there was a weekly act of worship then this could easily be the kind of meeting described in chapter 14 and does not need to take the form of a weekly meal (Smith's statement that 'we should imagine Christian meetings taking place at table most if not all of the time' (2003, p. 177) is utterly unfounded). How likely was it, therefore, that a community of about 50 individuals within a busy Greek city would have come together on a weekly basis for a shared meal?

In theory this is possible. There is some evidence of weekly meals among a number of Jewish communities within the ancient world (Smith 2003). I will come to look at this evidence in more detail in Chapter 4. If it is also assumed that this community is relatively new and, like all converts, the members still maintained a high level of enthusiasm for, and commitment to, their new-found faith, then the suggestion that they should come together once a week for a collective meal would not seem too burdensome. It is not the possibility of a weekly meal, therefore, that raises questions; it is the way in which Paul addresses the issue within the text.

In particular there are two points that suggest to me that what is being described is not a weekly event. The first relates to the disputes and arguments that form the primary reason for the text in the first place. Whatever Paul goes on to say about the link between the Lord's Supper and the Last Supper, and the eschatological nature of the meal, he is talking about it in this letter because some members of the Corinthian community have complained about the behaviour of other members of the community during the meal itself. While acknowledging the possibility that the reporters could have ulterior motives for passing on the information that they did, or that they may even have been falsifying their account for reasons of their own, for Paul the account of the disputes and the disruption is taken at face value and addressed as such within the letter. If, however, this is an accurate account, and if the meal was taking place weekly, then the resulting tensions would undoubtedly have made it very difficult for the community to continue in anything like a peaceful state. Theissen argued that it is not the Lord's Supper itself that was subject to disruption but rather a pre-meal or personal supper indulged in by the richer members of the community (1982, pp. 151–3). Theissen also suggests that this was accepted as a normal way of functioning in public meals of the time and would not have caused too much alarm or concern among the Corinthians (1982, p. 154). The problem with this argument, however, is, first, that it is clear that the divisions did cause alarm, at least for some, and enough alarm for them to pass this information on to Paul, and, second, that Paul, in his text, makes it clear that these divisions impact directly on the Lord's Supper even to the extent that it ceases to become the Lord's Supper and leads ultimately to judgement and death within the community (11.20, 30).

While other parts of the letter give the impression of a very divided and disturbed community, the divisions referred to elsewhere are different from those suggested for the meal. The divisions surrounding the meal are practical; each person is bringing their own meal and some are eating well while others are going hungry. It would have been very difficult to continue for any serious length of time to hold a weekly meal where there was such a level of resentment and utter disregard for the feelings of others. To say it would have been difficult does not mean, of course, that it was impossible. It is clear from chapter 14 that other gatherings of the community were also somewhat chaotic and this may have been accepted as the normal state of affairs. But why had the local leaders not sorted out what was, after all, a very practical problem much earlier? It is possible that the issue had only just arisen within the community, or had been developing only very slowly to the point that it had become a noticeable and serious issue at the time the reporters left on their journey to Ephesus. Either way, I think there is something about the nature of the dispute that makes the possibility of a weekly ✓ meeting very unlikely.

My other concern relates to the giving of the 'tradition'. Why should Paul's response to the divisions and discord present at the Lord's Supper take the form of a re-presentation of a tradition in the form of an account of the Last Supper? It is clear from the way the text is written that Paul does not really expect the Corinthians to remember the Last Supper narrative, he would not need to present it in full if this was the case. His usual way of referring to statements and rules from the 'tradition' is to allude to things, not to lay them out in full (1 Cor. 7.10; 15.3–8). In this case, however, he presents the whole narrative as he has received it. It is clear that he has already presented this narrative to the Corinthians while he was with them and that he has told them, in response to this narrative, to celebrate a meal, sharing in bread and the cup just as Jesus had done on the night before he was betrayed. If the instruction was to celebrate a weekly meal then this narrative could not have been repeated regularly as part of that meal. If it were, he would not need to repeat it in full within the letter. If what was instituted was not a weekly meal, however, then there is a possibility that the narrative might have been associated with the meal in some more direct way, although once again it is not possible to say whether or not it was read or spoken as some kind of warrant. Paul's felt need to restate the tradition in such detail, however, leads me away from the possibility of a weekly meal. As with all the other evidence, this is not conclusive in itself, it is part of a body of what might be called 'circumstantial' evidence. Before coming back to this question, therefore, it is necessary to look at other aspects of the letter beyond the account of the meal in chapter 11 and see what other 'circumstantial' evidence might exist.

1 Corinthians as a paschal letter

There are two other sections of 1 Corinthians that might have a bearing on the question of the meal and its frequency. The first relates to the question of meat offered to idols in chapters 8—10, and the second to a series of references throughout the letter that appear to point to a paschal context. The question of meat offered to idols is relatively simple in relation to the Lord's Supper, although the issues behind it are complex and have caused a great deal of controversy (Gooch 1993). I am only including it here because it deals with the question of eating and may have a bearing on whether the Corinthians shared a common meal on a weekly basis. It is also the context in which the other references to the bread and the cup are made.

Clearly there was some dispute over the eating of meat that was bought in the marketplace and that may have been offered to idols (10.25). Hurd suggests that Paul is tempering earlier advice that suggested that all meat could be eaten, either because it was causing difficulties for the Corinthian community or because Paul had realized that such a liberal attitude was not all that helpful (Hurd 1965, pp. 142–9). Gooch suggests that Paul never held the liberal position, and that he continued to maintain the traditional Jewish abhorrence of idol food that was accepted by the Corinthians and all other orthodox Christian communities at the time (Gooch 1993, pp. 129–33). It is not my concern here to tease out the exact meaning of the text. The question, in the light of chapter 11, is whether, if there was a common weekly meal, the source of any meat that might have been eaten at that meal was an issue.

If each household was providing their own food there may not have been a problem, but the question could, potentially, have been raised with some members asking others where they had acquired their meat. However, this is not stated as an issue, either in the account of the meal or, more importantly, at the time that Paul is discussing the eating of idol meat. The second of these points is significant. As Goulder comments, 'so many problems get an airing in the Corinthian letters that it is hardly believable that there was trouble over the meat at the agape without our hearing of it' (2001, p. 170). Paul talks in terms of members of the community being invited to the houses of unbelievers where potential idol meat was being served (10.27). If this were a concern in a weekly meal within the community then surely he would have said something about this as well. It is perfectly plausible, however, that the weekly meal did not contain meat on a regular basis. The poor at this time hardly ever ate meat and the richer members of the community would not have done so on a regular basis. Other evidence suggests that a meat-free communal meal, especially if it was a regular event, would not have been considered particularly unusual. Some broth and a few vegetables, or fruit and nuts with some bread, would have been perfectly acceptable (Smith 2003). I will come back to these issues in Chapter 4. For now, all I wish to note is that this discussion of meat offered to idols does not offer any further insight into the meal described✓ in chapter 11.

Within the wider discussion of meat offered to idols, however, following on from an account of Moses and the Israelites in the wilderness, there are a number of references to bread and the cup (10.14–17). These have always tended to be interpreted, without much critical reflection, as having a eucharistic referent. At the very least they are associated with the account of the meal in chapter 11, and are used as evidence that a symbolic discourse on the bread and the cup as the body and blood of Christ was central to the Corinthian community at this time. This, in turn, is used to suggest that the meal, with the blessing of the cup and of bread, was a regular, and potentially weekly event within the community (Mazza 1995, pp. 71–2). Fee, however, emphasizes that the main theme of this passage is not the eating of bread or the sharing of the cup per se, but rather the question of idolatry (Fee 1987, pp. 441–91). Indirectly, Paul is emphasizing the continuity between Israel and the Corinthian community, and only in passing is there a reference to bread and the cup. A core passage is in verses 15–21 where Paul refers to the 'cup of blessing' and also to the 'bread that we break', but goes on to talk about 'those who eat the sacrifices' (the Israelites) as participating 'in the altar'. Paul then extrapolates this to refer to the eating sacrifices offered to demons as participating with demons. Finally he tells the Corinthians that they cannot 'have a part in both the Lord's table and the table of demons' (10.21). Fee picks up the threefold structure of the rhetoric here and emphasizes the links between the sacrifices of the Israelites, the sacrifices to demons and the table fellowship of the Corinthians (Fee 1987, pp. 462–75). The Lord's Supper is being used here to say something about eating meat sacrificed to idols and not the other way round. It is an argument that draws on the Corinthians' own experience of the meal and it is not aimed at presenting any commentary on that meal in itself. Does this suggest, therefore, that the experience is so common, say weekly, that nothing more needs to be said?

The other point that is almost always made in relation to the phrases in verses 16–7 is that they have a ritual ring about them; they do not appear to be Paul's own words. The suggestion is that he is quoting a liturgical formula. Many of those who follow this line go on to point out that the nearest equivalent of these formulas, particularly the phrase 'the cup of blessing', appear in relation to the Jewish celebration of the Passover (Bruce 1971, p. 94). Very little is known about how the Jews celebrated weekly meals or festivals at this time, and so the phrases actually relate to later Jewish texts on the Passover. If there was no account of the meal within 1 Corinthians, however, and if there had been no future development of the Eucharist, it is very possible that these particular phrases would have been read metaphorically and would probably have led scholars to see the letter as being framed within a Paschal context (Bruce 1971). Paul would have been seen as using images and metaphors from the Passover liturgy to make wider theological points. Do these phrases, therefore, necessarily have to be seen as relating to a weekly meal?

There is a certain amount of other circumstantial evidence that points to a Paschal context for the letter, not least the reference to the place of unleavened bread at the feast and Jesus as the Paschal sacrifice (5.6–8), the reference to Jesus' resurrection as the 'first fruits' (15.20) and the fact that towards the end Paul comments that he intends to wait in Ephesus until Pentecost (16.8) (Bruce 1971, p. 145). The imagery and 'typology' of 10.1–13 has also been associated with the period surrounding the Passover (Carrington 1952, p. 42; Bruce 1971, p. 90). The comment at 16.8 would suggest that Paul is writing between Passover and Pentecost. If this is the case then he would have 'celebrated' Passover in Ephesus fairly recently and many of the images and practices associated with the Passover celebrations would have been fresh in his mind (Shepherd 1960, p. 22). It is not possible to know, of course, how Paul would have celebrated Passover. Nor is it possible to know in detail how any Jew of this time might have celebrated Passover, especially in the Diaspora. Even whether Paul, in his rejection of many Jewish laws and practices, would have celebrated Passover at all has to be guessed at. At one level this does not matter, and I will come back to the detail of the question in the next chapter. Paul, having been brought up as a devout Jew, and having been a Pharisee for much of his adult life, would have celebrated the Passover regularly before his conversion, and even if he did not continue to do so as a Christian, the way in which he conceived of time would still have been firmly rooted in the Jewish calendar, so the time of year, of itself, would have brought to mind Paschal imagery and practices, even if he was not celebrating them himself. I would want to suggest, however, that Paul probably had celebrated some form of Christian Passover with the community in Ephesus, and what is more, that the meal he refers to in 1 Corinthians was probably a Paschal meal celebrated by the community in Corinth.

Obviously this cannot be proved. Conzelmann, among others, goes out of his way to stress that, unlike Mark and the other Synoptic Gospels, Paul makes no reference to the Passover in his account of the Last Supper (1975, p. 197). However, if it were the case that the meal in question were a Paschal meal, then this would explain, first, the range of Paschal imagery throughout the letter, second, the particular association of the meal with the account of the Last Supper, which, I will argue in the following chapter, may have formed a part of a Christian Passover narrative that Paul may have heard once again in Ephesus, and third, it would explain the eschatological thinking that Paul associates with the meal, as for the Christians the Passover would have been associated with the death and resurrection of Christ rather than, or perhaps as well as, the liberation of the Jews from Egypt (Bruce 1971, pp. 113–14; Segal 1984). What is more, it may explain why the Corinthian community, many of whom were non-Jews, had such difficulties engaging with the meal. They did not really know how to celebrate it, and hence created such difficulties for themselves, with each person or household providing their own food and some even going without. It may also explain why those who were Jews were so offended by this behaviour and reported it to Paul. This does, at the very least, provide a plausible reading of the information contained within the letter.

The rest of Paul's letters

This explanation would also answer one other very puzzling element of Paul's other writings. If the meal, with its emphasis on bread and the cup, and its link in some way with the narrative of the Last Supper, was a regular, even weekly event that Paul had established in all the communities he founded and that he also shared in each week wherever he happened to be based (although probably not in prison or while travelling), then why is it that the only reference to it is in the first letter to the Corinthians? Not only does 1 Corinthians provide the only account of what happened at this meal (although it does not even do that), it is also the only direct reference to any kind of communal meal within the whole of Paul's output (whether that is measured by the traditional attributions or those of recent scholarship). Paul does mention baptism on more than one occasion, and makes a big play of the different ways of understanding baptism and the role it plays within the community and in the lives of individual Christians (Johnson 1999, pp. 22–32). Of course there would have been more baptisms at this time of expansion and evangelical activity than at many other times in the Church's history. However, baptism would not have been held as frequently as a regular weekly meal. Why is there no other mention of the meal? There is no easy answer to this question except to suggest that there was no regular weekly meal within the communities that Paul founded.

There are three other sections of the letters attributed to Paul where references to a weekly meal might be expected if it existed. The first two raise the question of who can eat with whom: the account of the divisions at Antioch that Paul provides in his letter to the Galatians (2.11–21) and a brief reference to a similar issue in Romans (14.1–23). The third relates to the issues raised by the Pastoral Epistles.

The Galatians material raises a number of complex issues. First, it is necessary to reconcile the account of the dispute at Antioch, as recounted by Paul, with the account in Acts. Having done that, it is important to decide what the real issues were in this dispute. It looks, on the surface, as if the issue concerned the question of whether Jews could share a meal with non-Jews (Esler 1987). Paul said that they could, his opponents argued that they could not. There is scholarly literature to suggest that both positions reflected the accepted position of the time, but the more general view in recent scholarship is that ordinary Jews in the first century, whether in Palestine or the Diaspora, would actually have shared meals with non-Jews with little concern (Sanders 1992, pp. 214–17; Barclay 2001). They would have become unclean in doing so, but this was easy to remedy. It would only be the nature of the food that would have caused problems, and if the Jews and non-Jews each brought their own food then even this could be avoided. It would only be the strictest Jewish groups that would have seen any real problem with this and so, once again, it is necessary to go back and ask what the real issues were in the Antiochene dispute. Unfortunately that is beyond the scope of this particular discussion and I will come back to it in Chapter 5.

Whatever the real issues, however, what is very striking in relation to the discussion in this chapter is that there is no mention of the 'Lord's Supper', or of any other regular cultic meal that the community is obliged to celebrate. The reference in Galatians 2.12 simply says 'before certain men came from James, he [Peter] used to eat with the Gentiles'. There is no further reference to indicate the context in which this eating takes place. This would be the ideal place to make reference to the regular weekly meal if such existed. Smith takes it for granted that the 'eating' in question represents the same basic meal tradition as at Corinth; 'in other words, what Paul calls "the Lord's Supper" at Corinth is also

40

what was being practiced at Antioch' (Smith 2003, p. 174). However, if that is the case then why is this not mentioned explicitly in the text? If Jesus really did institute a regular weekly meal, and if there were some in Antioch who found sharing food with others difficult if not impossible, then once again some reference to Jesus' command would surely have settled the issue once and for all.

The same argument can also be raised in relation to Romans 14, although this also relates back to the discussions in 1 Corinthians 8 — 10. As with Galatians 2, however, there is no reference to a specific meal within which, or around which, this discussion takes place. Once again Smith states, 'in Romans Paul also refers to a church fellowship meal' (Smith 2003, p. 177), except that he does not. He talks about what individuals feel it is appropriate to eat. At no point in the argument does Paul say that the Roman community should eat any particular thing at any particular meal, and the question that is raised over the wine in verse 21 (it is better not to eat meat or drink wine) would sit very strangely with the Lord's Supper as outlined in 1 Corinthians. Finally, there is reference in verses 5–6 to days kept sacred or not, depending on the consideration of each individual, making any suggestion that either Paul or the Roman community kept one day a week special with a celebration of a fellowship meal highly problematic.

Unlike the discussion of Galatians or Romans, there is very little scholarly discussion about the place of what might have become the 'Eucharist' in the Pastoral Epistles. This is not surprising as there is no direct mention of any meal, or anything that might be considered remotely eucharistic, within these texts. It is generally accepted by modern scholarship that these letters are not by Paul and represent a later development of a Pauline school or community (Pietersen 2004, pp. 4–26). They have features that indicate that the communities they represent are becoming more formal and more highly organized. In particular there is considerable discussion about the role of the overseers, deacons and elders within these texts (MacDonald 1988). Some have argued that these texts are proto-church orders (Pietersen 2004, p. 3), others suggest that this is misleading and that the texts are essentially written to challenge certain factions within the community and to bolster the position of Timothy and Titus (Pietersen 2004). If, however, these texts are concerned, in whatever way, with the role and practice of the leaders of the community, including their role in prayer (1 Tim. 2.1–8), in the public reading of scripture and teaching (1 Tim. 4.13; 2 Tim. 4.2) and in pastoral care (1 Tim. 5.1–25; Titus 2.1–15), why is it that they say nothing about meals (Rowland 1985, pp. 242–3)?

There is a condemnation of the 'hypocritical liars' who abstain from certain foods (1 Tim. 4.3) and a comment that if any food is 'received with thanksgiving' (εὐχαριστίας) then it should be considered good. This is not developed, however, into a statement about any kind of regular meal within the community. Timothy is also encouraged to 'stop drinking only water' (1 Tim. 5.23), which suggests that some of the ascetic practices that McGowan identifies in a later generation are already present here (McGowan 1999a, pp. 231–3). If a regular meal was taking place within this community, therefore, what might it have consisted of, and would wine have played any part in it?

The overwhelming lack of evidence for regular meals, with ritual significance, in the corpus of Paul's work, and those other texts that are a product of the school or community associated with him, must be important. I cannot accept that this silence is coincidental and that meals were occurring that had a special place for bread and a cup, blessings, and an eschatological or paschal meaning, but that they were not infringing on Paul's thinking enough to be mentioned in more than one letter. The only real solution is that they were not a regular or frequent part of the life of the communities Paul founded, or, by implication, of Paul's own practice. In my view at least, this lack of evidence suggests even more strongly that the meal in 1 Corinthians was probably an event that occurred less frequently than once a week and could possibly have been an annual event associated with the Passover. What I am proposing, therefore, is that the Lord's Supper was probably a part of the Passover celebrations of the Corinthian community. To justify this assertion, however, the Christian communities beyond Paul's own orbit need to be looked at much more closely, along with any evidence about the possible celebrations of the Passover within Christianity as a whole at this very early date. That will form the basis for the next chapter.

2

The Passion

At the end of the previous chapter I raised the possibility that the meal presented by Paul in 1 Corinthians was an early form of Christian ✓ Passover. This is not the first time that this has been presented, but the idea is usually dismissed, partly because there is very little positive evidence to support it, and partly because the presentation of the idea has often been too specific or too detailed. I am not, in this book, aiming to suggest that the form of an early Christian celebration at the time of the Jewish Passover can ever be known. I am not even suggesting that every Christian community in the middle of the first century must have celebrated a Passover. I am simply offering the possibility that the Lord's Supper, as outlined in 1 Corinthians, was an annual ✓ event, most probably associated with the time of the Jewish Passover. ✓ What I hope to do in this chapter, therefore, is to investigate the various texts and ideas that would be needed to support such a minimal contention.

There is one text in particular that is central to this argument and that is the text of the Last Supper. Paul quotes from this text when discussing the Lord's Supper (1 Cor. 11.23–25), suggesting that such a text, or at least an oral narrative that underlies the text, was available to him in the mid 50s of the first century. The various ous Gospel versions of the text were compiled, at the earliest, much not later in the first century. So what was the source of Paul's quotation? If it is assumed that the meal was a celebration at the time of the Passover, in some way associated with the death and resurrection of Jesus, then the quotation may have come from a larger narrative of the Passion recounted within the context of the celebration. One writer who has suggested this possibility is Etiene Trocmé in his 1965 book, *The Passion as a Paschal Liturgy* (1983). Trocmé's attempt to reconstruct a primitive form of the Paschal liturgy based on much later Christian and Jewish models must be rejected. However, the first half of the book, where he argues that the Passion narrative ✓ had an earlier life, before it was combined with other texts to form the Gospels, does deserve further investigation. If this presentation is considered to be possible, or even desirable, as an explanation of the narrative then that has consequences not just for the account in I Corinthians, but also for an understanding of the Gospel narratives of the Last Supper.

If Paul is quoting from a larger Passion narrative, whether that existed in textual form or as an oral presentation, then that Passion narrative must have included, even at this early stage, an account of the Last Supper. This probably suggests that the story of the Last Supper developed as part of the larger narrative and may never have existed in its own right as a separate unit. Practically all the studies of the 'institution narrative' within liturgical writing have tended to assume the opposite, that in some way the story of the Last Supper is related to the origins of a cultic meal within the Christian community which, while clearly linked to the death and resurrection of Jesus, only comes to be attached to the longer narrative because it has already established itself as the warrant for a weekly event. In this chapter, therefore, I want to propose that the narrative of the Last Supper must be seen as an integral and essential part of the Passion narrative, which in turn is probably independent of the later and longer Gospel accounts. If this can be demonstrated as a plausible reading of the evidence then the possibility of the Passion narrative being developed as part of a very early Christian celebration at the time of the Passover becomes more acceptable. It is in this light, I would suggest, that the accounts of the Last Supper in the various Gospels, as well as in Paul's letter to the Corinthians, need to be analysed.

In this chapter, therefore, I am going to begin with Trocmé's theory that the Passion narrative existed as a separate unit before the final editing of the Gospels. In particular it is necessary to look at the development and construction of Mark's Gospel, as this, according to Trocmé, is the place where the Passion narrative and the other elements of the Gospel first come together. I will then go on to look at the range of evidence that is available for the understanding of the Passover within the first-century Jewish and Christian communities. Unfortunately there is very little evidence for either community at this time, and the danger of reading back into this period material that relates to later developments must always be avoided. I will end the chapter by looking at the Last Supper stories as an integral part of the wider Passion narrative and ask what this says about the way in which they should both be understood from a textual and historical point of view.

Trocmé on the Gospel of Mark

Trocmé begins his analysis of *The Formation of the Gospel According to Mark* by looking at the possible sources of the material contained in the Gospel (1975, pp. 8–86). Having rejected various theories of a 'proto-Mark', Trocmé moves on to look at the kind of material that has gone to make up the current text. He identifies a series of sayings, which could be derived from the tradition (pp. 44–5). He notes the miracle stories, which Trocmé argues could only have come from eyewitness accounts or stories circulating among the Christian communities of Galilee (pp. 51–4). The legends surrounding John the Baptist probably come from the same source (pp. 54–6). There are then a series of narratives that contain sayings-type material: the baptism, the transfiguration and the entry into Jerusalem. These sayings are presented either in the form of a word from God or as commentary on Hebrew Bible sources (pp. 56–9). All this leaves the narrative of the Passion, chapters 14–16, which most commentators recognize as being a single coherent unit of a kind very different from the short, almost disconnected, elements of the first 13 chapters (pp. 59–63).

In discussing the Passion, Trocmé refers to the work of Carrington and Schille in order to explore a possible source for the narrative (Trocmé, 1975, pp. 60–1). Carrington argues that the Passion was 'put together as the *megillah*, or scroll for reading aloud in public, that was used by the primitive Church for the Christian Easter' (Trocmé, 1975, p. 61), while Schille 'thinks that it was the annual commemoration in Jerusalem of Good Friday and Easter that made it necessary to crystallize the memories of the passion' (Trocmé, 1975, p. 61). Both of these authors, as Trocmé rightly comments, provide too much detail for their theories, which are based on later Jewish or Christian models, and do not really fit the religious and social situation of the first Christian communities. However, Schille does suggest that the first day of the celebration may have consisted of an annual meal accompanied by an account of the last night of Jesus before the betrayal and crucifixion.

Trocmé moves on to look in more detail at what the compiler, or editor, of the Gospel appears to be opposed to and what he appears to support. In doing this Trocmé identifies that the compiler of the first 13 chapters of Mark is less antagonistic to the Jews than other Gospel writers, that he has difficulties with other Christians, especially the tradition identified with the disciples, and he has a serious problem with the family of Jesus that Trocmé identifies with James and the leadership of the Christian community in Jerusalem (see also Weeden 1971, p. 50;

Munro 1982, pp. 238–9). This, in part, leads Trocmé to the conclusion that many of the traditions that make up the first 13 chapters of the Gospel, as well as their original compiler, come from the north of Palestine and are in opposition to the community in Jerusalem (1975, pp. 136–7). The causes defended by the first section of Mark reinforce this understanding with a nascent ecclesiology rooted in the idea of Jesus as head of the Church, rather than any understanding of the disciples as leaders in any direct sense (1975, p. 214). The narrative of the Passion, however, presents a very different picture, being decidedly more favourable towards the disciples and more clearly rooted in the Jerusalem context.

Trocmé argues that the first section of Mark derives from a context in which the traditions of Galilee are brought together to form a continuous narrative by an individual who is sympathetic to the needs of the Christian community in that area, a view previously expressed by Carrington and others who tried to discover evidence for an early Christian calendar within the text of the Gospel (Carrington 1952, pp. 80–1). The Passion narrative, however, for both Trocmé and Carrington, existed as a separate document, probably originating within the community in Jerusalem. The two traditions are brought together, according to Trocmé, with a small amount of extra editing, possibly by an individual called Mark, and possibly in Rome, to form the Gospel as it exists today (1975, pp. 215–59).

Trocmé's analysis is detailed and, in its parts, convincing. Many other commentators have come to similar conclusions (for example, Johnson 1960, pp. 220–2). However, it is not a view that has been developed extensively in more recent literature on Mark, with most recent commentaries assuming that Mark is a single coherent document that originated in or around Palestine and/or Rome in about 70–75 CE (for example, Peterson 2000). Smith goes so far as to suggest that 'Mark's passion narrative has been shown in recent research to be largely a creation of the gospel writer' (2003, p. 225). Despite this, however, there are reasons to accept at least the possibility that a Passion narrative existed before the current Gospel was compiled and had been part of the tradition, at least in Jerusalem, from a very early date.

The origins of the Passion narrative

One of the few contemporary authors to raise the possibility of the Passion narrative forming a specific unit with a life prior to the compilation of Mark's Gospel is Gerd Theissen. In *The Gospels in Context* (1992), he notes the fact that many scholars have recognized that the Passion forms a coherent whole, unlike the first half of Mark's Gospel, which is made up of a series of sayings and stories that could be presented entirely separately and in any order (1992, pp. 168–9). However, Theissen asks whether the Passion narrative should begin at 14.1, which he recognizes as forming a natural break in the text. Alternatively it could begin with the arrest at 14.43, or perhaps from the account of the entry in Jerusalem at 11.1. Theissen then goes on to conduct the same kind of analysis of the Passion narrative that has already been described in relation to his work on 1 Corinthians. He begins to explore the people who are mentioned in the text and to ask why they are referred to in the way that they are (1992, pp. 170–89).

Pilate, for example, is referred to by name, but without his title. Meanwhile 'the high priest' is mentioned by his title, but his name is not given. Both of these would have been understandable if the text originated in Jerusalem only a few years after the events portrayed. Likewise, Simon is mentioned as the father of Alexander and Rufus, and Mary is referred to as the mother of the lesser James and Joses. In both cases it is the sons who are presumed to be known to the listener rather than the parents. This places the text within a particular generation, that of Jesus himself or the one immediately following. Third, the reference to places in people's names – Cyrene, Magdala, Arimathia, even Nazareth – are not to places that would have been well known outside of Palestine at the time (Theissen 1992, p. 179; Best 1992, II, p. 857; Miller 2004, p. 157).

Theissen then moves on to a discussion about Barabbas. Having noted that Mark gives no explanation of who he is when he first introduces him in the narrative – he is just 'a man called Barabbas' (Mark 15.7) – Theissen comments that Mark talks about 'the rebels' and 'the insurrection' suggesting that this has to be understood as the most recent insurrection. As there were further riots in Jerusalem under Cuspius Fadus (44–45 CE), Theissen asks whether the story of Barabbas must predate these riots (1992, p. 183). Finally, Theissen draws attention to two anonymous figures in the garden at Gethsemane. One strikes out with a sword and cuts off the ear of a servant of the high priest. The other, following a struggle with the guards in which he loses his clothes, runs off naked. Having looked at various interpretations for the role of these anonymous figures, Theissen suggests that the simplest explanation is that because of their actions these men are in danger from the authorities and therefore probably still alive at the time of the telling of the narrative (1992, pp. 186–7).

47

Drawing on these and other elements of the narrative, Theissen goes on to argue that it is possible that the Passion narrative, probably from 14.43, was developed within the Jerusalem community during the reign of Agrippa I, probably between 41 and 44 CE (1992, p. 198). This was a time, Theissen argues, when the community felt under particular stress with the ever-present possibility of persecution and the death of James. According to Theissen the Passion may have been compiled to enable the community to deal with this situation. As Theissen says,

> 'the life-situation of the oldest Passion tradition is that of a threatened minority whose confession of Jesus (Mark 14.62–63) constantly brings it into danger of denial and failure. The Passion account is a conflict *parenesis* in the form of a narrative of remembered events. (1992, p. 198)

Part of Theissen's argument relates to a specific tradition within biblical scholarship that tries to situate particular passages in their *Sitz im Leben*, the particular time and place in which, or the particular social or political situation against which, the author is writing. Even if Theissen's need to see each passage as being written for a very specific purpose with a very particular context is not accepted, the bare bones of his argument can still be recognized. The evidence that he presents strongly suggests that the Passion narrative, either as presented by Mark, or underlying the account in the Gospel of Mark, originated in Jerusalem within the first generation of the Christian community. This is exactly what would be expected if, as Trocmé (1983) suggests, the narrative may have originated as a Passover text to be read at an annual meal within the Christian community.

Other authors have provided different kinds of evidence that point in the same general direction. Kilpatrick, among others, has noted the Semitic structure of the phrasing in Mark's account of the Last Supper, especially when compared with Paul's account (1983, pp. 21–2). This can be accounted for either through Mark's own background, although most commentators do not stress his Palestinian origins, or through the possibility that he was drawing on a source that had originally been compiled in Aramaic rather than Greek (Black 1969). Sanders makes the comment, having analysed a vast range of the available evidence, that in the account of the trial within the Passion narrative, 'the system as the gospels describe it corresponds to the system that we see in Josephus,' and concludes that 'the trial of Jesus agrees very well with [Josephus'] stories of how things happened' (Sanders, 1992, p. 487; Rivkin, 1986).

48

This suggests that the authors of the Passion narratives knew more about the actual workings of the various authorities in Jerusalem at the time than, say, the compilers of the *Mishnah* some 150 or so years later. None of this evidence can stand on its own, and none of it really supports the position that the Passion and the rest of the Gospel originated as two distinct units, but they do point to the possibility of a very early date for the Passion narrative itself, even the possibility of a date only very shortly after the events it narrates.

Passover celebrations in the earliest Christian communities

Theissen points out that the narrative events of the Passion as provided by Mark assume that Jesus was crucified on the day before the Passover (Theissen, 1992, pp. 166–71). The Sanhedrin would not have met on the day of Passover for a trial, even in these exceptional circumstances. Simon of Cyrene is coming in from the fields when he meets the procession with the cross, again not something he would have done on the day of the feast itself. And Mark says that Jesus was laid in the tomb because it was the 'day of preparation', although he adds 'of the Sabbath' when it is more likely to refer, according to Theissen, to the day of preparation of the Passover (Theissen, 1992, p. 167). Why, then, is Mark, or his source, so keen to state that it is on the Passover, the first day of the feast, that the Last Supper took place?

There is a long and apparently never-ending debate within the literature about whether the Last Supper was, or was not, a Passover meal. Jeremias (1955) is perhaps the most obvious, and clearly the most quoted, advocate of the Passover theory and he argues that the Last Supper was clearly a Passover meal, dismissing all those elements that others have presented to demonstrate otherwise. However, there are others who are just as convincing in arguing the opposite position. This is usually done from the perspective of the Gospel of John, where the text does not even try to suggest that the Last Supper was a Passover meal and Jesus is killed at the same time as the sacrifice of the lambs in the Temple on the eve of the feast itself. Others look more closely at the texts in the other Gospels, and this is where the confusion lies. A more original solution comes from Jaubert, and those who follow her work, who suggests that there were in fact two dates for the Passover at this period in Jewish history (Jaubert 1957; Nodet and Taylor 1998, pp. 21–2). The Qumran sect, and those who followed the Jubilees calendar, aimed to fix each feast to a particular day of the week, and so the Passover begins on a

Tuesday evening. Meanwhile other Jews, following an older and more traditional calendar, celebrate the Passover on the Friday. There are a few hints in much later literature that some Patristic writers saw the chronology of the week as beginning with the Last Supper on the Tuesday (a celebration of the sectarian Passover) with the crucifixion on the Friday (to coincide with the majority Passover). This is interesting, and assumes that Christian communities, or some among these communities, followed the calendar of the minority Jewish sects, but the evidence for this tends to be fairly limited (Nodet and Taylor 1998). I would argue that there is a much clearer narrative solution to this problem.

We have to begin with the recognition, as Theissen does to a point, that the Gospel of Mark is unclear and even contradictory on this issue. Mark is keen to state that the Last Supper was a Passover meal and yet all the evidence from the narrative structure of the Passion suggests that it could not possibly be a Passover meal. Rather than trying to square this circle, it is better to acknowledge that the text itself is confused and then the question can be asked as to why that might be the case. I would suggest that if what I have been trying to propose within this chapter is correct, then at least one possible answer can be provided. If the actual events of the Passion took place around Passover (perhaps even with the timing that John presents, with the crucifixion occurring at the time of the sacrifice of the lambs) then this forms the earliest strata of the story, a simple retelling of what happened among those who were closely involved. If, however, the principal time for the telling of the story becomes the celebration of a Christian meal at the time of the Passover, then it would clearly be in the interests of the tellers of the story to suggest that the meal contained within the story was the Passover meal itself, as it is this meal that is being repeated and not the death and resurrection. The fact that this leaves glaring contradictions in the text is not an issue that would concern the first tellers of the story. By the time Mark gets hold of the narrative it is this combined, contradictory text that he discovers and, with minor editing in places to link it in with the first half of the Gospel, he uses it pretty much as he found it, complete with the confusion over the date (which he may not even have noticed). This is a plausible account of the text and, in a circumstantial fashion, may even add some further evidence to the case I am constructing. It does leave one further question, however: what kind of event might that very earliest Christian commemoration of the Passion at Passover have been?

In order to explore this further, the next stage in my argument must be to explore the evidence that is available relating to the celebration of the Passover within the earliest Christian communities. Like so much else in this field this evidence is not at all conclusive. However, the evidence that does exist shows that the possibility of a very early celebration of the Passover within Christian communities is highly likely, even if it is not possible to say what such a celebration might have consisted of.

The earliest evidence comes from the biblical texts themselves. Mark's insistence that the death of Jesus took place around the time of the Passover, and the agreement about this within all four Gospels, even if they do not agree entirely about the exact relationship between the feast and the crucifixion, suggests that the Passover was important to the early Christian communities (Shepherd 1960, pp. 34–7). There are other references to the Passover in the Gospels, and Paul picks up Passover themes in the first letter to the Corinthians and elsewhere. The first letter of Peter also picks up similar themes, as do one or two other texts within the New Testament. None of these texts, however, state explicitly that the Christian community celebrated a Passover and the themes can be related to general reflections on the Hebrew scriptures as well as they can to specific celebrations within the community. Galatians 4.10 suggests that Paul, at least, did not celebrate any Jewish feasts, whether annual or new moon. However, it is difficult to square this with his stated aim at the end of 1 Corinthians to wait till Pentecost before leaving Ephesus (16.8), and Acts 20.16 where it is stated that Paul wished to get back to Jerusalem to celebrate the feast of Pentecost (Talley, 1986, pp. 4–5). It is unclear what the Galatians passage actually refers to, but the weight of evidence certainly suggests that a significant proportion of the early Christian community continued to celebrate the Jewish feasts and Passover in particular.

We do have a 'Paschal sermon', the *Peri Pascha*, preached in the second half of the second century and attributed to Melito of Sardis (Cohick 2000). However, once again, this is simply a text that draws on paschal and resurrection themes, although interestingly it takes the traditional Passover text (Exodus 12.1–30) as its starting point. Many authors have pointed to this to show that in the first few centuries of the Church Pascha, or Easter, was celebrated as a feast which covered the whole of salvation history and in particular both the cross and the resurrection (Talley 1986, pp. 12–13; Bradshaw 2002, p. 83). Pascha, therefore, is stated in books on the history of the Christian calendar as the earliest, and originally the only, specifically Christian feast, although some recent scholarship has suggested that Pentecost might actually have been the primary feast, at least for the Christian community in Jerusalem (Ray, 2004, pp. 3–30; Nodet and Taylor 1998). Either way, the Pascha of the latter half of the second century is clearly not a Christian Passover and may or may not have much to do with the practice of the first-century communities.

Another text that is dated to the middle of the second century and that scholars suggest originated in Asia Minor is the *Epistula Apostolorum* (Elliott 1993, pp. 555–88). Among other things, Talley suggests that this text appears to be arguing for the observance of the Passover against some communities that don't observe it and probably never have done. There is a claim for apostolic authority for the celebration and therefore a suggestion that some of the Christian communities in Asia may not have developed the practice (Talley 1986, p. 5). Chapter 15 of the Ethiopic edition of the text provides details of a celebration of the Passover in which an all-night vigil is followed by the celebration of 'my agape and my remembrance' (Elliott 1993, p. 565). Talley, along with most other commentators, assumes that this *agape* and remembrance is a Eucharist, but in many other texts from the same date '*agape*' is treated as a charitable meal rather than a Eucharist as such and the reference to remembrance is difficult to interpret, so the exact nature of this event is very unclear (Talley 1986, pp. 5–6). I will come back to look at this text again in Chapter 6. What is clear, however, is that what the *Epistula Apostolorum* describes is not what Paul presents in 1 Corinthians. Over 100 years separate the two documents and many things had developed in that time, not least the worship of the Christian community.

Also, in the later half of the second century a dispute arose over the dating of Easter and this is the first real evidence for the celebration of a Christian feast at, or around, the time of the Jewish Passover (Talley 1986, pp. 18–27; Bradshaw 2002). Put very simply, the debate focused on whether Easter was to be celebrated on the 14/15 Nissan, which is the traditional dating of the Passover within the Jewish tradition, or on the Sunday following. Again, very loosely, it appears that the Christian community in Asia Minor stuck to the Passover dating, while Rome and the rest of the Christian world preferred the Sunday option (Martimort et al., 1983, pp. 33–4). A letter from Irenaeus, preserved by Eusebius in *Ecclesiastical History* (*EH* 5:24:14), can be read to suggest that before Soter (165 CE) there may not have been any celebration of the Pascha in Rome at all, but I will come back to this letter in more detail in Chapter 7.

In itself this debate is far too late to read back any specific suggestions relating to the first 50 years or so of Christian history. However, Eusebius also records a letter from Polycrates, the Bishop of Ephesus, who claims that the Jewish dating can be traced back to Melito, Polycarp, Philip and the Apostle John, so claiming apostolic authority for the practice (*EH* 5:24:2–7). As Talley notes, Victor, the Bishop of Rome who opposed this practice, offers no similarly ancient tradition for celebrating Easter on the Sunday (1986, p. 19). In fact Talley suggests that the origins of the Sunday Pascha are to be dated to the first non-Jewish bishops of Jerusalem in around 135 CE (1986, pp. 20–7). The suggestion that there is a tradition, therefore, within the Asian communities that wishes to celebrate the death and resurrection of Jesus on the same day as the Jewish Passover, implies that this was a date that was taken over from Jewish practice into the Christian communities of this area at a very early date.

What none of the texts can tell us, however, is how the earliest Christian communities actually celebrated their Passover, or the commemoration of Jesus' death and resurrection at the time of the Passover. There is circumstantial evidence for the inclusion of a meal but no evidence, or even any suggestion within the evidence that this was a Passover meal in the Jewish sense of that term. This is important. It is easy to assume that any reference to a Christian Passover meal must have been similar, if not identical, to the meal outlined in later Jewish documents complete with lamb, bitter herbs and other items as well as bread and wine. There is no good reason why this should be the case. All the evidence that is available (the Last Supper accounts themselves and Paul's comments in 1 Corinthians among others) suggest that the meal Christians shared at the time of the Passover did not include meat, and may not have included the bitter herbs or the other items associated with a Jewish Passover. As Paul says, 'Christ, our Passover lamb, has been sacrificed' (1 Cor. 5.7) and John's Gospel goes out of its way to stress that Jesus died at the moment the lambs were being sacrificed. There would be no need of a lamb at a Christian celebration at Passover. Jesus is the lamb and he has already been sacrificed. What is needed is some means of sharing in the sacrifice, in the body (and blood?) of the lamb, and that is achieved through the reinterpretation of the bread. At this point the feast becomes something very different, a meal centred on the breaking and sharing of bread. I will come back to this discussion in Chapters 3 and 5, but I do want to stress that when I talk of the possibility of an annual Christian commemorative meal at the time of the Jewish Passover, I am not, in the usually accepted sense of the term, talking of a 'Christian Passover'. Here I do very clearly part company with Trocmé.

Finally, therefore, it is unfortunate for my purposes that while it is possible to argue that the emphasis on the Passover, which is so strong in the Passion narratives, encouraged a later Christian community to use this feast as a time to commemorate the events of the crucifixion and resurrection, it is equally possible to argue that the early example of Christian communities celebrating these events within the context of a Christian commemoration at the time of the Jewish Passover led the Passion narratives to emphasize the date. Either is possible, both are plausible, and it is not really fruitful to go any further with this discussion at this time. All that is left, therefore, is the possibility that some kind of Passion narrative was originally composed, within Jerusalem shortly after the events themselves took place, to be proclaimed as part of an early Christian commemoration, which probably included a shared meal, on an annual basis, at the time of the Passover. None of the evidence rules such a possibility out of hand. The question of the role of the account of the Last Supper within the Passion narrative as a whole, however, still remains and this is what I wish to turn to in the final sections of this chapter.

The accounts of the Last Supper

The accounts of the Last Supper within the Passion narratives have probably generated more scholarly comment than any other single passage, especially within that literature that deals with the origins of the Eucharist. The main problem is that there are four accounts, each of which is very similar, but all of which, in their own small way, are different from the others. It is in attempting to reconcile these differences that most scholars have been engaged. Essentially there are three distinct issues. These relate to the similarities and differences between the four accounts, the relationship between these accounts and the meal that Jesus might have shared with his disciples on the night before he was betrayed, and the relationship between these accounts and any meal that the community for whom the texts were written might have celebrated. I have already dealt with some aspects of the second of these issues in my discussion of the Passover, although I will restate the arguments again very briefly in what follows; it is the first and third issues that I wish to explore in more detail in this section.

When the texts themselves are analysed there are both similarities and differences. These can be summarized as questions of order, and the differences in what is said over each of the elements, more specifically the use of the words 'this is my body/blood' and 'do this in remembrance of me'. It is in relation to these details that many authors aim to explore which of the four accounts is the oldest or more original (Jeremias 1955; Léon-Dufour 1987, pp. 157–79). There are four accounts. However, in practice Matthew follows Mark so closely, only really adding 'for the forgiveness of sins' after the words over the cup, so for practical purposes there are only three versions. The Mark/Matthew text has bread then wine and 'this is my body/blood' with a covenantal elaboration of the blood imagery (Mark 14.22–25; Matt. 26.26–29). Paul also has bread and a cup. The words 'this is my body which is for you' are used over the bread but the words over the wine refer only to the 'cup', which 'is the new covenant in my blood'. In both cases Jesus tells the disciples to 'do this in remembrance of me' (1 Cor. 11.23–25). Luke, depending on the text that is followed, has a cup, then bread and then another cup. The words are similar to those used by Paul, although there is no command to do this in remembrance in relation to either cup (Luke 22.17–20).

Léon-Dufour identifies two 'tendencies' behind these different presentations: the Antiochene tradition that links Paul and Luke, and the Markan tradition that links Mark and Matthew (1987, pp. 96–7). While it might be necessary to question the link between the Paul/Luke tradition and Antioch, as well as the exact nature of the relationship between Paul and Luke, the division into two different traditions is relatively clear and unproblematic. Léon-Dufour also identifies two other 'traditions' that cut across the four accounts in a slightly different way (1987, pp. 82–95). He distinguishes between what he calls the cultic tradition, the words over the bread and the cup, and the testimony tradition, the claim from Jesus that he will not eat of the meal again or drink of the fruit of the vine until the end of the age. This distinction helps to show how the texts have been put together and Léon-Dufour provides a very detailed analysis of the various words and texts used by each of the four accounts. What is interesting, however, is that each of the accounts combines both the cultic words and the testimony, and Léon-Dufour's own, very tentative, attempt to uncover the original words of Jesus also combines a cultic statement over the bread with a testimony statement over the wine (1987, pp. 175–6). This may seem to make the division rather irrelevant to a deeper analysis.

The most hotly debated issue in the scholarly literature concerns the place of the first cup in Luke's account (Kilpatrick 1983, pp. 28–42). This sets Luke apart very significantly from the other three narratives and is clearly at odds with later eucharistic practice. The other issue is that the manuscript traditions do not agree at this point, with some manuscripts leaving out the first cup, some having both, and a small number, the so called Western tradition, leaving out verses 19b–20 and so making no reference to the second cup (Kilpatrick 1983, pp. 28–9). It is clear that the earliest transcribers and copyists of the manuscripts also had difficulties with this aspect of Luke's account.

There are a few scholars who would want to suggest that the first cup is a later addition to the text, but the majority opinion today is that the original version of Luke's account either contained a reference to two cups, one before the meal and one following it, or that the original version only had one cup before the meal (Kilpatrick 1983, pp. 28–34). This is primarily based on the view that there would be no good reason for a later redactor to add the first cup if it was not already there, but it is clear why some copyists may remove it if they wished to bring Luke's account into line with the other narratives from Matthew, Mark and Paul. The question of whether two cups may have been original, or just the first, depends on whether verses 19b–20 are written by Luke or are an interpolation based on 1 Corinthians (Kilpatrick 1983, pp. 33–4).

The next question at this point, therefore, is to ask why Luke may have talked about a cup before the meal at all, and here the literature is divided and no clear consensus emerges. Some claim that this reflects the practice of the community that Luke belonged to, a practice that died out shortly after the writing of the Gospel. Others, with slightly more evidence, have suggested that Luke was trying to make the narrative fit the model of the Passover meal, which begins with a cup of blessing (and also ends with a cup) (Kilpatrick 1983, pp. 39–42). If this is the case then such an argument would probably support two of my general contentions within this chapter: that the narratives of the Last Supper do not reflect any current practices, either of the author or their communities, and that the narrative is essentially to be seen as part of a wider Passion narrative that is associated with the Passover in some sense. If this is the case, however, then why is it that the other institution narratives do not refer to a number of cups, or follow the pattern presented by Luke? Kilpatrick simply suggests that Mark only made a couple of minor changes to suggest that the meal was a Passover, primarily adding 14.12–17, while Luke, who had Mark's text in front of him, chose to go further and to adapt the structure of the meal as well (1983, p. 39). This is certainly plausible but can never be finally demonstrated one way or the other.

The questions raised by the first cup in Luke's account, therefore, remain open. This leaves two points that need to be stressed. The first concerns the hesitancy in the Luke/Paul version to say 'this is my blood'. This is unusual because while a Jewish reluctance to claim that we are drinking blood, which is forbidden under the law, is understandable, it is the traditionally less Jewish texts that seem to be most concerned about this. Kilpatrick argues that Luke-Acts, of all the texts in the New Testament, is most concerned about avoiding blood in food and that this may be reflected in the Last Supper account (1983, p. 35). For Paul, however, the idea of the cup being associated with the blood of Christ is not an issue elsewhere in 1 Corinthians. Both 10.16 and 11.27 make explicit reference to the drinking of the 'blood of Christ' or the 'blood of the Lord' (Kilpatrick 1983, p. 25). It may, therefore, be Paul's source, whatever that might have been, that is responsible for the lack of reference within the tradition. Léon-Dufour relates this distinction to the importance Paul and Luke place on the idea of covenant within their presentation of the cultic tradition, and the difference between this understanding and that of Mark (1987, pp. 144–54).

The other issue is that it is, in fact, only the Luke/Paul version that adds 'do this in remembrance of me', although if Luke 22.19b–20 is not part of the original text then this removes Luke as well. This is important because it is this statement which leads most authors to suggest that the text reports Jesus' own command to perform the rite on a regular basis or, alternatively, that the text reflects the author's current practice in the repetition of the rite. Léon-Dufour, among others, claims that the command to perform the rite is implicit in the Markan tradition. This is presented in the form of a dialogue that assumes a response. No such response is mentioned within the text and therefore, it must be assumed, within the hearers of the account. It is this that makes this a cultic text for Léon-Dufour (1987, pp. 195–6). However, there is nothing explicit in the Matthew/Mark version to suggest that the meal should be repeated at all. This is significant as such a command would not be necessary if the whole narrative was constructed to be read at a celebration of the death and resurrection of Jesus. In this case the meal is not the real focus of the text, it is not the dramatic highlight that the compiler wishes to draw attention to, it is simply part of the build-up. Certainly, I am suggesting that the text may have been read within the context of a meal even from the very earliest times, hence the need for the account of the meal within the text, but at this point it is not the meal that is the focus. Therefore there is no need for an explicit statement making reference to repetition. In the context of Paul's argument in 1 Corinthians, however, this is not the case. Paul has chosen to focus on the meal and it is the repetition of that meal which is precisely the point at issue. If this were the case, therefore, then it might suggest that it was Paul, or potentially the source that Paul is drawing on, that has added this command and that it never was a part of the original narrative. This also suggests that verses 19b–20 in Luke's account are a later addition based on a reading of Paul's account in 1 Corinthians.

This leads on to the final issues in this section. How far does the account represent a true account of a meal that Jesus had with his disciples before his death, or, alternatively, does it reflect a rite that is performed within the community that the author either belongs to or is writing for? Alikin is very blunt in dismissing the possibility that the Last Supper account reflects an actual meal that Jesus shared with his disciples (2009, p. 108). This is suggested on two main grounds. First, it seems strange to Alikin that if Jesus had instituted a meal with reference to his body and blood and a strict instruction to do this in memory of him, others, such as the compilers of the *Didache*, would have ignored it. Alikin's second argument relates to Jesus' own foreknowledge of his death and the saving power of that death, which is implied in the texts of the Last Supper but which, in Alikin's view, cannot reflect the understanding of the historical Jesus. The second argument is more theological and difficult to engage with in a direct sense. The first can be tackled much more easily. Jesus may well have held a meal of the form Mark suggests, but that it never occurred to any of those present to repeat it as such, as in Mark's account there was no command to do this in his memory. Even if there was a command to 'do this' it is possible that Jesus was not assuming that a weekly meal would result. As Higgins says, 'the fact that the Church came to remember the Lord at the weekly breaking of bread and not an annual Passover should not be brought against the strong possibility that what Jesus expected to happen was the latter' (1952, p. 55). Of course, it is impossible to know what Jesus intended and from my point of view the question is largely irrelevant. If the Last Supper narrative is, and always was, an integral part of the Passion narrative and not a separate unit that was related to any weekly meal within the early Christian community then the historicity of the whole Passion is what needs to be questioned, not the specific details of the meal itself.

Alikin is very clear, however, that the account in Mark reflects the practice that Mark knew, that the account in Luke reflected the practice Luke knew and that the account in Paul reflected the practice of the Lord's Supper in Corinth (2009, pp. 104–16). It is probably the Pauline version that other scholars have seen as being a clear reflection of the practice, either at Corinth or within some other community that Paul is associated with, perhaps Antioch, if that is where this account originated. I have dealt with this in the previous chapter and do not wish to repeat that material again here. It is important to look, therefore, at those authors who claim that the Markan or the Lucan accounts may, in some way, reflect the contemporary practice of their communities. I will explore this in more detail in the following chapter.

Overall, the discussions about the Last Supper are inconclusive. The vast majority of commentators have looked at this text through the two thousand years of history associated with the Eucharist and there is clearly not enough evidence within the text itself to be able to make any clear statement about whether it is based on a factual meal or even whether it had any specific relationship to any meal shared within the earliest Christian community. Any attempt to relate these texts to specific meals must, ultimately, be speculation, like so much else in this field.

One thing that is clear, however, is that practically all those who have argued about these texts and their significance have done so by first of all removing them from their wider textual context. It is as a distinct textual unit, covering just the details of the meal, or more specifically, the sharing of bread and wine at the meal, that this narrative has concerned commentators, especially those with a liturgical interest. There has been little attempt to widen that context and to ask whether these accounts take on a different complexion if they are considered within the account of the Passion as a whole. This, however, is the logic of Trocmé's position and it is to this way of understanding the texts that I wish to return in the final section of this chapter.

Retelling the Passion

Smith says of the account of the Last Supper, 'in Mark . . . the text is enclosed in a narrative context, just as are the other Jesus stories, without any obvious sense that it is intended to mirror liturgical practices in the Markan community, or, if it is, how it is to do so' (Smith and Taussig 1990, p. 40). What I want to do in this final section is to ask whether it is legitimate, on textual and narrative grounds, to see the Last Supper account as an integral part of the Passion narratives and, if so, what this says about the role of the Last Supper as a distinct element within that text.

It is obvious that Mark, or who ever edited the final version of the text, drew together the various sources and linked them together in an almost seamless fashion. This will inevitably have led to some reworking of a Passion narrative that might have existed alone. Miller, for example, following Barton, raises the question of whether the story of the anointing of Jesus (14.3–9) is a freestanding story within the tradition that is slotted into the narrative by Mark to add extra commentary to the events (Miller 2004, p. 129; Barton 1991, p. 231). There may, of course, be other such elements that were added, or adapted by Mark when he prepared the final text. It is impossible to get back, therefore, to the narrative that might have existed before Mark edited it and it is not a reconstruction as such that I wish to achieve.

A number of attempts to provide a structural analysis of the Markan Passion narrative have also been provided. Léon-Dufour, for example, treats the first half of the narrative, what he describes as the 'private passion', as a distinct unit (Mark 14.1–52). This sees its climax in the story of Gethsemane and recounts the slow realization of the inevitability of Jesus' death and his own free acceptance of that death (1987, pp. 186–7). The Last Supper falls into this structure as one stage on the journey towards full realization. This is followed by the 'public passion' of the trials and the crucifixion (Mark 14.53 – 15.47). Such a reading, and many others like it, does make sense of the text and provides a narrative logic to that text. It does not, however, really answer the question of why the account of the meal is an important part of the narrative or how the structure of the narrative may relate to the wider context of reading as part of the meal itself.

One possible solution to this problem, albeit a highly speculative one, is offered by Feely-Harnik in a book originally published in 1981 (1994). Feely-Harnik is an anthropologist and her purpose for writing the book was to set the Eucharist in the early Christian community within the wider context of food, and ideas about food, within the contemporary Jewish communities. There are some very interesting and impressive elements to the book, but it suffers from two major flaws. It is essentially a structuralist analysis and therefore fails to contextualize the texts that are being discussed. This allows Feely-Harnik to draw together quotes and references from across the New Testament and beyond to support various different assertions, without ever analysing one particular text in any great depth. Second, Feely-Harnik writes as though the obsession with food and who should eat with whom is something distinctive to the Jewish community and that is clearly not the case. As Douglas points out in one of the papers that Feely-Harnik quotes as a founding text for her own methodology, food, eating and other natural processes are used as symbolic markers by most, if not all, societies the world over (Douglas 1972).

Accepting these critiques, however, Feely-Harnik raises a number of interesting questions about the account of the Last Supper and its relation to the Passover (1994, pp. 107–48). She presents a model for the Passover ritual derived from the *Mishnah*, which she acknowledges was compiled some 150 or more years after the events described in the Passion (1994, p. 121). However, she claims that the basic structure of the rite probably did not change although the texts, and particularly the *Haggadah*, the telling of the events that are commemorated in the Passover, would clearly have developed and would probably have taken a number of very diverse forms at the time of Jesus depending on the different group or family involved. The most important element of the ritual structure that Feely-Harnik identifies is the use of four glasses of wine and the order of the various foodstuffs eaten at the meal (1994, p. 121).

According to the *Mishnah Pesahim*, and supported by other documents from the same kind of period, there would have been a glass of wine at the beginning of the meal, a second to accompany the laying out of the food, a third at the end of the meal and a fourth following the singing of psalms (Feely-Harnik 1994, pp. 121–4). Each of these would have been accompanied by a blessing. In relation to food, alongside the unleavened bread and the lamb there would have been lettuce, a mixture of fruit, nuts and spices, and the dish of bitter herbs. The point that Feely-Harnik makes is that all of the accounts of the Last Supper, even those that are insistent on the fact that this is a Passover meal, only ever include one and at most two glasses of wine, and the only food mentioned is the bread (1994, p. 126).

This causes some problems. What happens to the rest of the ritual? If the first cup of wine and the bread are the only elements that Jesus actually engaged with, and changed in terms of their meaning, then this is all that the narrator needs to say. If the meal was not really a Passover, and therefore did not have all the other ritual paraphernalia as outlined in the *Mishnah* (the blessing of bread and wine was an important part of all communal meals), then again this kind of detail does not need to be mentioned. If the ritual of the Passover developed over the hundred or so years from the Last Supper to the *Mishnah* then what is seen in the text may be an earlier, simpler version. All of these are possible explanations and have been offered by scholars within the literature. Feely-Harnik, however, notes two other elements of the account that are at odds not just with the *Mishnah*, but also with scriptural laws on the eating of the Passover. First, it is stated that the Passover should be eaten within the family unit and, while Jesus had clearly redefined what a family unit should be in his earlier teaching, it is unusual to see the Passover celebrated by a group of unrelated men in this way (1994,

p. 144). Second, the scriptures are clear that nobody should leave the house following the eating of the meal, in remembrance of the original Passover night, and yet Jesus, after the singing of the final psalms, leaves with his disciples and goes to the Garden of Gethsemane (1994, p. 145).

Once again it is possible to counter both these points with a statement that the Last Supper cannot have been a Passover or that Jesus was deliberately flouting the law here as at other times, or that the law was not as fixed and clear at this time as it was to become (Jeremias 1955). Feely-Harnik, however, offers another, literary, solution. She claims that the insistence on the Passover allusions are important and she argues that the Passion narrative has to be seen as a whole as a possible Passover *Haggadah* structured around an extended meal which includes the trials, crucifixion and resurrection (1994, pp. 144–8).

Feely-Harnik structures her analysis around the four cups of the Mishnaic Passover. What is presented in the Last Supper, she suggests, is only the first of these cups. The second comes in the Garden of Gethsemane, the third in the rejected cup of bitter wine at the crucifixion and the fourth in the vinegar drunk just before Jesus dies. Jesus himself is the lamb at the centre of the meal and the bitter herbs and other dishes fit in and around the rest of the narrative (1994, p. 145). This is an ingenious and interesting approach to the narrative and one that fits well with the kind of analysis that I am trying to present. It cannot, however, be offered as proof that the Passion existed in a distinct form or that it ever acted as a *Haggadah* to any Christian Passover. An analysis such as Feely-Harnik's, however, does indicate that scholars do have to take the text seriously and does offer one way in which the Last Supper can be seen not as an account of an actual event, but rather as an integral part of a wider literary structure. There are no doubt other ways in which this could be constructed and as it is impossible to know what a pre-Markan Passion narrative may have looked like, and that there would inevitably have been a number of different versions of this essentially oral narrative, then it is impossible to say definitively, this is how it should be. What is offered, through Feely-Harnik's work, is just one possibility among many.

This brings me back to my final point. The phrase that is quoted most often from Paul's account of the Last Supper to suggest that the Lord's Supper was a weekly meal is his closing sentence, 'For whenever you eat this bread or drink this cup, you proclaim the Lord's death until he comes' (1 Cor. 11:26). The question has often been asked about why the eating and drinking is in some way a 'proclaiming'. How is the proclamation as such being understood? However, if this account was read within the context of a retelling of the full Passion then this sentence makes perfect sense. As Bruce suggests, 'the verb you proclaim (Gk *katangellete*) cannot be satisfied by anything less than a public narration of the death of Christ as the *haggadah* or *heiros logos* which explained the act' (1971, pp. 113–14).

The account of the Last Supper, therefore, does not suggest that the meal in 1 Corinthians has to be understood as a weekly meal. In fact the opposite may even be true: it adds extra weight to the possibility that this was an annual event. The Last Supper, however, is not the only account of a meal in the Gospels and Acts, and these other accounts have often been presented as evidence of a weekly, or at least a reasonably regular, meal within the earliest Christian communities, so it is to these accounts that I turn in the next chapter.

3

Other New Testament Texts

While the majority of the debates about the Eucharist in the New Testament focus on the narratives of the Last Supper and the Lord's Supper, these are not the only texts that are referred to. Many commentators note that meals play a significant role in the development of the Synoptic Gospels and have an important place within the Acts of the Apostles. The sixth chapter of John's Gospel is also understood by many scholars as being explicitly related to eucharistic themes, although there is considerable debate about how these themes related to actual practice. Finally there are references to sacrificial imagery in both the letter to the Hebrews and the Revelation of John, which some scholars relate implicitly or explicitly to ideas of the Eucharist. To limit the discussion, therefore, to just four passages does not do justice to the full range of texts that are available. Also, while many other writers may agree that the evidence from 1 Corinthians and the accounts of the Last Supper do not of themselves suggest a weekly meal, it is often asserted that the wider emphasis on meals in the Synoptic Gospels, specific references in Acts, and the wider discussion in John and other texts all come together to provide a convincing case for a weekly cultic meal within the earliest Christian communities (Smith 2003).

In this chapter, therefore, I wish to look at the other evidence and to ask what it does and does not indicate for the practice of meals within the various Christian communities that developed within 100 years of the death of Christ. There are two points, however, that I would want to stress before I look at the specific details. The first is that even within the New Testament the different texts come from very different times and places, and while a discussion of Luke, or John, for example, may indicate something of the practice of the community for which that specific text was written, it cannot automatically be made to speak for the whole of the Christian community for a period of over 100 years (Bauer 1971). Each item of evidence must be judged on its own terms before the different items can then be brought together in order to explore some possible common themes. The other point I need to stress is that not every account of a meal must be read as though it related to what was later understood as being 'eucharistic'. All references to meals, or other forms of eating and sharing food, must be judged entirely in their√ own terms.

Meals in the Gospel of Luke

There are a number of meals mentioned in the Gospel of Luke that punctuate the narrative of the ministry of Jesus (Heil 1999). McGowan points out that, according to Luke, Jesus is rarely the host at the various meals he attends during his earthly ministry (2004, pp. 101–15). This leads him to argue that there is probably no immediate link between these formal meals within the Gospel and the Eucharist. Having made this point, however, McGowan does suggest that the feeding of the five thousand and the resurrection meals are influenced by church practices and may, therefore, have eucharistic overtones. This raises the question, however, about the nature of the community the author of Luke is familiar with and whether a regular cultic or fellowship meal was part of the practice of that community. It is necessary to take one step back, therefore, and ask what scholars have said about Luke's community before coming back to look at the various meals within the Gospel.

The authors of the Gospels attributed to Matthew and Mark are usually assumed to come out of the same social context, and to be writing for Christians within the same social context as would have been familiar to Jesus and his disciples (Trocmé 1975; Sim 1998; Peterson 2000). This is generally understood as being essentially Jewish, probably rural, and led by itinerant 'charismatic' preachers. At some level there is a certain amount of circular argumentation going on here. The nature and form of the community of the author is developed through an analysis of the internal evidence of the text and so the community of the author is bound, in many respects, to reflect the community portrayed in the text. Having said this, the geographical and social setting of the communities from which the authors of these two Gospels are usually said to have come is never that far from the Galilee of Jesus himself (Theissen 1989, pp. 236–52). In the case of Luke, however, things are very different.

If, for example, the Luke of the text is assumed to be the 'Luke' whom tradition has presented as the author of the text, then the discussion begins to focus on a single individual, and one with a considerable range of different social experiences, rather than on the 'community' that is often seen as the origin of the Gospels of Matthew and Mark (Peterson 2000). If the authorial Luke was including the practice of his own community within the text then it would be necessary to ask which community, and at what time in the author's life? If the author is the Luke of the text then he would have witnessed considerable changes over time from his first links with the Christian community through to the time of writing, and he would have experienced a wide range of probably very different practices in many different cities, from Jerusalem, through Antioch, to the cities of Asia Minor, possibly Crete and certainly Rome. It is part of the argument that I am presenting in this text to suggest that there was no common practice at this very early time, and so which practice is it that this Luke is reflecting? If this is true of a potential 'authorial Luke' it must also be true of any anonymous author who may have compiled the text many years later. This author, like those of Matthew and Mark, also had a history, would potentially have experienced a number of different communities, and may have had a choice as to which kind of meal practice known to him to include in the text. This fact is often overlooked in the more simplistic assertions of the influence of the communities of Matthew, Mark or Luke on the texts of the Gospels.

A number of commentators, however, make a very clear distinction between the Luke of the text and the author of Luke-Acts, situating the text clearly within a Christian community, probably consisting of both Jews and Gentiles, within an eastern city of the Roman Empire, although there is no evidence within the text to suggest which city this might be (Esler 1987). If this is the case then it is possible to argue that the social context of that community, and its own concerns about sharing in a fellowship meal, can be seen to underpin many of the meal stories within Luke-Acts. Esler takes this position to an extreme to argue that the question of whether Jews and Gentiles can share in 'table-fellowship' is one of the guiding features of the whole double text (1987, pp. 71–109). Esler's argument is convincing, but only if Jews of the first century would have had a serious problem in eating with Gentiles, and more recent literature on this issue is much more ambivalent than Esler's very rigid position suggests (Barclay 2001).

What is clear, however, is that whether the author of the Gospel is the Luke of the text, or whether he is simply claiming a pseudonym and is rooted in an eastern Roman city, it is very likely that he would not have had any real experience of the kind of social world inhabited by Jesus in the rural surroundings of Galilee. This can be shown through careful textual analysis of the Gospel itself (Theissen 1992). It also means that the meals presented in the Gospel are unlikely to reflect anything that the author might have experienced. These are stories that he has inherited from other sources and he is either faithfully reflecting those sources (in their social and cultural context at least) or is inventing a tradition, and probably making significant errors based on a lack of shared experience. Given the way Luke develops the one source that is known, that of Mark, it is probably fair to accept that Luke is not reflecting his own experience, but rather that of his sources, and to that extent the same experience as that of Matthew and Mark. Luke's meal stories, therefore, cannot really indicate anything directly about Luke's own experience of meals within the various early Christian communities that he inhabited, whoever the author of Luke might have been. This must be true of the feeding of the five thousand just as it is of many of the other meal stories presented. It is unlikely, therefore, that these stories reflected later practice associated with the author's own community.

Smith identifies four kinds of meal within Luke's Gospel and asks which, if any, might reflect the practice of the historical Jesus (2003, p. 223). He dismisses those that are shared with Pharisees, and also those relating to miraculous feeding, while focusing much more attention on the meals Jesus shares with his disciples and those that relate to eating and drinking with tax collectors and sinners. While recognizing that Jesus must have shared meals with his disciples and, following recent critical opinion (2003, p. 222), suggesting that meals with tax collectors and sinners must have played some part in Jesus' life and teaching, Smith concludes that all the meals of the Gospel are essentially literary constructions that draw on the wider banqueting ideology of the period (2003, pp. 253–72).

What this ideology highlights, according to Smith, is, on the one side, the tradition of the messianic banquet and the image of the wedding feast, and on the other the tradition of eating with the outcast and marginal in Jewish society (Esler 1987, pp. 189–93). These traditions are clearly linked in the way that Luke presents his material. The messianic banquet is an important image for understanding the nature of the apocalyptic within Second Temple Jewish thought and in early Christianity (Smith 2003, pp. 166–71). This imagery is developed in those meal stories where Jesus is either a guest at banquets held by others, or, more commonly, in those parables where meals are central to the story. It is an image of the 'kingdom' that is being developed here, within a specific eschatological discourse. The 'kingdom' is also central to the meals where the poor, the sinners and other marginal people are included in the feast. Smith is undoubtedly correct to see these as literary tropes. This is not to say that these traditions do not reflect actual meals that Jesus may have shared with such people. Perrin argues that the idea of eating with sinners and tax collectors would have been so shocking that it must reflect a practice undertaken by Jesus rather than a story constructed by the Christian community (1967, pp. 102–8). This does not detract, however, from the fact that within the context of the Gospel these meals form a literary genre and do not necessarily reflect the practice of the earliest Christian communities.

This leaves those meals that are hosted by Jesus, beginning with the feeding of the five thousand (Luke 9.10–17). This narrative certainly has more of the feel of a cultic event than many of the other meals mentioned in the text. There is a thanksgiving, a breaking, and a sharing of bread and fish. Luke, however, did not pluck this story out of the air; he developed it from Mark. For Mark this story, or rather these stories, as there are two of them, are also borrowed from an earlier tradition and are presented, along with the calming of the storm and other similar miracles, as a demonstration of the power of Jesus over nature (Kee 1977, p. 33). These are miracle stories. They have a clear narrative structure, and the various numbers involved (five loaves, two fishes, twelve baskets etc.) would suggest that this story has deeper theological significance, once again with messianic or apocalyptic overtones, but they have no necessary connection with any real practice, either within the context of Jesus and his disciples or within the community of Mark or Luke. This still leaves the apparently ritual elements of the story: the thanksgiving, the breaking and the sharing. The thanksgiving, or blessing, does not distinguish this meal from any other Jewish meal. The breaking and sharing will be picked up later when I come to look at the Acts of the Apostles, so I do not wish to develop this further here.

This does, however, leave the question of fish. There are two meals within the Gospel of Luke that involve fish – although the post-resurrection feeding on broiled fish (24.42) is hardly a meal – and a series of related meals in the other Gospel traditions. Fish has developed a particular symbolic association within the early Christian communities and Vogel has even suggested that an early form of 'Eucharist' consisted of bread and fish, based in part on these stories (Hiers and Kennedy 1976, p. 21). The word 'Eucharist' can be ignored in this analysis, but the question has to be asked as to whether the various stories in the Gospels that do include fish might reflect a regular pattern of meals within the earliest communities, and particularly among those that compiled the

Gospels. Hiers and Kennedy argue that there is a gradual diminishing
of the importance of fish through the different Gospel texts if they are ✓
placed in chronological order. Mark mentions fish five times in his discussion of the feeding of the five thousand, while Luke has far fewer
references. This leads them to argue that what is reflected here is a tradition of bread and fish meals that was already dying out and being sup-
pressed by the time that the Gospels were written (1976, pp. 20–47).

This is unlikely, and McGowan provides a coherent critique of this
argument based primarily on the fact that there is no reference to bread
and fish meals outside of the Gospel tradition (1999a, p. 130). Having
said that, it is clear that the cooking and eating of fish does have an
important place within the Gospel traditions, and primarily, with reference to McGowan's other point above, in those meals where Jesus is
the host. It is possible to argue that this is merely symbolic, and the use
of fish symbolism is very widespread, especially in early Christian art
(although the only examples that remain date from the beginning of the
third century onwards (McGowan 1999a, pp. 132–4)). Alternatively
it could reflect the memory of the meals shared between Jesus and his
first followers, many of whom were fishermen, but that had no place
beyond this original community. It is not, however, a tradition that is
ever developed within the earliest Christian communities where records
are available.

The final story in Luke is the post-resurrection narrative of the meal
on the road to Emmaus (24.13–35). Here again Jesus is the host, but it
is the significance of the breaking of bread that draws attention to this
meal as having a potentially eucharistic context. I do think that this is
more significant, but I would want to link this meal to other references
to the breaking of bread throughout Acts rather than seeing it as something distinctive in itself. I will therefore move on to look at the Acts of
the Apostles, and I will include the Emmaus narrative within that wider
discussion.

The breaking of bread in Acts

Throughout the narrative of the Acts of the Apostles, therefore, reference is made to the 'breaking of bread'. These references form what
are practically the only reference to eating and drinking within the narrative, although there are a few exceptions such as Peter's vision in
chapter 10 (Heil 1999). In most cases these references to bread have
been seen as eucharistic. This is particularly true of the narrative that

follows the story of Pentecost where the text states that the community 'devoted themselves to the apostle's teaching and to the fellowship, to the breaking of bread and to prayer' (2.42). Other references are to the breaking of bread in the middle of an all-night prayer meeting in Troas, where the meal follows the rather traumatic accident in which a young man falls out of a window (20.7–12), and the breaking of bread by Paul in the middle of a storm on a ship bound for Cyprus (27.33–38). At first sight these accounts do not appear to have very much in common. Their contexts, their characters and their roles within the text are very different. All that they share is the phrase τῇ κλάσει τοῦ ἀρτου, 'the breaking of bread', whether this is as a noun or a verb (Higgins 1952, p. 56), and it is this that links these stories with that of Emmaus, as well as to the feeding of the five thousand and the Last Supper (Heil 1999, p. 238).

In all these cases it is the reference to bread, and more specifically the breaking of bread, that is seen to be eucharistic. However, the first thing to note is that there is no equivalent reference to the drinking or sharing of a cup. It could be that this was not needed, as the 'breaking of bread' was clearly understood by Luke and his audience as shorthand for both bread and cup. It could be that at this very early stage the use of wine was not universal (McGowan 1999a). The third option, raised by Jeremais and others, that the cup was not mentioned as part of some kind of *arcanum*, is now generally accepted as being highly implausible (Higgins 1952, p. 56). However, if the 'breaking of bread' can be seen as shorthand for the use of both bread and cup, then it is also possible that the 'breaking of bread' may also be shorthand for the inclusion of a full meal (Conzelmann 1987, p. 23). It is perfectly reasonable to see the full meal as being possible in all the cases where the 'breaking of bread' is used, apart perhaps from the Emmaus story where it appears that the very action of breaking bread is the important point.

There is no direct evidence for the term 'breaking of bread' being used for a full meal within Jewish contexts of the time (Higgins 1952, p. 56). However, as it would have been normal to bless, break and share bread in any meal that involved more than the immediate family then some commentators assume that the term would have had a Jewish origin. To refer to eating of any kind, therefore, as the 'breaking of bread' would have been perfectly reasonable, and if the breaking of bread was the first act of the meal then this could also explain its specific use within the Emmaus story. Barrett suggests that even at the time of writing the 'breaking of bread' might have had an archaic feel to it, but this assumes that Luke was already familiar with a full-blown Eucharist and this cannot be sustained (2002, p. 34). At one level there is no real reason to pursue this further, except to say that some sharing of meals was a part of some early Christian communities as attested by Luke.

What is quite striking, however, is how few references there are, even to the breaking of bread, within the overall narrative. Apart from the post-Pentecost reference, where eating communal meals appears to be part of the construction of the community along with prayer and sharing all goods in common (2.42–47), the other references are incidental and no significant meaning is attached to any of the accounts, or to sharing communal meals in any regular fashion throughout the narrative (Heil 1999). Baptism is mentioned much more frequently and, if there were regular meals, then baptism must have been much less frequent even at this time in Christian history. Once again it is the lack of evidence that is significant rather than an excess of evidence that needs to be interpreted. It is important therefore to look at each of the three references in Acts in a little more detail.

The narrative of the post-Pentecost period is a difficult passage to interpret. Some commentators see the whole of Acts 2 as the result of a combination of various sources that have been brought together and associated with the feast of Pentecost by Luke (Shepherd 1960, pp. 24–5). Most of the commentary on verses 42–47, however, deals with the question of sharing all goods in common and stresses that even if this did occur, it is clear from the text that it would not have lasted for very long. The meeting in each other's houses and the sharing of regular meals are similar kinds of activity that point to a similar idealistic community. Acts 2.46 could be seen to suggest that there was a daily sharing of food (Heil 1999, pp. 239–41). However, Kilpatrick argues that καθ ημέραν (daily) refers only to the first phrase, and the passage should read 'and they continued together daily in the Temple and they broke bread in houses' (Kilpatrick 1983, p. 37). Either way, what is being presented is the activity of a small highly enthusiastic community in its first flush of energy, which would gradually die away as the community grew in size and began to become more institutionalized. At the other extreme the whole of this narrative has been seen as an idealistic account of what such a community should have been like in its purest and most ideal form (Conzelmann 1987, p. 24). Whatever position is taken, it is fair to assume that the small common community either never existed at all or only survived in this highly enthusiastic form for a few years at most. And, if the sharing of all goods in common died out fairly rapidly, then there is no evidence to suggest that the meeting in each other's houses and the shared meals did not go the same way.

The event in Troas is clearly an account of worship within the early Christian community (20.7–12). It is worship that is dominated by preaching and prayer. There is no mention in this text of the ecstatic elements of 1 Corinthians 14 but the whole feel of the narrative would suggest that they would not have been out of place. The event lasts all night and the meal, whatever form it might have taken, occurs about halfway through. For this reason alone, this story has to be dismissed as an example of the widespread use of the symposium model in early Christianity (Smith 2003). It is the disruption caused by Eutychus falling out of the window that appears to trigger the meal, a kind of forced break, rather than any sense that at this point in such meetings a meal would always take place. Conzelmann, however, suggests that both verses 7 and 11 are later incursions into what is otherwise a coherent narrative (1987, p. 169). These verses, therefore, should not be used to suggest any specific sequence of events.

What distinguishes the Troas account, however, is verse 7, which says, 'On the first day of the week we came together to break bread.' This raises the question of 'the first day of the week' and the importance of this as a time for the Christian community to gather. What is not clear is whether Luke is referring to a Saturday evening here, following Jewish practice in seeing the day as running from sunset to sunset, or a Sunday evening, following wider Hellenistic practice (Shepherd 1960, p. 15). The text also suggests that the breaking of bread was a regular and significant element of that gathering: 'we came together to break bread'. Again, however, this does not specify what 'breaking bread' actually implies and, more importantly, it says nothing about what might have been eaten or drunk alongside the bread. Having said that, I would recognize that this is the only point in all the New Testament texts that offers fairly unambiguous evidence for a weekly sharing of food among at least some communities of early Christians.

Finally, therefore, there is the breaking of bread on the boat (27.33–38). Here there is a specific reference to 'giving thanks', and Paul is in a state of agitation and concern. The meal is part of his response to the storm and, in the context of the narrative, part of what leads to the ending of the storm. This is a much more ritualistic kind of event, and yet it is also a very private one, although there is some confusion of the text at this point that might point to a more communal activity (Kilpatrick 1983, pp. 36–7). In most accepted versions Paul is not sharing this meal with the crew or even his fellow travellers, whether Gentile or Jewish, although he is encouraging them to eat. This is an odd event, of which McGowan says:

The only real issue we can address is whether the author presents the story as related to other early Christian or eucharistic meals; and the answer to this must be 'yes', or at least that this is as much a Eucharist as we find anywhere else in the Lucan corpus or the New Testament as a whole. (McGowan 2004, p. 113)

Perhaps it is as much a Eucharist as is found anywhere else in the Lucan corpus, or the New Testament as a whole, but as such it is not really eucharistic at all.

Having said that, this story is another example of the use of the 'breaking of bread' formula. It is the third such account in Acts and, if the Emmaus story, the feeding of the five thousand and perhaps the Last Supper are also included, the sixth account in the writings attributed to Luke. In four of these accounts the host 'gives thanks' before breaking and sharing the bread. The use of the word 'thanksgiving', εὐχαριστεῖν, needs some elaboration in these contexts. It has been noted by a number of scholars that Christian material tends to use the term εὐχαριστεῖν, while, admittedly later, Jewish meal prayers emphasize blessing, εὐλογεῖν (Talley 1976; Betz 1996, pp. 258–9; Rouwhorst 2005, p. 149). It is not known when this formula became the norm within Jewish prayers as it is primarily attested to in the third-century rabbinic material. It has even been suggested that the Jewish emphasis on blessing emerged as a reaction to the Christian claims to thanksgiving (Leonhard 2007). The use of the word 'thanksgiving' in a number of these breaking of bread texts, therefore, has to be significant and I will come back to this in later chapters.

What is very clear, and may appear to be stating the obvious, is that all the accounts of the 'breaking of bread' in Luke focus almost entirely on the bread. The fish, as Hiers and Kennedy outline, are played down in Luke's narrative of the feeding of the five thousand (1976, pp. 20–47), and if, following Kilpatrick (1983), only the first cup is accepted as authentic in Luke's version of the Last Supper, then this also places the climax of that meal at the breaking of bread. It is possible that there is some kind of tradition here, and it could well reflect the practice of one or more of the early Christian communities that the author of Luke-Acts is associated with. This tradition does not give any significance to the cup and yet it does suggest, from the Troas example at least, that a weekly event of some kind may be involved, even if it is just the breaking and sharing of bread. It is also clear that there is very little symbolic development associated with this practice. There is no reference to body and blood except in relation to the Last Supper. The Emmaus story simply focuses on the recognition of Jesus in the act of breaking the bread, not to any other kind of presence. The stories in Acts have no further elaboration of any kind, and Barrett sums these up by saying that 'what was important to Luke was not the symbolic significance of what was done . . . but the shared life that commensality represented' (2002, p. lxiii). Unfortunately it is not possible to take this discussion any further at this stage. It is almost impossible to link these texts with a specific community in the way that can be done, for example with 1 Corinthians, and unless that can be done, or it can be shown that this tradition is much more widespread through other kinds of evidence, then this is probably as far as the current argument can go.

Finally, therefore, is it possible to read 1 Corinthians 11 in the light of this tradition from Luke? Possibly. It is clear that there are connections between the communities Luke engages with and those that Paul worked with or founded. These two traditions are seen to overlap on many occasions despite some minor differences in narrative history between Acts and Paul's own writing. If Luke, or the compiler of the Gospel and Acts, knew of a weekly meal focused on the breaking of bread is it not possible that Paul did as well? Again this is possible, and if the meal had such little symbolic elaboration as is suggested in Acts then that may explain why Paul pays so little attention to it in any of his other writings. But if this is the case, then it is still necessary to explain why he would suddenly want to relate this elementary breaking of bread to the full Last Supper account, with all the symbolic elaboration that this includes, in his letter to the Corinthians. I would still want to argue, therefore, that the best explanation of the Lord's Supper is that Paul is referring to an annual meal held at the time of the Passover to commemorate the Passion. There is nothing to prevent both the annual Paschal meal and the weekly breaking of bread existing side by side, but I will come back to this in Chapter 5.

The Gospel of John and the eating of flesh

Moving on to the Gospel of John there are a very different set of problems. John does not mention meals in any direct way to the same extent as Luke or the other Synoptic Gospels. Even the Last Supper is not presented in terms of a meal as such. On the other hand, chapter 6 does lay out an extended meditation on eating the flesh of Jesus and drinking his blood. This is put into the context of the feeding of the five thousand, but clearly has theological links to the Last Supper narratives in the other Gospels. Whether there is a direct link between these two passages, the similarity of eating the flesh/body of Christ and drinking his blood must be seen to point to a common source. This idea is so shocking within the context of first-century Judaism that for both John and the Synoptic tradition to come up with it independently does not make sense. However, having made that point, the differences between the Synoptics and John are probably just as significant as the similarities. Bradshaw notes the difference in language: the synoptics' 'body' against John's 'flesh' (2004, pp. 87–91; Morris 1971, p. 375). The setting for the statements must also be recognized as a difference, and it is important to see whether this may be significant in itself.

The first thing to do, therefore, is to look at chapter 6 in the context of the wider narrative of the Gospel to see what can be learnt from this within its own framework. As with all the other texts that have been looked at, it is necessary to begin by asking about the community within which the text originated, the community of the author and the community assumed by the text of the audience. There has been a great deal of work on the community associated with John and the community associated with the text. All these works agree that the question of a Johannine community is important, but few agree as to its exact form and history (Ashton 1991; Fuglseth 2005). Meeks (1972) provided a significant impetus by asking about the 'sectarian' nature of the community. This analysis, however, is rooted in a fairly rigid sociological understanding of the 'sect' (Fuglseth 2005). Martyn offered a wider, developmental understanding of the community (1979; Ashton 1991, pp. 166–74) and Wengst did most to situate the community in a specific time and place, on the northern fringe of Galilee at the very end of the first century (1981; Ashton 1991, pp. 196–8). Perhaps the most complete study is Oscar Cullman's book on *The Johannine Circle* (1976), although it is the very completeness of this work that often generates most criticism.

Cullman, like all other scholars, points out that the first problems arise from the nature of the text itself. There is clear evidence of editing and redaction within the text and many different scholars have suggested numerous different elements that should or should not be included in the writing of the original author or the work of one or more redactor (Cullman 1976, pp. 1–9; Ashton 1991, pp. 160–6). Having noted this Cullman goes on to look at the relationship between the language of the Gospel and that of non-mainstream Jewish writing at the time. Cullman argues that the Greek of the Gospel shows clear signs of Aramaic roots (1976, pp. 26–9; Barrett 1975, pp. 20–39) and the emphasis on Judaea and Samaria within the text leads Cullman to place it within a marginal Jewish tradition based in one of these two regions (1976, pp. 30–8); in particular he links it with the Hellenists mentioned at the beginning of Acts (6.1, 1976, pp. 55–6). Most other scholars are less precise and follow Brown who proposes an ejection from the synagogue much later in the century as the initiating point for the community and the first edition of the Gospel (Brown 1979). This leads Ashton, following Wengst, to situate the text in an area where the rabbinic structures were becoming fixed following the fall of Jerusalem (Ashton 1991, p. 197; Wengst 1981, p. 80).

Cullman ends his text by asking about the question of authorship, or in his terms the primary influence on the community. Cullman is fairly clear to distinguish 'the beloved disciple' from John the son of Zebedee, and suggests that the beloved disciple is the primary author of the text, making him an eyewitness to at least some of the events that are being presented (1976, pp. 71–85). Most other scholars would not be prepared to go so far and situate the writing and editing of the text so far away from the events of the Gospel as to make eyewitness accounts implausible. The nature of the 'beloved disciple', however, remains a significant problem. Other scholars have, of course, questioned many other aspects of Cullman's analysis (Smalley 1978; Hengel 1989), but the link with non-mainstream Jewish thinking, the focus on Judaea (if not always on Samaria) and the possibility of an eyewitness account lying somewhere behind the Gospel have often been considered.

What is important for this analysis is the idea that the Johannine community could represent a distinct strand within early Christian thought that, from a relatively early date, followed a different path from the kind of Christian development that has been seen in the Passion narrative of Mark and the works of Luke or Paul. It will have originated in Judaea, had possible links with non-mainstream elements of Jewish thought and practice, including perhaps the Essene community in Jerusalem and the Samaritan tradition, and it possibly moved, over time, from Judaea to Syria or northern Palestine, and ultimately to Asia Minor (Hengel 1989, pp. 109–35). The Gospel itself probably arrived in its final form towards the end of the first century and took some time to be as widely accepted as that of Matthew and perhaps those of Luke and Mark (Hill 2004).

Is there anything in the text, therefore, that gives any sense of ritual activity, or forms of worship, within this community? This is a much more difficult task. One of the problems is that there has been a significant debate among biblical scholars in the middle of the twentieth century about whether John's Gospel reflects a certain level of 'sacramental' thinking and retains constant and regular references to baptism and the Eucharist (Smalley 1978, pp. 128–30, 204–6), or whether the Gospel is essentially anti-sacramental (Bultmann 1971; Morris 1971). I do not wish to pursue the baptismal imagery within this text, but the elements that are commonly linked to the Eucharist begin with the miracle at Cana (2.1–11) and work their way all through the text (Higgins 1952, pp. 78–88). Much of this analysis, however, is clearly a case of reading later practice back into the text. If the text is not looked at through a eucharistic lens then many of these examples of supposed eucharistic reference might need to be analysed differently. The wedding at Cana is a good example of this. Here there is a miracle story in which Jesus, somewhat reluctantly, changes water into wine. The wine is given no symbolic interpretation within the text and the story is presented, as stated in verse 11, simply as an instance of the way in which Jesus 'revealed his glory' (2.11). It is only the reference to wine that leads scholars to assume that the text must be referring to the Eucharist. All that can be said, however, from this text is that the Johannine community did not belong to the ascetical tradition that has been identified by McGowan (1999a); it clearly did not have a problem with drinking wine.

McGowan, however, does suggest an alternative reading based on the number of allusions throughout the Gospel to the drinking of water (1999a, pp. 236–7). Just as it is not appropriate to assume that any and every reference to bread and wine must be eucharistic, so every reference to water must not be seen as being baptismal. John in particular emphasizes the drinking of the living water rather than being washed in it, and the story of the Samaritan woman at the well (4.1–26) could be read as eucharistic if it is assumed that the Eucharist known to John was of the bread and water kind that McGowan wishes to identify. As with the wedding at Cana, however, the evidence is not clear and while it has been argued that a water-drinking tradition can be traced from John, through to Justin Martyr and others (Daly-Denton 2007), this needs to be supported by other evidence and cannot be read out of the text of the Gospel of John alone.

Finally, therefore, coming back to chapter 6, what could this mean within the context that has just been laid out? Most commentators begin by asking whether the whole of chapter 6 is in the right place (Ashton 1991, pp. 200–1). Some scholars have seen the longer passage relating to the bread of life (6.25–71) as a later interpolation, an attempt by a later editor to add something eucharistic into the text (Bultmann

1971). Others have argued that it is only the section from verse 52 to 58 that is an interpolation and that the rest of the text can be read in a spiritual sense where no reference to the Eucharist is implied (Wilkens 1958). If more or less of this passage is a later editorial addition then it would be necessary to argue that the earliest form of the Johannine community never did know any kind of regular meal that related the bread and wine to the flesh and blood of Jesus. This position, however, is probably unsustainable and recent commentators do tend to see John 6 as an integrated whole, however complex their understanding of that whole. Léon-Dufour, for example, says, 'the discourse on the Bread of Life, including vv. 52–58, thus proves to be very carefully structured. It is pointless to fragment it by assigning different parts to different "sources"' (1987, p. 257). This is a position supported by a number of other more recent scholars (for example, Borgen 1996, pp. 205–30).

The most important point to make about John's Gospel is that the argument is essentially theological; it is designed to say something about who Jesus was rather than to provide a blueprint for the life of the Christian community (Smalley 1978). If this is the case then this passage must also be seen as a reflection on the nature of Jesus and the individual Christian's relationship with Jesus, rather than a reflection of practice. This still does not account for why John chose specifically to link the discussion to the feeding of the five thousand rather than the Last Supper, except to suggest that he probably already had other ideas for the Last Supper account and needed some other hook on which to hang this debate (Léon-Dufour 1987, pp. 249–52). Higgins argues that the emphasis on eating the flesh must be related to John's decision to situate the death of Christ at the moment of the sacrifice of the Passover lamb. If this is the case then the flesh of the lamb/Jesus cannot be eaten before the sacrifice and hence the sharing of bread and wine cannot be part of the Last Supper account (1952, p. 77). Remnants of the original Passion narrative can, however, still be seen in the account in chapter 6. Verse 4 says that the Jewish Passover feast was near, and at the very end of the chapter there is reference to the betrayal by Judas (6.70–1). Gärtner develops this Passover link much more explicitly showing parallels between John 6 and the later Jewish Passover Haggadah (1959, pp. 25–9). Gärtner notes the references to manna or the 'bread from heaven', and the walking on the water (which he associates with the crossing of the Red Sea) as images associated with the Passover (1959, pp. 14–19; Guilding 1960).

What this leaves open, however, is whether there was a weekly meal within John's own community and how this might have related to the text. If there is a symbolic association between bread and wine and flesh and blood then it is logical to assume that there must have been some sharing of bread and wine that underpins this. Brown even goes so far as to suggest that the rejection of Jesus in verse 66 refers to 'Jewish Christians who are no longer to be considered true believers because they do not share John's view of the eucharist' (Brown 1979, p. 74). Some kind of meal could have occurred on a weekly basis. It could also have occurred on an annual basis, as the feeding story is clearly associated with the time of the Passover. It may have been more or less regular, more or less infrequent. It is impossible to know. However, if John's text does demonstrate the development of a link between the sharing of bread and wine, associated with the flesh and blood of Jesus, and the Passover, this may be another tradition that, like Paul in 1 Corinthians, begins with an annual Passover meal.

Finally, a great deal of space is given over in the scholarly literature to the use of the word 'flesh' throughout John's Gospel and the importance of this within John's wider theological purpose (Barrett 1978, pp. 164–5, 297–8; Morris 1971, pp. 102, 373–6). From the very opening of the Gospel ('the word became flesh', 1.14) through chapter 6 and beyond, John is emphasizing the fleshly nature of Jesus against an embryonic Docetical position (Higgins 1953, pp. 82–3; Morris 1971, p. 102). If this is the case then the passage may simply be a piece of theological rhetoric developed in an imaginative way on the basis of an early attempt to understand the incarnation (Morris 1971, pp. 373–6). There is, however, too much emphasis on eating within the text for this to be comfortable. Higgins translates τρώγειν in verses 54 and 56–58 as 'munch', with the comment that 'it is a real eating that is meant' (1953, p. 82). It seems reasonable to acknowledge, therefore, that the author does reflect a tradition in which there is a regular (potentially annual) sharing of bread and wine and that this has some symbolic associations for his community with flesh and blood, although there is little more of a practical nature that can be said at this stage. I will come back to this in Chapter 6.

This only leaves the Last Supper account itself and the other meal stories associated with the resurrection appearances. There is no indication from the Gospel's account of the Last Supper as to what kind of meal was involved or whether it was ever intended to be repeated. Higgins refers to the washing of the feet as an 'allegory of the Eucharist' (1952, p. 84), and in 13.15 Jesus does tell his disciples that 'I have set you an example that you should do as I have done for you', but this action does not appear to have been repeated in any rite within the earliest

Christian communities. Moving to the resurrection appearances, 20.19 says that 'on the evening of the first day of the week . . . Jesus came and stood among them'. One week later the same thing occurred, although this time Thomas is present (20.24). Lunny assumes that, as this is an evening gathering, this must have taken place at a meal and argues that the Jerusalem tradition of the resurrection accounts (including both Luke and John) is that of a meal tradition (1989, p. 124). The meal, however, is not mentioned in chapter 20, although the reference to the 'first day of the week' does refer back to the discussion of the meeting at Troas in Acts 20. The appearance by the Lake of Tiberius (21.1–14) does occur within the context of a meal but is in itself a retelling of a story of a miraculous catch of fish that is reminiscent of Luke 5 (5.1–11). The meal itself consists of bread and fish (21.13), although the emphasis here is not on the breaking of bread as it is in the Lucan traditions. Overall, therefore, it is clear that these other meals cannot take the discussion any further forward.

Other texts

In 1960 Massey Shepherd noted that there had been a recent spate of works trying to show how different texts of the New Testament could be understood as relating to the worship of the earliest Christian community (1960, pp. 27–8). Most of these aimed to demonstrate how the calendar had influenced the writing of a Gospel (Carrington 1952; Kilpatrick 1946; Schilling 1953; Guilding 1960). Others have tried to see other texts as part of, or encapsulating, a specific liturgical act, most commonly the Paschal vigil. Cross presents 1 Peter as a Paschal liturgy (1954). Carrington refers to 1 Corinthians as a Paschal letter (1952, p. 42) and suggests that Hebrews is a Christian *megillah* for the Day of Atonement (1952, p. 44). Shepherd's own work presents the theory that the Apocalypse is also rooted in, and structured by, the Paschal vigil (1960, pp. 77–97). All of these fail because, like Trocmé's analysis of Mark's Passion, they all presume a far too highly developed Paschal liturgy for the time that the relevant texts were written. Whether any of the Gospels, or other texts, were read within the context of regular Christian worship from the date of their production can never be known, but it is probably fairly safe to assume that they were. However, to go further and to say that the content and structure of the texts themselves, as they exist today, is determined by that liturgical use is probably taking the argument far too far. Shepherd provides a clear defence of the

80

possibility that not all early Christian worship was informal, as in Acts 2, or chaotic, as in 1 Corinthians 14, and that some element of orderly practice may have been inherited from Jewish practices associated with the Temple, the synagogue or the community at Qumran (Shepherd 1960, p. 79). This may be true, but there are few today who would take this as a justification for reading the structure of the Paschal vigil as outlined by texts from the end of the second century back into the texts produced by visionary Christians at the end of the first.

When looking at these other texts, therefore, it is important to see what, if anything, they have to offer to an understanding of early Christian meal practices among the communities where they were authored. This, however, is not an easy task. The letter to the Hebrews presents a commentary on the high priesthood of Christ and his sacrifice, but as Rowland comments, 'there is no attempt to link this to the eucharistic meal of the assembled Christians' (Rowland 1985, p. 243). In fact there are very few references to food of any kind. Baptism is alluded to a couple of times (6.2; 10.22) and the 'blood of Christ' provides a leit-motif for the whole letter. This, however, is associated with the blood of sacrificial animals and not related in any way to meals or to bread and wine.

The epistle of Jude talks about 'certain men whose condemnation was written about long ago' (4) who are 'blemishes at your love feasts, eating with you without the slightest qualm – shepherds who feed only themselves' (12). The reference here is to the *agape* (love feast), which is almost certainly a reference to a meal. However, despite the later use of this term to refer, in a technical sense, to a non-eucharistic meal, there is no supporting evidence within the letter to suggest what the *agape* was for Jude, or what it might have meant to the author or his community.

A range of different authors have linked the book of Revelation with the worship of the early Christian communities and with the Eucharist (Shepherd 1960). The most common way of doing this has been in terms of structure, matching the structure of the text onto the structure of Paschal vigil or of some other ritual. The possibility that such so-phisticated, highly structured rituals existed in the first century is, as I have stressed, highly unlikely. This does, however, raise the question of the dating of Revelation and the community associated with it, both of which have proved very difficult to pinpoint with any kind of accuracy (Morris 1969, pp. 15–41). In very general terms scholars are agreed that it originates from the western coast of Asia Minor, probably in the early years of the second century (Hengel 1989). There are also clear connections with other Johannine texts, although it is clear that the author of Revelation is not the same John identified as the author of the Gospel or the letters. Situating this text in its wider sociological context, therefore, does not really help to provide any further information relating to possible meals.

In fact meals, as such, play little or no role within the text as it stands. There is clearly an image presented of the worship of heaven, and it is possible that this is related in some way to the worship of the community known to the author. Some of the prayer structures are related to known Jewish prayer structures, although it is not possible to reconstruct any kind of 'order of service' and it is unlikely that the author had a specific act of worship in mind. The only reference to meals comes either from the idea of the sacrifice of the lamb (5.6), which in any sacrificial system would be associated with a meal even though the meal element is not mentioned in this text, and the image of the wedding of the lamb (21.2, 9), which again is associated with feasting in other traditions. The question of sacrifice will be taken up in Chapter 7, but as with Hebrews references to sacrifice at the end of the first century cannot be assumed to be related to eucharistic thought. The wedding imagery, however, simply picks up the literary image of the messianic banquet that has already been seen in the stories and parables of the Gospels and will be seen again in some of the Jewish material (Smith 2003, pp. 168–70). Again there is no necessary link between this literary image and any specific meal.

Conclusion and summary

From this general review of the relevant material it is possible to divide references to meals within the texts that make up the New Testament into four loose groups if, for the moment, the Last Supper narratives are put to one side. These groups are not exclusive to each other, and nor should they be seen as totally exhaustive. They can provide a model, however, that will help me to explore other references to meals that occur in some of the other early Christian texts that are analysed in Chapters 5–7.

The first group consists primarily of literary allusions to meals, most of which are clustered around the idea of the messianic banquet or the eschatological wedding feast. These can be seen in the parables told by Jesus about the nature of the kingdom, and also in the stories told about Jesus attending meals as a guest, or as the context for the telling of the parables. Finally, these literary allusions are developed in later writing such as the book of Revelation. None of these allusions suggest very much about the nature of the meals that were shared by the communities behind the various texts, despite some references to reclining at table, the washing of feet or anointing within the stories about Jesus sharing in meals. These features are common to many meals of the time and are telling details within the story rather than a specifically Christian activity (Smith 2003). Even the fact that the meal is such an important literary image in so many different traditions within the New Testament does not of itself say anything about the actual meal traditions of the communities. All human beings have to eat and it would be surprising if eating and drinking, like marriage or farming or commerce, were not one of the images drawn upon by these writers, or by Jesus himself. There is also little evidence in these texts for any suggestion that these stories and images are being used to inform and give meaning to actual practice, although it is inevitable that they did once the stories began to circulate more widely. In the texts themselves the meal is being presented as an image of some other element, whether that is the kingdom of God or the nature of the last things, rather than these other elements being used to inform meal practices. This is an important distinction and one that I will come back to in the final chapter.

The second group of references, therefore, concerns those comments about who can eat with whom and what a Christian is, or is not, allowed to eat. These are associated with the underlying rules and practices of the Jewish community at the time and there is considerable debate about just how strictly such rules were taken by different Jewish communities (Barclay 2001). It is very clear, however, that at least at Antioch in the early years of Christian development, and probably in Corinth, Rome and other places, the question of who can eat with whom, and what can and cannot be eaten remained an issue within the communities concerned throughout the first century and probably beyond. These issues are associated with other related matters such as circumcision and reflect a developing negotiation of the distinctive identity of the Christian communities as they interacted with Jewish and Gentile members (Lieu 2002). There was clearly no consensus on this issue and even Paul is not entirely coherent in his views (Gooch 1993). It is an ongoing discussion, and different groups, or different individuals within a specific community, continued to hold differing positions for many decades to come. What is important to note about this group of references, however, is that none of these discussions are ever associated with a specifically Christian cultic meal. If, as I suggested in Chapter 1, the sharing of a formal supper with strong christological overtones (whatever they might have been) had been an important part of the life of the Christian community in Antioch when the debate over food laws arose, then surely those who discussed or recounted the debate would have linked it to this central cultic activity. This is not to say that the Antioch community was not sharing meals; they obviously were or else the dispute may not have arisen in the first place. It is just that the way in which the dispute is presented gives no suggestion that these meals had any other significance than simply shared food. For me this offers strong evidence for the absence of anything 'eucharistic' among these communities at this time.

Third, therefore, there is the account of the Lord's Supper in 1 Corinthians, the only detailed account of an actual meal within the New Testament literature. I have discussed this at length in Chapter 1 and would simply want to restate the conclusion that I developed in that chapter, that the Lord's Supper, as discussed by Paul, was probably an annual meal held by the community at, or around, the time of the Passover, at which the events of Jesus' death and resurrection were remembered and very probably retold within a Passion narrative. It is important to reiterate that I am not suggesting that this was a 'Christian Passover', and there is no evidence in the text, or in the accounts of the Last Supper that are associated with this meal tradition, that Christian communities took over any of the ritual and food practices of the Jewish Passover. This was a common shared meal (which may have been very simple, although there is no evidence of its content or its actual form) during which the community remembered the death and resurrection of their Lord and perhaps looked forward to the coming end of the age. The development of ideas presented in John 6 may also have belonged to this kind of tradition as I have suggested earlier in this chapter.

The fourth group of references contain the phrase 'the breaking of bread', or variants on this, which have also been looked at in more detail in this chapter. These are focused in the works attributed to Luke, in both the Gospel and in Acts. In Acts it is clear that the breaking of bread, whatever that consisted of, was important to at least one early Christian community and that Luke saw it as taking place on a regular basis, either daily or weekly. It was taken for granted by Luke as a regular part of the community's activity, but it is not clear whether it could ever be described as 'cultic' or as part of a wider act of worship. What else was eaten alongside the bread is not clear from the texts and there is no basis on which to speculate as to whether the breaking and sharing of bread in itself could have been enough to form a small ritual. Given the circumstances in which it is mentioned (daily among the earliest

84

community, in the middle of a meeting for preaching and prayer, on a ship in a storm, or even in the context of the Emmaus story), it is unlikely that the breaking of bread formed the opening of a substantial meal, but some kind of drink or other minor foodstuffs may have been included. The breaking of bread is linked in the text with giving thanks or blessing and this is significant as it allows the feeding of the five thousand to be brought within the same group, as here also thanksgiving is offered and bread is broken and shared. However, it must be realized that the feeding of the five thousand provides a literary link rather than being seen as the root or starting point for this tradition. Little is said about the significance or meaning of the breaking of bread in the texts except for its association with the Emmaus story where the disciples recognize Jesus in the breaking of bread. This may indicate some kind of sense of the presence of the risen Lord at the meal in a way that is similar to Matthew's comment that 'where two or three come together in my name, there am I with them' (18.20). This association of the breaking of bread with thanksgiving and the idea of the presence of the risen Jesus within the community is one that shall occur again in later texts.

The evidence that is available, therefore, is very limited and is very diverse, with very few of these groups of texts being found in more than one specific author within the New Testament. This suggests considerable diversity, but also very little specific development, and reinforces the view that I have expressed on a number of occasions over the last few chapters, that there is very little evidence for any kind of regular cultic meal within the communities underpinning the texts of the New Testament. If ritual meals were not a significant part of the life of these communities then much of the discussion about the importance of meals within the culture of the time and the form that such meals might take probably seems irrelevant. However, I think that it is useful to review this material briefly in Chapter 4 before going on in the next three chapters to see how any of the groups of ideas found in the New Testament are developed in later literature, or whether completely new ideas and practices begin to emerge.

4

Non-Christian Meals

Many works on the place of the Eucharist in the New Testament or the early Church state what they assume is a commonly known fact, that communal meals play an important role in the classical world. Very few of them, however, set out to explore the evidence. Even fewer state just how limited that evidence is. Liturgists are very used to stating that there are only half a dozen or so direct references to something that could be considered 'eucharistic' within the first 150 years of the Christian community (Bradshaw 2004, p. vii). This is considered to be very limited evidence. It is very difficult to say anything very specific on the basis of it. It is also the case that the literary evidence for dining practices within the wider Roman and Hellenistic society of the same 150-year period also consisted of no more than 16 or 17 texts, which puts the whole discussion into some kind of perspective (Gooch 1993, p. 28). It is clearly the case that the general texts have far more detail and are often far longer than the brief references that are available within the Christian corpus, but the fact remains that the literary evidence that is available for communal meals is also very limited. On the basis of this wider evidence, however, great claims are made which occasionally do not appear to be based entirely on the texts that are available.

In working through the evidence that is available for communal meals in the ancient world I will begin with the literary texts. I will look at their context and their content and draw a number of general conclusions. I will then move beyond the literary to the archaeological and the epigraphical evidence. The evidence from the archaeological record of buildings and spaces is also limited, although it can offer a number of hints as to the kind of spaces that were available, even if it cannot say much about the way those spaces were used. The epigraphical evidence, or the evidence from inscriptions, is much more useful. It is also much more extensive (although many of the texts do need some level of interpretation and cannot stand on their own as evidence). It was common practice throughout the Roman and Hellenistic worlds at this time for inscriptions to be raised to honour benefactors, or for the rules of societies and clubs to be carved in stone and written out on the walls of their meeting rooms. These can provide a significant number of important insights into communal eating practices during the first 150 years of the Christian era. I will end this chapter with some reference to the specifically Jewish contexts. Here, again, evidence is very limited for the time period covered by this book and once again many of the confident conclusions of commentators, especially those who are interested in the Eucharist, cannot really be supported from what little evidence is available.

The evidence of the New Testament material, and particularly that of 1 Corinthians, relates primarily to meals that were held outside of the familial context, shared by people from a wide range of social statuses and attended by both men and women. One question that needs to be addressed from the wider evidence, therefore, is whether this was a common practice within the wider society or something of an anomaly. More specifically I want to try and answer those questions that the Corinthian data cannot answer. I want to get some kind of sense of what size of community might have been involved in Corinth on the basis of the range of gatherings common within the ancient world. It may also be interesting to ask about the content of the meal, beyond the bread and wine, but I am not sure this can be determined, or is ultimately of much significance. Finally, and perhaps most importantly from the direction of the argument in this book so far, I want to know how frequently such communal meals were held, and whether it is plausible for a community to come together every week to share a common meal within the ancient world.

Jews and the wider society

Before going on to look at the literary and other evidence in more detail, however, I will begin by looking at one specific area, that is, the relationship between Jews and the wider society. This is of direct relevance to the theme of this chapter: did Jews eat with Gentiles during the first century or not? Looking at the debates surrounding this issue, however, may also help to articulate in more detail the relationship between the kinds of data that I will be looking at in this chapter, particularly the complex relationship between literary and archaeological data from this period.

In 1987 Philip Esler, in his book on the social context of Luke-Acts, was able to put together a substantial argument to suggest that Jews did not, and could not, mix easily and regularly with the wider society (1987, pp. 71–86). In doing this he draws partly on the anthropological literature, particularly Mary Douglas and Edmund Leach, to demonstrate a generalized principle of purity and distinctiveness (Douglas 1966; Leach 1969). This is reinforced by literary evidence including that of Hecataeus of Abdera, who visited Egypt during the reign of Ptolemy I (323–285 BCE), Apollonius Molon, who made Rhodes the centre of his teaching in the first half of the first century BCE, Diodorus Siculus who wrote a world history in the period *c*. 60–30 BCE and Pompeius Trogus who lived at the end of the first century BCE and the beginning of the first century CE (Esler 1987, pp. 78–9). Esler quotes Tacitus who says that the Jews 'take their meals apart, they sleep apart, and, although they are as a race much given to lust, they abstain from intercourse with foreign women' (*Historiae* v 5:2; Esler 1987, p. 80). Finally, Esler quotes from a number of Jewish texts, from the Maccabean revolt to the destruction of the Temple, to support his contention that 'it is difficult to imagine how it would be possible for any genuine table-fellowship to occur even between Jew and Gentile in a Jewish home' (1987, p. 86). This allows him to go on to argue that the core theme in Luke-Acts is the development of an argument in favour of Jews and others eating together at the eucharistic meal.

Even when Esler was writing, however, it was clear that there was some evidence, and considerable debate, that tended to question the clear distinction between Jews and others. Esler constructs his whole argument in reaction to the position held by Dunn and Wilson (Dunn 1983; Wilson 1983). Esler was also severely criticized by Sanders, among others, who argued that the literary evidence that Esler was drawing on did not represent the widespread views of the Jewish community and was in certain important respects distorted by bias (Sanders 1990). For the ordinary Jew, Sanders argued, purity only became an issue when visiting the Temple or taking part in feasts such as the Passover. Esler defended his position in his subsequent book, *The First Christians in their Social Worlds* (1994), and in a subsequent article (1995) in which he went back to the anthropological literature, this time to focus on questions of shame and the maintaining or breaking of agreements.

By the turn of the millennium, however, the evidence that had emerged from the archaeological record began to make Elser's stance very difficult to sustain. The evidence from the Roman catacombs suggests a highly integrated community (Rutgers 1995). There is evidence from Asia of non-Jewish supporters of the synagogues, and more importantly there is also evidence of Jews taking an active role in city life and even reserving for themselves seats in the local amphitheatre (Treblico 1991). Jews in Cyrene had their names written on an inscription to Hermes and Heracles, and an inscription in Upper Egypt suggests that Jews worshipped a god in the temple of Pan (Borgen 1996, p. 31). It is now very difficult, on the basis of this wider evidence, to sustain the rigid distinctions and distances between Jews and others that are central to Esler's argument. Barclay emphasizes the incredible diversity of relationships between Jews and the surrounding communities from city to city and region to region in the ancient world (1996, 2001, p. 59) a point subsequently developed further by Harland and other more recent scholars (Harland 2003, pp. 200–10; Zetterholm 2003).

From the point of view of this discussion, therefore, it is important to be clear that a purely literary study of eating in the ancient world will only provide a fraction of the evidence that is required, and it may well provide a distorted picture. The archaeological record is extensive, but I have barely scratched the surface of what is available in this presentation. This account, therefore, has to be partial and it must always be noted that while it may be the case that the literary record provides fairly clear-cut views, as with Esler's statement about the distinctions between Jews and others, the archaeological record inevitably leads to ambiguity, confusion and diversity.

Literary accounts of meals

Peter Gooch lists 24 literary sources on communal meals in the period from 200 BCE to 200 CE, of which about 17 originate within the period 0–150 CE (1993, p. 28). Gooch does not include fragments or papyri in this list and is not concerned with historiographical writings as he argues that these tend to represent great events rather than the ordinary lives of people in the ancient world (1993, p. 27). From these texts Gooch argues that there is a standard picture of a typical communal meal (1993, p. 29). It tended to take place in the early evening. It began with food but almost always contained some kind of 'entertainment', whether this was dramatic or musical or whether it was some kind of discussion or debate. This, it appears, was as true of the poor as it was of the rich, although the nature of the entertainment might change. It is the entertainments, Gooch argues, that had the clearest religious connotations (1993, p. 30).

One of the points that Gooch makes, and that is reinforced by many other commentators on this period, is that there is no clear distinction between 'sacred' and 'profane'. The meals concerned are not either religious or non-religious. All the meals described contained religious elements and many also contained very vulgar or sexual entertainment as well. It appeared to be normal, in meals that were of social significance, to sacrifice the meat before the meal, especially at weddings, family feasts or religious holidays. Gooch also makes it clear that meals were an important feature of social intercourse and the marking of social status. He draws on the letters of Pliny to illustrate the way in which the dining room is seen as a public space (1993, p. 41) and quotes from the Stoic philosopher Musonius Rufus to demonstrate the social importance of shared eating through a list of 'table vices' (1993, p. 41). These, and a number of other texts, show that for all classes invitations to share meals, and what is done at the meal itself, who sits where and how the guests are expected to interact, are an essential part of daily life. In particular, friendship is often presented as being closely associated with shared meals.

Gooch begins his conclusion to the analysis of the texts by saying, 'First, the contexts in which sacred food was consumed at homes or temples among guests were many' (1993, p. 45). However, what Gooch is concerned with is chapters 8—10 of 1 Corinthians and the question of whether eating meat sacrificed to idols was a real concern to the community. What this evidence does not show, however, is that regular gatherings for shared meals among a specific group or society was common. The vast majority of the texts referred to deal, as I have indicated, with family meals, with celebrations, or with meals where the host invites a group of friends or colleagues to share in good food and good company. These may be common and important to the social life of a city such as Corinth, but they do not of themselves help to answer the question of how often a meal such as the Lord's Supper may have been held within a particular community. For that it is necessary to look to other evidence.

Smith (2003) draws on a similar range of literature to develop the idea of the 'banquet' in the Graeco-Roman world. In this case Smith is clear in stating that he is drawing on material from 300 BCE to 300 CE with the justification that there were very few significant differences across this period (2003, pp. 18–20). All the examples he draws on, many of which are also explored by Gooch, tend to focus on high-status contexts although he does note, like Gooch, that some of the principles can also be applied to other status groups. What is most important for Smith, however, is the division of the typical Hellenistic banquet into two, and later three, distinct courses (2003, pp. 27–31). The first of these, which developed within a Roman context, consisted of appetizers, the second was the meal proper and the third was the drinks party or symposium, which, in Roman meals, was generally accompanied by fruit, nuts and sweets. It is this division into the meal and the symposium that is central to Smith's overall argument. He is not suggesting, however, that this was a common pattern for the practice of all or even most meals within the ancient world. The structure, at its most ideal, was probably only present within a small group of high-status events. It was the idea of the symposium, as a literary form and a social ideal, associated with what Douglas calls a 'social code' (1972), that is most important for Smith. It is this ideal, with its accompanying social code, that is adapted and developed by philosophical groups, collectives within the ancient world, by Jewish communities and by Christians, as a central concept underlying the cultural interpretation of the meal. This does not, however, take the argument very much further in asking what communal meals may have looked like, beyond the social elite, or how frequently collective, non-familial meals may have taken place.

Architecture: Pagan, Jewish and Christian

Turning from the literary accounts of meals in the first two centuries of the Christian era to the architectural record there is a similarly limited range of any real evidence. The earliest identifiable Christian space is the Church House in Dura Europus, on the edge of the Roman Empire and dated to the first half of the third century (White 1990, pp. 21–5). There are some hints at other possible spaces, particularly under the titular churches of Rome, but none of this is conclusive (Rutgers 1995; Lampe 2003). In many ways, however, this is to be expected, as any account of the earliest Christian communities will stress the fact that they met in the houses of rich patrons and maintained a low public profile until well into the third and fourth centuries. What then can the architectural evidence tell us? One possibility is to look to Jewish as opposed to specifically Christian spaces. Unfortunately there are almost as few of these as there are Christian ones for the period covered by this text, but a few do exist and most of these are in the Diaspora. These could, therefore, throw some light on the context in Corinth, and I will come back to these later in this section (White 1990, pp. 60–101).

The other option is to look at pagan architecture of the time. At first sight this may not offer anything very helpful, as many contemporary scholars insist that Christianity took its shape and form from within a specifically Jewish milieu and any previous attempts to link Christian ritual with, for example, rituals of Mithraism have been shown to be distinctly off the mark (Lieu 2002). By looking at pagan religious architecture, however, I do not want to suggest that Christian communities followed any of the practices or architectural patterns of the pagan world. I want to explore this body of evidence to answer two specific questions. The first relates to the prevalence of meals within pagan religious practices. What evidence is available for the spaces created for communal meals at pagan religious sites? Can anything be said about the numbers catered for, and the kind of meals that society at large would have expected to accompany religious activity? More importantly, what evidence is available for the frequency of such meals? Michael White raises a further issue in his book *Social Origins of Christian Architecture* (1990). This is the fact that the religious spaces of many of the newer cults in the first-century Hellenistic and Roman worlds were developed within, and as adaptations of, existing buildings; most frequently it appears, out of the houses of the patrons of these communities.

Peter Gooch opens his discussion of 1 Corinthians 8—10, and the question of eating food offered to idols, with a detailed exploration of the temple complex of Demeter and Kore on Acrocorinth and other temple complexes in the area around Corinth (1993, pp. 1–26). In each case Gooch's purpose is to demonstrate that the various complexes all contained spaces that are clearly designed as dining facilities. These each have a series of benches around the walls and a central space where food could be served. Similar dining facilities have been found all over the ancient world and exist in domestic as well as communal and religious contexts. Gooch suggests, from the architectural evidence at these Corinthian complexes, that food would be offered to the gods in the central part of the temple, either in sacrifice for meat or by other forms of offering for other foodstuffs (1993, p. 22). It would then be prepared in a central kitchen area and either offered to the priests, taken to the dining facilities for those who brought the offering to share with family and friends, or carried home for a private meal (1993, pp. 22–3). There is some suggestion that this is as much a social occasion as a religious one, as it is clear that these dining facilities could be hired out for special occasions by those who could afford them, and some even existed with little or no obvious link to the temple cult that housed them (1993, p. 17).

What interests me is the size of these dining facilities. On the whole they are small and intimate, only big enough for a maximum of eight to eleven diners (Gooch 1993, pp. 3, 17). Some of the larger shrines had many such rooms, or what Gooch refers to as banqueting halls, and so could, in theory, cater for fairly large numbers, but the halls were divided into smaller rooms and each room held a similar number of guests (1993, pp. 18–19). This is not to say that there were not large public feasts or that dining did not take place in larger units. Other archaeological evidence suggests the possibility of dining halls that could hold up to 70 individuals (the Hall of Benches at the meeting place of the 'cowheards' of Dionysius in Pergamum, for example; Harland 2003, pp. 78–80). This, however, is still a relatively low number and the style of banqueting, reclining on benches around the walls of the room, is inevitably going to limit the size of the gathering.

What is clear, therefore, is that sharing food, or even dining, within the context of a religious event would not have been considered unusual within Corinth during Paul's mission. The only real question is whether anybody would have considered a Christian gathering a religious event. It did not take place at a temple. There was no sacrifice. There was probably no specific libation to speak of (we have no record of such within the literature). There was probably a blessing, but that was not unusual, and that was all that could have made any shared meal within the Christian community 'religious' so far as the ancient world would have seen it: that, plus the references to sharing in the body and blood of the god as referenced in 1 Corinthians.

Michael White's (1990) discussion demonstrates another aspect of pagan architectural practice that might have an impact on the kind of argument being developed. What White demonstrates, through an extensive survey of archaeological sites across the Roman and Hellenistic world, is that many of the smaller, newer cults in the Roman Empire around the first century of the Christian era, began by meeting in the houses of those richer members of the community who acted as patrons to the community. He talks specifically of Mithraeums in Ostia, many of which were built either within domestic property or through the adaptation of other buildings (1990, pp. 47–59). The patronage system is important here as identified in the many inscriptions that accompany these sites (Chow 1992). What is also evident from these inscriptions is that many of these religious or cultic communities were made up from the members of one single household, including the slaves and freedmen of that household, and that the hierarchical structure of the cult community would often match that of the household itself.

Once again, however, the size of these communities is important, around ten to thirty individuals (White 1990, pp. 48–53). These were not large public cults with large public communities. In many cases they were small familial and household-based communities, or communities that were made up of the members of a particular ethnic group within a city, people who shared the same origins. In the case of the Mithraic communities it was common, as in Ostia, to have six or seven such communities within a single city rather than one large community (White 1990, p. 48). This would suggest that the idea of the small, family-based, household community would not have been unknown to the early Christians. If the Corinthian community was only ten or twenty members strong then the way in which the text is read, and the possibility of a weekly meal at which the death of Christ was remembered, becomes much more realistic. What White himself suggests is that there were probably six or seven such communities within Corinth, each of which was associated with a different household, and he draws on the names from the letters to Corinth, Acts and the letter to the Romans to indicate who might have acted as patrons to the different communities (1990, pp. 105–6).

White also lists only five synagogue buildings from the Diaspora during the period covered by this book that have been extensively excavated (1990, pp. 62–77). Of these four, Priene in Asia Minor, Stobi in Macedonia, Delos in the Aegean and Dura Europos in Syria, were all converted from previous domestic buildings. The last, in Ostia, may also have originated in this way but the evidence is less conclusive. The spaces themselves consist primarily of a large hall, usually with stone benches around the walls and in most cases with a niche for the Torah against one of the walls. All the buildings also have other rooms, whether these are the remains of the domestic space that may continue to be inhabited or whether they are rooms that could be used for community use or hospitality. In none of these cases, however, is there any specific reference to rooms set aside for regular dining within the community. It must be assumed that if such regular meals occurred they would have done so at the domestic residencies of the members.

The Collegia: inscriptions and rules

It is the material that is available on clubs and other social groups, however, that is perhaps most relevant for an understanding of the earliest Christian communities. Throughout the ancient world there were gatherings of individuals for various purposes that formed themselves into clubs, or *collegia* to use the standard Latin term of the time (Stambaugh and Balch 1986, p. 125), and provided themselves with rules and regulations. Many of these rules have been preserved through the widespread practice of inscribing the rules on the walls of the building where the *collegia* are to meet. It is very difficult to generalize about this material or to argue that because one such *collegium* undertook certain activities then they all must have done the same (Harland 2003). It is also important to recognize that most of these *collegia* came together for very specific purposes, not all of which were strictly religious, and therefore the Christian communities are probably not to be compared with many of the *collegia* for which there is evidence. The Christian communities were not *collegia* in themselves. It is possible, however, that in some ways they behaved like the *collegia* and may have been understood as such by those outside the Christian community (Harland 2003, pp. 210–12).

Collegia existed for many purposes (Stambaugh and Balch 1986, p. 126). One clear subgroup consisted of benevolent societies (*eranoi* in Greek) where individuals came together to offer financial assistance to members and to share the burden of funerary expenses (McDonald 1998, p. 152). Members also came together to share food and wine, particularly on the anniversaries of the death of their members. Some commentators have noted the similarities in the way members of the *eranos* each bring food to share at their meals with the account of the meal offered in 1 Corinthians (Bradshaw 2004, p. 44; McDonald 1998, p. 152). Other *collegia* gathered around a particular ethnic group within a city, or among members of a specific trade, or through devotees to a particular god (*thiasoi*) (Harland 2003, pp. 28–52). Others again, especially within the higher-status groups, were probably little more than drinking clubs, a chance to get together to share good food and good company. It is not the function of the *collegia* that makes them interesting; it is their membership and their practices.

It is often assumed that the kind of community that is portrayed in 1 Corinthians and other Pauline works, with its wide diversity of social status and mixture of men and women, is either unique to Christianity at the time or at least should be considered as unusual. Esler stresses that rich and poor within the Hellenistic city did not interact on the social level (Esler 1987, pp. 171–9) and others have stressed the limited role of women, especially in Greek society (Barton 2001). However, there is some evidence to suggest that Christian communities may not have been all that unusual (Harland 2003, pp. 180–2). Horsley provides evidence of a first-century fishing association whose members had set up a custom's house near the harbour in Ephesus (1989, pp. 95–114). As McDonald states, 'the social mix of the group, from Roman citizen to slave, is remarkably similar to that shown in the list of church members in Paul's writings' (1998, p. 153). Many of the inscriptions associated with cult groups also make it clear that they are open to both men and women and in some cases slaves are expressly included (Barton and Horsley 1986, p. 25). Christian communities would not have appeared all that distinctive in terms of membership when compared to such groups.

According to the inscriptions that have remained, almost all the *collegia*, whatever their primary purpose, met at least once a year for a feast or shared meal (Smith 2003). The religious *collegia* tended to meet on the feast day of their particular deity and some of these could have been rather large gatherings. Other *collegia*, those focused on a particular trade or ethnic group, might have met on a monthly basis. The rules of the society of the *Iobacchoi*, for example, whose meeting house was excavated in Athens, state that feasts are to take place 'on the ninth of each month, on the annual festival, on Bacchic holidays and if there is any occasional feast of the god' (lines 42–6) and they also engaged in wine feasts at the death of a member (lines 159–63). Harland describes this group as gathering quite frequently (Harland 2003, p. 83). The funeral societies, apparently, met less frequently depending on the specific dates on which they commemorated past members or their founders. Esler can say in relation to the possible charitable function of these societies that 'although they held regular meetings at which the members enjoyed a banquet . . . such meals were too infrequent to be a permanent solution to the problem of hunger' (1987, p. 176). In all these lists of meetings, however, there is no clear evidence of a *collegium* or association of this kind that met weekly. On the whole the week was not a unit of time that held much significance for the Roman world (Rordorf 1968, pp. 24–38). It was designated by the names of the seven planets, but there was no break in work routines on a weekly basis and the week was not a unit of time for regular gatherings of the associations. If the early Christian community, therefore, functioned on the model of a *collegia* then there would be little expectation of a regular weekly meal.

Another point worth noting relates to the food that was served at gatherings of the *collegia*, as this may provide some sense of what a 'meal' would have consisted of among a reasonably large gathering where different social classes mixed within the same social unit. There is not a great deal of evidence for the menu at the meals of the *collegia*, but what there is suggests that, except among the high-status drinking clubs, excessive feasts were not common. They consisted of simple food served to a reasonably large group of people (Harland 2003, pp. 74–5). It was the company and the underlying purpose of the club that mattered not the lavishness of the food served. Despite some criticism of *collegia* in general for drunkenness and excess in the literature of the time, the overall impression of the associations as outlined by their rules is one of simplicity and sobriety (Harland 2003, pp. 74–86). If this is the case for many of the *collegia* then, when the texts talk of a shared meal within Christian contexts something equally simple – bread with either fish or stock and some wine or water to drink – may be all that was on offer (McGowan 1999a). The idea of an elaborate meal with multiple courses was clearly not the nature of many of the events being discussed. In these contexts the question of whether there was a full meal or just bread and wine, may have been the addition of some fish, a light broth or perhaps even nuts and dried fruit. It is the bread and wine, or bread and water, that formed the basis for the meal and so to talk of bread and wine being separated from the wider meal may not be as significant as some earlier scholars have suggested (Dix 1945).

The final point that I would want to make in relation to the lists of rules relating to the different *collegia* is the emphasis on order. If the main activity of the *collegium* is to eat and drink then some level of disorderliness would be expected. It is not all that surprising, therefore, to see rules outlining how members are to behave and the fines that are meted out for drunkenness and other forms of disorder (Harland 2003, pp. 82–3). This is only really of interest in relation to the Corinthian context where Paul is performing the same task as the rules of these *collegia*, insisting on order within the context of a shared meal. This does not, however, suggest that the Corinthian meal was some kind of communal feast for a Christian *collegium*. It certainly does not suggest that the Corinthian meal was a regular event. In fact it probably suggests exactly the opposite. If the meal had been regular, say weekly, then somebody within the community would probably have followed the example of the *collegia* around them and imposed a rule insisting on orderly behaviour long before Paul had to interfere with his letter from Ephesus. While there are some interesting points, therefore, that can be learned from the *collegia* meals, they do not offer anything like a single model for the meals within the earliest Christian community.

Jewish meals

Dennis Smith begins his exploration of the banqueting tradition in Jewish sources with reference to the writings of Ben Sira, approximately

200 BCE, and the *Mishnah*, approximately 200 CE (2003, pp. 134–50). In this way he claims to show that a common ideology or 'code' has been present within Jewish meal traditions for over 400 years. Unfortunately neither of these texts can easily be claimed to be 'typical' of their period; the information contained in both only partially supports Smith's arguments, and neither can suggest very much in terms of an understanding of Jewish meal practices in the first century of the Christian era.

There are only two texts that are roughly contemporary with the New Testament and that have something to say about Jewish meal practices. These are Philo's account of the *Therapeutae* in Alexandria and the range of codes and disciplines available from the Qumran community. Philo's account of the *Therapeutae*, whoever they might have been in practice, provides very little in relation to 'typical' practices, as even Philo recognizes that they were unusual within Jewish terms and hence his reference to them in the first place (*Da Vita Contemplativa* 64–90). They share a regular meal of an ascetical form that links them in many ways to the *collegia* tradition that I have already explored. Men and women are treated equally although they eat in separate spaces (*Da Vita Contemplativa* 68, 83–7). The form of the meal, as recounted by Philo, also appears to follow that of the symposium as outlined by Smith, but even Smith recognizes that this does little more than reflect Philo's own knowledge and use of the symposium literary tradition (Smith 2003, pp. 158–9; Harland 2003, pp. 72–3).

The Qumran material is also controversial and difficult to interpret (Hempel 2001). It is not always easy to assess whether the texts are referring to a quasi-monastic group living in the desert or a body of followers scattered throughout society. Two of the texts appear to deal with meals within the community itself, the Rule of the Community (1QS) and the Rule of the Congregation, or the Appendix to the Rule (1QSa). It is unclear whether these rules ever related to specific communities or reflected actual practice, but they do provide accounts of communal meals that can be compared with those from Christian literature. Both rules appear to come from a community set apart from the rest of society with a strong emphasis on purity and boundaries. Josephus suggests that communal meals took place twice a day among Essene communities following on from purificatory rituals (*Jewish War* 2:129–32; Smith 2003, p. 153). The rules, however, do not offer any suggestions as to the frequency of the communal meals.

Presence at, and participation in, the meal outlined in the Rule of the Community is clearly restricted and new members have to wait a year before they can participate even partially and two years before they can be full participants (1QS 6:16–17). The texts also say that one of the punishments for disobedience within the community is to be excluded from the meal (1QS 6:24–5). The meal, therefore, is an important community marker and essential to the understanding of the separated community itself. The content of the meal is not specified in detail but reference is made to the blessing of the 'first-fruits of the bread and new wine' (1QS 6:6). Smith suggests that 'new wine' in this case is partially fermented wine or even simple grape juice (2003, p. 154; Nodet and Taylor 1998, pp. 99–100). It is clear from archaeological excavations at Qumran, however, that at least at this site meat was eaten in some meals. The Rule of the Congregation matches this description very closely, with a similar reference to bread and new wine (1QSa 2:11–22), but with a specific mention of the role of the Messiah at the meal. It is difficult, therefore, to see how this could relate to actual practice among any specific community. As a model for, or even a reflection of, early Christian meals, therefore, these rules cannot really take the discussion very far as, at this period at least, Christians did not form the kind of closed community envisaged by this text and would not have shared a meal on anything like as regular a basis as suggested by Josephus. The emphasis on bread and wine, however, must be noted and I will come back to this in the conclusion to this chapter.

This suggests that it is necessary to consider what little evidence there is for other communities within Jewish society at this time. There is clearly a considerable interest in meals, in purity, and in who is able to eat what, and with whom. None of this material, however, actually provides clear information about who was eating what, or whether groups with any kind of religious affiliation met on a regular basis to share a meal. Where scholars in the past have asserted with confidence that the Last Supper was an example of a common Jewish meal among friends or followers of a particular religious figure, then the source for this information tends to be the *Mishnah* or other rabbinic literature (Rouwhorst 2007 p. 298; Leonhard 2007). It is not at all clear that what was codified in the second and third centuries, following the destruction of the Temple and the recreation of rabbinic Judaism, could actually be said to exist for first-century Jewish life.

E. P. Sanders is very interesting in this respect. In his book *Judaism, Practice and Belief, 63BCE–66CE*, he states with confidence that the Sabbath was a 'joyous occasion' and that the 'Friday evening meal was as festive as people could afford to make it'. 'We may also assume', he continues, 'that the Sabbath meal included a special dish, probably fowl or fish; that is, not red meat as at a full festival, but something better than the ordinary' (1992, p. 210). Little or no evidence, however, is provided for this statement and it is recognized by Sanders as an 'assumption', probably a correct one in the circumstances. Elsewhere in the book, however, Sanders questions the idea that the Pharisees met in closed associations called *havûrôt* that met for regular communal meals (1992, p. 440). This is an idea that sits behind a number of the earlier understandings of the origins of the Eucharist (Oesterley 1925; Dix 1945). 'The only evidence', Sanders says, 'is that those who happened to live in the same courtyard or alley ate together on the sabbath' and that this was related to the distance individuals were allowed to carry their food (1992, p. 442). The evidence for Jewish associations in Palestine, therefore, that had an institutional form and met regularly for communal meals simply does not exist (Leonhard 2007). The only collective meal that is clearly evidenced within this literature is the idea of friends and family within a particular neighbourhood coming together to share the Sabbath supper.

Moving on to the Diaspora, Josephus provides a series of texts in Books 14 and 16 of the *Jewish Antiquities* that purport to be quotations from a number of decrees from Roman authorities and by Greek cities of the East on the rights of the Jews (Winter 2001, pp. 288–93). Most of these texts are not directly relevant here, but a number do present, as part of the series of rights offered, the right to meet for common meals (Esler 1987, p. 212; Zetterholm 2003, p. 40). This is set alongside customs, rites, prayers, keeping the Sabbath and so on and it is never made explicit what kind of event these 'common meals' might have been or how often they might have met. It is not even clear that the Roman compilers of these documents understood what practices the Jewish communities had, as there is also talk of 'sacrifices', which were unlikely to be taking place among Jewish communities in provincial cities (Winter 2001, p. 288). Having said that, it would probably be fair to guess that the common meals were modelled in some sense on those of the *collegia*, although there is not enough evidence to suggest that they followed a strict symposium format (Harland 2003, pp. 219–37; Runesson 2001, pp. 467–70). It is also highly likely that they consisted primarily of men, although again it is clear that there is no evidence to support this and some of the inscriptions that have remained also refer to women in prominent positions as patrons to the communities or even as leaders (White 1990, pp. 80–1). All that can be said, therefore, is that some kind of 'common meal' was expected in Diaspora Jewish communities and this could have provided the model for subsequent Christian meals (Sanders 1992, p. 202).

That Jews did meet regularly, as part of *collegia*, or more frequently as family groups to celebrate festivals and probably the weekly meal associated with the Sabbath, must be acknowledged. Sanders is fairly confident in assuming that these probably included fowl or fish and he outlines a long list of the kind of foodstuffs that were available to Jewish communities in Palestine and in the Diaspora (1992, p. 129). There are also some later examples of blessings that were used in Jewish meals, especially over bread and wine and at the end of the meal (Leonhard 2007). What cannot be known, however, is how these later (second/third century) examples, from a specifically rabbinic, and therefore probably Pharisaic, tradition might have related to blessings that were, or were not, used by a wider cross section of Jews in the first and early second centuries.

Leonhard (2007) makes an interesting observation in a recent paper on the relationship between blessings in Judaism and early Christianity. He uses a careful analysis of the rabbinic literature to show that subsequent to the fall of Jerusalem the use of blessings, *berakha*, were related to rules on tithing that were redeveloped to take account of the destruction of the Temple. In particular he suggests that the saying of a *berakha* allowed the Jew to reclaim a product that, because the tithed element could not be removed from the rest of the foodstuff, was entirely given over to God. The *berakha*, therefore, was part of a process of desacralization, while the thanksgiving in the Christian tradition, especially by the time of the *Didache*, Ignatius and other writers in the second century, had become a means of making sacred something that would otherwise be available to all people. It was this thanksgiving that set the meal apart and made it impossible to be a partaker of the meal without first undergoing baptism. The Jewish forms of blessing, therefore, and the tradition of thanksgiving that developed in Christian communities, despite their use of similar words and imagery, are according to Leonhard performing very different functions within the meal (2007, p. 309). The two traditions must, therefore, have had very different origins.

What the Sabbath meals consisted of in the mid first century, what prayers or blessing were used, and who was involved in such meals, cannot be ascertained for certain from the literature as it exists today. It is, however, very likely that the earliest Christian communities did, in some shape or form, follow local Jewish practices. Until scholars develop a much clearer idea of what these might have been then the limited evidence that is available cannot take the discussions very much further.

Conclusion

One thing that becomes clear when early Christian meals are looked at in relation to the use of meals within the wider society is that there is very little within the wider material that is of any real use to us. At one level there simply is not enough evidence of what was happening more widely. At another level, and despite the argument put forward by Smith and others, there was actually very little consistency or pattern to the day-to-day practices associated with meals across the Mediterranean and through the century or more that is being investigated. It is also very important to distinguish between evidence for actual eating habits and evidence for literary genres associated with meals. There are three points, therefore, that I wish to make in conclusion to this particular discussion.

The first conclusion is suggested by the final point of the previous paragraph. While there may be common literary motifs associated with meals in the ancient world, of which the symposium tradition is undoubtedly an important feature, this has very little value in trying to understand the actual practice of early Christian meals. It is very probably the case, as Smith argues, that Luke, for example, in his Gospel, draws on a wider literary tradition in describing meals and table talk (2003, pp. 253–72). This, however, provides no evidence, in and of itself, for the practices of the community that Luke was associated with. Where there is evidence for actual meal practices within the pages of the New Testament, then it is also clear that the symposium with its two parts does not provide the model for those meals. In 1 Corinthians, for example, the discussion of the meal in chapter 11 and the discussion of the meeting for worship in chapter 14 are dealing with two distinct events and it is only if the model of the symposium is taken as the starting point that it would be possible to consider them to be connected. The 'breaking of bread' tradition in Luke-Acts does not reflect a two-part symposium meal either as there is no discussion or table talk in two of the contexts, and in the other two (Emmaus and Troas) the discussion precedes the breaking of the bread and does not follow it. It is necessary to look beyond the symposium, therefore, for an understanding of early Christian meals.

A more helpful model may be the nature of the *collegia* in the ancient world. The evidence from the rules associated with *collegia* meals can certainly help to throw some light on the Corinthian context. It is also possible that the *collegia* can be seen as a model for some of the Jewish examples that have been touched on. What must be recognized here, however, is that the *collegium* does not provide a clear and precise blue print; something that is always the same everywhere it is enacted. The nature of social groupings and their gatherings for meals varies considerably across the ancient world, and the *collegium* is only a very loose category that allows scholars to bring together a whole series of sometimes very different examples. In some senses to describe the *collegium* as the basis for early Christian meals is something of a circular argument. The *collegium* is defined as any group that meets regularly, under rules, for social or religious purposes, and therefore the Christian communities, like all other such communities within the society, must inevitably fit within this category. It is possible to suggest that, at least outside of the Jewish community, there is very little evidence for *collegia* that meet on a weekly basis. Most of the examples that are known meet monthly or less frequently. Most also have very limited membership and do not tend to provide a context where different social classes and different genders can mix, whether over a meal or for any other purpose, although as I have shown there are some notable exceptions. If the Christian community of the time, therefore, is considered to be a *collegium* of some kind, then it is important to recognize that it is a very unusual and very distinctive one, especially in relation to its assumed meal practices.

The final conclusion that I wish to note from this wider discussion of meal practices is the perhaps obvious point that for much of the ancient world bread and wine would clearly have been seen as a meal in itself. Modern commentators have been conditioned to think of meals in modern western societies as consisting of a wide range of foodstuffs and being relatively complex activities. This led scholars such as Dix (1945) to pose the question of when the eucharistic elements became separated from the meal itself. However, if the meal, or any meal held on a regular basis for a relatively large crowd of mixed social status, would have consisted of little more than bread, a drink (probably cheap and diluted wine) and perhaps a broth, or some nuts and fruit, and occasionally, in some places, a little fish and so on, then the idea that the bread and wine has to become 'separated' for some other kind of meal begins to look rather unlikely. It is particularly the work of McGowan (1999a) that has made this clear, although he was looking primarily at ascetical traditions. Christian 'meals' however, at whatever frequency they may have been held, were most probably very simple affairs for which the term 'breaking of bread' was probably a very apt and accurate title.

In the next few chapters, it is necessary to move on from the New Testament material to look at other evidence from the first 150 years or so of the Christian communities. In order to do this I want to focus on three regions and explore these in more specific details. I will begin in Syria, and more specifically in Antioch, and then move on to Asia Minor, or Anatolia, before finishing up in Rome.

5

Antioch

Lietzmann, in his classic text *The Mass and the Last Supper* (1979), argues that he can identify two eucharistic traditions in the New Testament. The first is based on the breaking of bread in Acts and takes the form of a fellowship meal, possibly following the example of Jesus and his disciples in the post-resurrection meals. The other is an adaptation of this by Paul who brings the Eucharist narrative into association with this fellowship meal and reinterprets it in the light of sacrificial language and the idea of sharing in the body and blood of Jesus. The older fellowship meal tradition continued, according to Lietzmann, in and around Jerusalem and Antioch and can be seen in works such as the *Didache*, the Apocryphal *Acts* of the Apostles and later in the Egyptian material. Meanwhile the Pauline tradition was developed in Rome and can be traced through the writings of Ignatius, Justin and Hippolytus. Many scholars over the years have rejected this theory, either because they are uneasy with two or more origins for the Eucharist, or because they cannot see Paul as an innovator rather than one who, as he says in his own words, passed on the tradition that was given to him (1 Cor. 11.23). Others have noted that the subsequent texts that Lietzmann draws on do not really offer the weight of support that is needed for his theory to work. In recent years, however, the idea of two or more origins of the Eucharist has been widely acknowledged and a far wider range of possibly relevant texts has been studied in detail (Bradshaw 2004). Perhaps, therefore, it is time to revisit Lietzmann's theory.

At the end of Chapter 3 I presented four groups of texts within the New Testament that deal with eating and drinking, or with meals more generally. Of these I identified two that might be related to the possible practices of the early Christian community. The first is the proposed annual Paschal meal underlying Paul's comments in 1 Corinthians, and perhaps also relating to John 6, and the second focused on the 'breaking of bread' texts in Luke-Acts. On the surface these relate quite well to Lietzmann's dual origin theory, although my understanding of the Pauline material is very different from Lietzmann's. Lietzmann, like so many other 'comparative liturgists' developed his argument by moving back through history, beginning with the later texts and moving on to the earlier ones (Baumstark 1958). I have chosen to move in the other direction and to work forwards in time to see where the various ideas and practices I have identified in the New Testament texts may emerge within the writings of the next generation (Brown and Meier 1983).

I will begin at Antioch and look at a series of texts associated with Syria, Palestine and the area east of Antioch. This will focus primarily on the *Didache*, a central text for our understanding of meal practices in the Christian communities of this region, and a text that Lietzmann associates firmly with the fellowship meal tradition. I will also look at a range of other texts that scholars have associated with the Syrian/Palestinian area to see what other discourses about meals and eating can be identified within these texts, and whether anything can be said about the practices that underpin them. In Chapter 6 I will move on to look at the literature from Asia Minor, with a specific focus on the writings of Ignatius, and in Chapter 7 I will move on to Rome with a primary focus on Justin Martyr. I am not suggesting that these are distinct regions that have no influence on each other. Nor am I following Lietzmann in saying that different traditions are associated with different regions. The fact that Ignatius, for example, travelled from Antioch through Asia Minor to Rome, and that Justin was born in Samaria and travelled widely before settling down in Rome, where his *Apologies* were written, must indicate considerable movement and interaction between the regions. The choice of geographical focus, therefore, is not intended to imply any regional differences; it is simply an aid to the investigation of the material available. Having traced this material forward, it will be possible to ask whether the dual tradition that I have identified in the biblical material can be sustained with anything like the certainty that Lietzmann provides for his own presentation.

Assessing the Christian presence in Antioch

Antioch was clearly a very important city at the time of the emergence of the Christian community. It acted as the regional capital and as the administrative centre for the Roman authorities of the time. It had already had a significant history up to this point and had had a Jewish community for more than 300 years (Stambaugh and Balch 1986, pp. 147–8; Zetterholm 2003, pp. 31–40). There is not much real evidence for the nature and organization of the Jewish community in Antioch, but

Meier suggests that the community was made up of a series of smaller communities linked together by a general council of Jews, leading to a significantly more centralized organization than is found in other parts of the Jewish Diaspora (Brown and Meier 1983). Zetterholm does not endorse this view as he sees the Jewish community as being split between a number of different synagogues, many of which may have reflected specific Jewish factions (2003, pp. 38–9).

From a Christian point of view Antioch is central (Stambaugh and Balch 1986, p. 148). It is the main centre, outside of Jerusalem, where the first followers of the teachings of Jesus developed a distinctive voice and organization. It was also, if the narrative of Acts is accepted, the springing-off point for the mission to the rest of Asia, both into Anatolia and towards the East. That there was at least one Christian community in Antioch from a very early period after the death and resurrection of Jesus is beyond dispute (Zetterholm 2003, p. 93). Acts 11.19–30 suggests that some of those scattered from Jerusalem following the stoning of Stephen went to Antioch. Those associated with Stephen are described as 'Hellenists', although it is a matter of dispute among scholars as to what this meant (Wedderburn 2004, pp. 67–9). If the first community in Antioch was Greek-speaking then the later dispute over eating with Gentiles and the delegation from Jerusalem is perhaps more understandable. It is also claimed that it was in Antioch that the term 'Christian' was first used (Acts 11.26). How this community was organized, its relationship with the local Jewish community, and how unified it was in its thought and practice, are all open to question and have been discussed at length within the literature (Zetterholm 2003).

Antioch is also the site of the first reference to eating in the Christian literature, the dispute over who was able to eat with whom that led to the dispute outlined in Paul's letter to the Galatians (2.11–14). I have already touched on this dispute in Chapter 1 and noted at that point that there is no reference here to anything that could link it to Paul's concerns over the Lord's Supper in 1 Corinthians. Many authors want to assume that this passage suggests that 'communal meals were already a regular part of the various early Christian communities' (Smith and Taussig 1990, p. 59). Magnus Zetterholm provides a very detailed analysis of the literature and the various arguments that have surrounded this incident, many of which I have already discussed in the previous chapter when looking at whether Jews were able to share food with non-Jews, but concludes that there is no evidence within the text that Paul is talking about anything that might be called eucharistic, and is probably not even talking about communal meals within the Christian community (2003, pp. 149, 163). The emphasis appears to be on those people who share meals with others on a more informal and social basis, and Zetterholm stresses that the eating itself is probably not the issue. The argument for him is one of covenantal theology (2003, pp. 140–9). If Zetterholm's position is accepted then it is clear that this text cannot offer any evidence for the presence, or otherwise, of regular communal meals within the earliest Christian communities of Antioch.

Léon-Dufour (1987) is one of a number of authors who suggests that the tradition Paul received about the Eucharist, which is reproduced in 1 Corinthians, must have originated in Antioch. He develops this, alongside his own analysis of the texts of the Passion narratives of Matthew, Mark and Luke, to suggest that there was an Antiochene tradition which is seen in the texts of Luke and Paul, as opposed to the Markan tradition seen in Mark and Matthew (1987, pp. 96–8). I have discussed these texts in some detail in Chapter 2, and it is clear that Léon-Dufour's association of the 'tradition' with Antioch is incidental rather than rooted in clear evidence. While it may be possible, therefore, that Paul received a tradition about the Last Supper, associated with a Passover meal while in Antioch, we have no specific evidence to support this.

Meier identifies Antioch as the source of a range of Christian literature from Matthew's Gospel in the first Christian generation through to Ignatius' letters in the third (Brown and Meier 1983). Jefford asks whether it is possible that one town could have been the source of such a wide range of important Christian texts, and comes to the conclusion that Matthew, the *Didache* and Ignatius all originate in this milieu (Jefford 2005). What is also clear, however, is that apart from Antioch itself, many of the earliest Christian communities existed outside of the main urban centres. The evidence provided by the Gospels of Matthew and Mark suggests small, rural communities scattered across the Galilean landscape. There is an almost deliberate attempt to avoid the large Hellenistic towns of the area within the Gospels (Theissen 1992). How far north these communities existed is very difficult to assess, but the *Didache* is also often said to originate from a rural community outside of Antioch, that is, in southern Syria rather than in northern Palestine.

The *Didache* as a text

The *Didache* is a very different kind of text from any that have been considered in relation to the New Testament. Not only is it clear that there is no single author, it is also very apparent from the document itself that this text is an amalgam of a number of different elements that have been brought together for the benefit of a particular community. Different strands have been brought together and combined into one document with little or no significant editing. Having said that, it is not always easy to separate these strands out and their nature and content are as contentious as almost every other aspect of the text (Niederwimmer 1998).

The text of the *Didache* first came to light in modern times towards the end of the nineteenth century (Niederwimmer 1998, pp. 19–21) and immediately caused controversy within the academic world. There is only one almost complete manuscript of the text and this is very late (tenth century), so the first problem is to ask whether this does reflect the original form of the text. Scholarly opinion is divided on this but the consensus is that the text as it exists is probably very close to the original (although it is possible to ask what is meant by 'original' in this context). There are, however, elements that are very clearly later interpolations (Niederwimmer 1998, pp. 19–29). Second, the text contains a number of points that reflect an early stage in the development of a Christian community. The discussion of leadership, for example, shows a transitional position between a peripatetic charismatic leadership of prophets and teachers moving towards a fixed leadership of bishops and presbyters (*Didache* 11–15). Other elements demonstrate a much closer relationship to earlier Jewish discourses than to later Christian ones and this again appeared to suggest an early dating for the text. However, there also appears to be some dependence on the Gospel of Matthew, and perhaps other New Testament texts, within the document and this has led some scholars to suggest that the text is an ancient forgery that used biblical material to give it an 'apostolic' feel (Vokes 1938). Niederwimmer argues that those references that do exist only relate to the Synoptic tradition, and are probably the work of the redactor (1998, pp. 46–51). He therefore proposes that the core elements of the text might reflect an earlier strand that shows no relationship to the New Testament, but that the text as a whole could be quite late, probably in the early decades of the second century (1998, pp. 53–4).

More recently it has been proposed, in a very detailed and careful study of the text, that many elements of the *Didache* may predate the compiling of Matthew's Gospel and that Matthew may be dependent on the *Didache* and not the other way around (Garrow 2004). Garrow's analysis does depend on identifying a number of different strands within the text and on tracking a fairly complex textual history for the *Didache*, but the overall thesis is quite convincing and provides a plausible explanation of the relationship between the *Didache* and the Gospel. If this were the case, then the *Didache* would rival Paul's letter to the Corinthians as offering our earliest account of a meal tradition within the emerging Christian communities. As there is no obvious textual relationship between the *Didache* and Paul's own writing, the relative dates of these two texts does not make a great deal of difference for this analysis. What is important is to note that the *Didache* was probably compiled in southern Syria, or northern Palestine, any time from 50 to 150 and it is in these terms that the text has to be studied.

Before going on to look in more detail at the specific references to meals within the text it is important to place these in the wider context of the document as a whole (Niederwimmer 1998). The *Didache* opens with a series of moral injunctions set out as a demonstration of the way of life and the way of death. These injunctions follow a common and well-attested model. It is clear that the same kind of framework was developed in other Jewish and Christian material and it is found in a number of variant forms in a series of documents (1–6, Niederwimmer 1998, pp. 30–41). There then follows instruction on baptism (7.1–4), on the meal (9–10) and on leadership within the community (11–15). This material is very sketchy, partly contradictory and probably compiled from a number of different sources offering a series of repetitive elements and different understandings. The baptism material is perhaps the most straightforward, emphasizing the importance of baptism in running water (7.1), but the meal and the leadership sections do present considerable problems of interpretation. Finally, the document concludes with an apocalyptic section that has close associations with the apocalypses found within the Synoptic tradition (16.1–8).

It is important to note that this is not a theological work. It is not aiming to set out a specific understanding of Christian ideas. It is clearly aiming to draw together the practice of a small, probably rural, community at a time of great transition within that community (Niederwimmer 1998, p. 3). The compiler, therefore, brings together both older traditions and newer ideas and possibilities. It is an attempt to draw together and perhaps even to fix the tradition in a form that would be useful to the community (Niederwimmer 1998, pp. 42–4). Some of the internal evidence might suggest that the community itself was divided and in dispute, perhaps with younger members wanting to move on while older members preferred to hold on to cherished traditions. The prayers in the meal, in particular, emphasize the need to come together in unity (9.4; 10.5), but how much can be read into this for the context of the text is difficult to determine. The current text presents a snapshot in time and place. It is only unfortunate that the exact time and place cannot be known.

The meal(s) in the *Didache*

The main problem facing scholars when they come to look at the *Didache* is that there are two accounts of meals within the text. Some scholars have assumed that these must be two distinct rites within the community, one a Eucharist and the other an *agape*, for example, although this is to impose later terms on the events described. Others have seen the two accounts as being contradictory or complementary and have attempted in different ways to reorder the parts of the text to make them fit into whatever theory they propose. There are almost as many solutions to this problem as there are commentators on the text and to list all the possibilities and proposals would take too long (Niederwimmer 1998, pp. 139–43; Garrow 2004, pp. 13–25; Rouwhorst 2005).

Most earlier commentators were keen to fit the text into later models of what a Eucharist was, either by claiming that the texts reflect a eucharistic pattern or that they were not eucharistic in any sense. The possibility that the 'eucharistic' element might have been combined with a meal (Vööbus 1968), that the earlier text reflected a communal meal, possibly held on the Saturday, with the later one referring to a Sunday morning celebration (Klein 1908), or that they were just an ordinary meal (Wengst 1984) have all been proposed. More recently questions have been raised about the relationship between the *Didache* and the pattern of the Eucharist assumed by the Last Supper. Rouwhorst identifies two further proposals in the literature (2005, pp. 153–4). Betz and Mazza both suggest that the meal in the *Didache* is an early form of the Eucharist that predates the institution narratives, which are based on later practice (Betz 1996; Mazza 1996). Bradshaw and McGowan argue that the institution narrative does not reflect any kind of practice at all and so follow Lietzmann in seeing the *Didache* as part of a tradition of fellowship meals that eventually developed into eucharistic practice, while the institution narrative developed within a catechetical context (McGowan 1999b; Bradshaw 2003). Rouwhorst positions himself more closely with Bradshaw and McGowan. However, in a similar line of argument to my own, he sees the institution narrative as rooted in an annual Paschal meal (1996, 2005, pp. 154–5). Almost all these difficulties and problems, however, come from later expectations of what a Eucharist is and very few previous scholars have been prepared to accept the texts as they stand and to ask what kind of event (or events) they actually portray.

From the perspective of discovering an underlying practice the double account may not be important. If it is assumed that the text is made up of a series of elements brought together by a single editor who was not all that concerned about consistency and coherence, but rather wished to collect together the various elements of the text into one place, then the presence of two accounts is of little relevance; they offer two examples of practice that may or may not have originally belonged to one community. Each one has to be treated separately to begin with and only then is it possible to ask what issues may arise if they are brought together and it is proposed that they both originate from the same event, or perhaps from different events within the same community. I will therefore take the two accounts in order.

Chapter 7 opens with the phrase 'as for baptism' (reminiscent of the phrases in 1 Corinthians when Paul is addressing the elements of the letter sent by the Corinthians (Hurd 1965, p. 63)). Instructions are then given on how to baptize. Chapter 9 begins with a similar phrase 'as for thanksgiving' (εὐχαριστεῖν) (9.1). It is unclear what 'thanksgiving' in this context refers to. Is it the whole meal, the sharing of cup and bread, or is it, given that the rest of this chapter and the one following consist entirely of prayers, simply what it appears to be – when you give thanks, do it in this way?

There follow short prayers over the cup, with reference to the 'holy vine of David' (9.2), and over the bread, which gives thanks for the 'life and knowledge which you have made known to us through Jesus your servant' (9.3). The second prayer goes on to talk about the broken bread being scattered upon the mountains and becoming one when it is gathered and asks for the same for the church (9.4). The language of these prayers (the use of 'our Father', the reference to the kingdom, and the closing line 'for glory and power are yours for ever') is reminiscent of the Lord's Prayer that is offered in chapter 8. The prayers are followed by a rubric which says, 'Let no one eat or drink your thanksgiving save those who have been baptized' (9.5), and a reference to Matthew 7.6. The term 'thanksgiving' is used at this point in a much more technical sense to refer either to the whole meal or to the specific sharing of bread and cup. It is partly for this reason that Niederwimmer argues that verse 5 is a later interpolation (1998, pp. 152–3).

This is followed in chapter 10 with a longer thanksgiving to be said after 'you have had your fill' (10.1). Most commentators point out that the language at this point makes it clear that a full meal is involved. The prayer after the meal gives thanks for 'your holy name which you made dwell in our hearts' (10.2), and for knowledge, faith and immortality. The second section begins with creation, and particularly the giving of 'food and drink to human beings for enjoyment so that they would thank you' (10.3). Finally God is thanked for all things and is asked to be mindful of the Church, once again being asked to gather it together, this time from the four winds (10.5). There is a short doxology: 'May grace come, and may this world pass away. Hosanna to the God of David! If anyone is holy, let him come. If anyone is not, let him repent. Maranatha! Amen' (10.6). The chapter ends with a short statement saying that prophets should be allowed to give thanks as much as they like, which leads on, in chapter 11, to a discussion of teachers, apostles and prophets.

There are many difficulties with this text that various scholars have picked up, but the first thing to note is that this does not say very much about what this community actually did. These two chapters present a series of prayers or thanksgivings. The rubric at the start of chapter 10 suggests that they should be said at either side of the meal, and the thanksgivings over the cup and the bread at the start suggest that these were an important element of that meal. Commentators have noted a strong correlation between these texts and similar prayers said over meals in later Jewish sources. The prayers in chapter 9 are likened to the *qiddush* prayers before a meal and that in chapter 10 is often linked to the *birkat ha-mazon* (Rordorf 1978, pp. 10–13; Mazza 1996, pp. 277, 288). The earliest versions of both of these prayers come from the *Mishnah* at the beginning of the third century. The links between the text in the *Didache* and the later rabbinical texts, however, are not straightforward, especially for chapter 10 and the *birkat ha-mazon* (Rouwhorst 2005, p. 149; Garrow 2004, pp. 17–19). While each prayer has three parts it is only in the second part of the *Didache* prayer that the themes of the first prayer of the *birkat ha-mazon* are developed, and while the themes of the third part of the Jewish prayer are picked up in the third part of the *Didache* prayer the main thrust of the latter looks back to the second part of the prayer over the bread in chapter 9. Garrow suggests that the prayers in chapter 9 and those in chapter 10 are structurally identical, with a great deal of common text (2004, pp. 26–7). This can be accepted, without moving on to Garrow's conclusion that these must represent two versions of the same prayer. There is no doubt, however, that the *Didache* prayer and *birkat ha-mazon* both inhabit the same discursive field. To place too much emphasis on their links and associations, however, is probably going too far. The language of the *Didache* prayers, as I have suggested, is very similar to that of the Synoptic tradition and the Lord's Prayer, more so perhaps than to any Jewish equivalents.

The most controversial element, however, is perhaps the doxology at the end of the prayer in chapter 10 and what exactly this could mean. It is not even clear whether it is a part of the prayer at all, or another kind of rubric limiting those who can come to the meal. However, if the meal has already taken place then this clearly causes problems (Garrow 2004, pp. 21–5). Niederwimmer, among others, suggests that this is the beginning of the 'eucharistic' rite and should be followed by the sharing of bread and wine, but there is no evidence for this within the text (Niederwimmer 1998, pp. 161–3; Rordorf 1978, pp. 13–14). There is no question that these short phrases are of a different kind from the prayer itself, and they could well, as Lietzmann has suggested, form a dialogue between the leader of the celebration and the congregation, although he sees this as a supplement to the main prayer and not really part of the celebration at all (Lietzmann 1979, p. 193). Bornkamm notes that these few phrases match very closely to the series of similar statements at the end of Paul's first letter to the Corinthians (16.22) and he links both to an anathema that he claims introduces the eucharistic rite (1966, pp. 169–76). This leads him to make links to a very wide range of similar anathema statements throughout the New Testament and in other early Christian writers. If Bornkamm's view is accepted, that this kind of structure is widespread, and it is noted, unlike Bornkamm, that it is only in the *Didache* that there is any direct association with a meal, then it may be possible to recognize that some kind of dialogue, including an anathema, is involved, but that it may be more closely associated with more general Christian worship and not specifically linked to the meal itself. What these phrases do achieve, however, is to set the text within an eschatological frame and in this there is once again a link through to Paul's account of the Lord's Supper in 1 Corinthians (Bruce 1971, p. 114).

Having talked about itinerant prophets and hospitality for travelling Christians there are instructions on the distribution of first fruits, which lead directly, in chapter 14, to the second account of a meal. This is a much shorter statement that reads:

Assembling on every Sunday of the Lord, break bread and give thanks, confessing your faults beforehand so that your sacrifice may be pure. Let no one engaged in a dispute with his comrade join you until they have been reconciled, lest your sacrifice be profaned. (14.1–2)

The section concludes with a quotation based on Malachi 1.11 and 14. Chapter 15 then goes on to ask the community to select bishops and deacons worthy of the Lord.

This short passage clearly has similarities to the Luke-Acts passages on the breaking of bread, especially that relating to the prayer service at Troas, where the community is said to meet on the first day of the week to break bread (Acts 20.7–12). It is clear that what is being talked about here is a weekly event and there is no reason why the thanksgivings offered in chapters 9 and 10 could not relate to the same kind of event. If this is the case then it cannot be assumed that references to the 'breaking of bread' do not include a cup, and this may well affect the way in which the references in Luke-Acts are also considered, although I will come back to this at the end of this chapter.

The other important point here is the reference to reconciliation and to sacrifice and the suggestion that this meal is in some senses to be seen as a sacrifice (Milavec 2005, p. 79). The context is the idea, from the Torah, that a sacrifice cannot be offered until the parties are reconciled, and likewise the breaking of bread must not happen unless the community is one and sins have been confessed. It is the emphasis on the 'pure sacrifice' in the quotation from Malachi that is important here, not the idea that the bread (and wine) are to be seen as sacrifices in themselves. If there is a sacrifice then it is one of praise and thanksgiving (Rordorf 1978, p. 17). Niederwimmer suggests that the whole section is not really about the meal at all, but rather the need 'for confession, or reconciliation, as precondition for the purity required for the carrying out of the sacrifice' (1998, p. 194). More importantly, however, the people need to be prepared and ready to partake in such a sacrifice. This has some reference back to the statements at the end of chapter 10 and the demand that if anyone is holy they are to come, and if not then they should go. This suggests something of a closed community that is being very careful about its own boundaries and who it allows to share the meal (Milavec 2005). I will return to this idea again in later texts.

This comes back to the question of the relative dating of the *Didache* and other documents. I have already mentioned Garrow's (2004) work that discusses the relationship between the *Didache* and the Gospel of Matthew. What becomes more significant from my analysis is the relationship between the *Didache* and the Acts of the Apostles on one side, and with Paul's first letter to the Corinthians on the other. Betz also raises the question of the relationship between the language of the *Didache* and that of John's Gospel, but I will leave that to the following chapter (1996, p. 255).

I raise the question of the letter to the Corinthians not because of any direct textual relationship, but because a number of themes – such as eating food offered to idols, reconciliation in relation to the meal, offering payment to travelling apostles and the sense of the fragile unity of the community – are all common to both documents. Is this entirely coincidental? These are issues that are likely to have concerned many different communities struggling to develop their own Christian identity over and against a wider Jewish and Hellenistic culture. Whether there are more substantial links than this I am not able to say. The commonality of themes, however, is worth noting even if only in passing. On the other hand, while there is a significant amount of prayer-related material that allows scholars to see not only what the community did, but also something of how they interpreted what they did, a detailed analysis of this material shows that there is a significant lack of any reference to the Eucharist. It was for this reason that Lietzmann saw the *Didache* as reflecting a development of the breaking the bread tradition in Luke-Acts rather than as part of the Pauline body and blood sacrificial tradition.

In relation to Luke-Acts the question really revolves around the phrase 'breaking of bread' and the association of this with 'thanksgiving', a link that was seen in a number of the passages in Luke-Acts and is explicit in the *Didache*. If, as Garrow suggests, the *Didache* is to be dated before the Gospel of Matthew then this indicates a use of the term 'breaking of bread' that is earlier than Luke and raises the question of where Luke, or his community, derived the term. If, however, the *Didache* is dependent on the Gospel of Matthew then is it possible that this phrase originated from the editor's knowledge of the Acts of the Apostles or related material. The main difference between these two traditions is that chapters 9 and 10 of the *Didache* clearly identify both bread and the cup as part of the meal. Are we, therefore, talking about two independent sources for the term 'breaking of bread' (along with its relationship to thanksgiving) or is there a textual link? I would probably have to conclude that there are two distinct sources, and this will be important for further discussion.

The texts of the James tradition and the Pseudo-Clementine literature

The *Didache* is often seen as evidence for the development for a specifically Jewish form of Christianity within Syria, and its strong links to Jewish themes and ideas is stressed. This is seen as distinct from the Pauline tradition where a more Hellenistic thought world is developed, a view that is implied in Lietzmann's two-traditions theory, although not stated explicitly. The clear distinction between Jewish and Hellenistic thought has, however, been challenged in recent years (Lieu 2002). Having said that, there is still considerable evidence for the development, in Palestine and Syria in particular, of a form of Christianity that maintained much closer links with its Jewish roots and clearly followed elements of the law, including purity rules, some level of exclusivity, and circumcision, well into the third or even fourth centuries. The theological and practical traditions of the churches east of Antioch also continued to have a much more clearly Jewish ethos throughout their history.

In looking more closely at this strand of Jewish-Christian thought there are a number of texts that need to be looked at in more detail. Unfortunately none of these is easy to place or to date, and none offers the kind of detailed account of meals that is seen in the *Didache*. There are two bodies of literature in particular that I would want to look at briefly from the middle of the second century, and then I will move on to a more substantial body of material which dates more frequently from the third century. Unfortunately, as this is material that never found its way into the New Testament and was therefore considered to be suspect by the majority of the Christian community, either at the time it was written or at least by the time that the 'orthodox' writers of the late second and third centuries were writing, much of this literature is only known through the writings of orthodox theologians who were opposed to it.

The first body of literature relates to Palestine and Samaria and is linked to the names of James and Peter. James, the brother of Jesus, soon became the leading figure in the Jerusalem church until his martyrdom in 61 CE. Trocmé (1975) provides some evidence from the first 13 chapters of Mark's Gospel that the community where these stories originated was opposed to the authority of James in Jerusalem. James, however, became very influential beyond Jerusalem and was generally well respected throughout the Christian communities. He developed a clear reputation for piety and for his ascetical practices. He also appears to have maintained a close allegiance to the Jewish law. Towards the end of the second century, Hegesippus presents James through the image of the Nazerite (*EH* 2:23:4–6; Lapham 2003, p. 23), shaving his head and avoiding wine and meat. If the leader of the Jerusalem community did not drink wine, then what role could wine have played in any regular meal within that community? Unfortunately this simple statement does not really provide any solid evidence either way for the practice of the community. Hegesippus could simply be drawing on a stereotypical image, or James could have refrained from wine while the rest of the community shared it. No definite statements can be made based on this tradition (McGowan 1999a, pp. 149–50). There are, however, a number of texts that bear James' name or relate to his community beyond the letter contained within the New Testament (Lapham 2003, pp. 50–65). These generally offer a Jewish and early Gnostic perspective on Christianity and present a strongly ascetical stance.

One interesting text from the James tradition, quoted by Jerome and others, derives from a work that Jerome refers to as the 'Gospel According to the Hebrews' (Klauck 2003, pp. 38–43). Traditionally this text was understood to be the Hebrew original of the Gospel of Matthew but modern scholarship sees it as possibly a mid second-century document that provides a harmony and paraphrase of at least Matthew and Luke, although there are so few quotations from the text available that it is difficult to make any firm conclusions. The passage Jerome quotes says:

And when the Lord had given the cloth to the servant of the priest, he went to James and appeared to him. For James had sworn that he would not eat bread from that hour in which he had drunk the cup of the Lord until he should see him risen from among those who sleep. And shortly thereafter the Lord said: 'Bring a table and bread!' . . . He took bread, blessed it and broke it and gave it to James the just and said to him: 'My brother, eat your bread, for the Son of Man has risen from among those who sleep.' (Jerome, *De viris illustribus* 2; Klauck 2003, p. 42).

This passage is clearly an attempt to bolster James' authority within a Jewish-Christian community drawing on a tradition known to Paul in which Jesus appeared to James (1 Cor. 15.7), although also placing James at the Last Supper. It also appears to be based loosely on the Emmaus story in Luke, particularly in the reference to taking bread, blessing it and breaking it. The meal offered to James does not explicitly involve a cup, despite references to a cup in relation to the Last Supper, and nor does it make any direct link with the body and blood element of the Last Supper tradition. It is, therefore, very much of the 'breaking of bread' tradition, despite the use of 'blessing' rather than 'giving thanks', although this may only be a fault of translation as Jerome is claiming to be working from a Hebrew original. If the story is dated to the middle of the second century, and if it is suggested that this is more than simply a literary variation on the Emmaus text, then it might provide some useful evidence for the development of a 'breaking of bread' tradition, but this must be very tentative.

Another body of texts has become known as the Pseudo-Clementine literature as they claim to be written by Clement who was noted by Eusebius as being an early Bishop of Rome and who was more likely to have been the secretary to one of the Christian communities in Rome. These texts, which have a complex and rather confused history and internal relationship, are said to relate to Clement's travels with Peter in Samaria (Lapham 2003, pp. 43–4). They consist of an exchange of letters between Peter and James and a series of other texts usually referred to as the *Homilies* and the *Recognitions*, which partly overlap in content although they have originated from different sources. Some of the material consists of the preaching of Peter, others stories of Peter's conflict with Simon Magus and the Martyrdom of James and others, again of a more speculative nature. There is no certainty about when this material was brought together, what form the original texts might have taken, or where the material originated, although the general view is to place it in Samaria and northern Palestine probably at the beginning of the third century (Lapham 2003, p. 77). What is clear is that in their current form the texts reflect a strong Jewish-Christian perspective and are even anti-Pauline in their stance.

Like the James material there is a strong emphasis on asceticism in this material and what evidence there is for ritual meals tends to focus on bread and salt. McGowan identifies a section in the *Contestatio* where the person receiving the teaching stands next to baptismal waters and makes a solemn declaration prior to eating bread and salt (*Cont.* 4:3, 1999a, p. 118). The baptism of Clement's mother, as recounted in the *Homilies*, also involves Peter in breaking the bread with thanksgiving and then putting salt on it before sharing it among those present (14.1.4), although in the *Recognitions* the same story is told with a full family dinner (7.38.2). Finally, elsewhere in the *Homilies*, as well as in the letter of Clement to James, the eating of salt stands, as in much of Greek literature, for the eating of a full meal (*Hom.* 14.8.3; *Ep. Clem.* 9.1–2; McGowan 1999a, p. 119). McGowan recognizes these as possibly eucharistic, but goes on to say, 'It must be admitted that the Pseudo-Clementine works lack not only a Eucharist consisting of the recitation of the institution narrative over bread and wine, but also any one meal radically distinguished from all others for its sacral qualities' (1999a, p. 121).

In a later discussion McGowan stresses the way in which these texts present an ascetical perspective that emphasizes the use of food to define the boundaries of the community and their rejection of meat and wine (1999a, pp. 181–2). While bread and water is mentioned in an ascetical context (*Hom.* 15.7.6; *Recog* 9.6.6), the same stance is elsewhere presented in terms of bread and olives (*Hom.* 12.6, *Recog.* 7.6.4). Despite Elliott stating that 'water alone is permitted in the Eucharist' (1993, p. 430), this reference to bread and water as an example of asceticism cannot be taken to suggest the presence of a ritual meal consisting of bread and water. In fact drink is not mentioned in any of the meals that could, possibly, be described as cultic, that is, those associated with baptism. The one positive reference to a semi-ritual meal that can be isolated, that of the baptism of Clement's mother, fits neatly into the 'breaking of bread' tradition without reference to a cup, although admittedly with the addition of salt. However, unless it can be argued that any of these texts date back before the middle of the second century they may have little to contribute to the argument.

Before concluding this section I need to look at a number of references not to texts as such, but rather to communities who are associated with this region in the first and second centuries. The Nazarenes and the Ebionites were, according to the 'orthodox' literature, fairly strict Jewish-Christian communities active in Palestine and Syria in the second and third centuries. Elliott suggests that the survival of the Pseudo-Clementine literature was due to its popularity among Ebionite communities (1993, p. 430).

Although the term 'Nazarean' is used in the Acts of the Apostles (24.5), and Justin Martyr does refer to some communities in Samaria and Palestine that appear to have similar views to the Ebionites and the Nazareans (*Dialogue* 10.17), the substantial evidence for these groups comes towards the end of the second century and into the third (Lapham 2003, p. 28). Both show signs of Jewish practices and values and both appear to have had a strongly ascetical approach. Irenaeus says that the Ebionites use only bread and water in their Eucharists and he relates this to a rejection of the divine and human natures of Jesus (*Adv. Haer.* 5.1.3). Origin adds that the Ebionites kept the Passover at the same time and in the same way as the Jews (*Matt. Comm. Ser.* 79) and Epiphaneus, in his *Panarion*, says of the Ebionites, 'beside the daily bath they have a baptism of initiation and each year they celebrate certain mysteries in imitation of the church of the Christians. In these mysteries they use unleavened bread and, for the other part, pure water' (*Panarion* 30.16; Lapham 2003, p. 29). However, as McGowan and others note, it is not at all clear from the references that these three authors are dealing with the same community or what kind of evidence they are drawing on (1999a, pp. 144–7). While many scholars argue that the Ebionites or the Nazareans reflect a form of Jewish Christianity that goes back to the earliest days of the Christian community, and the report of an annual meal involving unleavened bread and water is very suggestive of some of the ideas that I have already developed, using evidence from such a late date to read back into the earliest communities has to be treated with great care. The possibilities raised by this account, however, are interesting.

The Apocryphal *Acts*

The second body of literature that I wish to look at are the so-called Apocryphal *Acts* of the Apostles. A number of authors have noted over the years that the Apocryphal *Acts* of Peter, Thomas, Paul, Andrew and John contain references to what appears to be a eucharistic meal that contains only bread and water (Lietzmann 1979; Cirlot 1939, pp. 232–5). It was McGowan (1999a), however, who developed this idea and saw the bread and water tradition as more than simply an alternative to the bread and wine tradition. Rather, he saw cultic meals consisting of bread and water as a practice that reflected an ascetical, anti-sacrificial stance among the communities that developed it. McGowan sees elements of this tradition in the Pseudo-Clementine literature that was discussed in the previous section (1999a, pp. 176–83) and some possible references to a similar tradition in the texts of the New Testament, although these are mostly opposed to such a tradition (1999a, pp. 219–39). It is important, therefore, to investigate whether the evidence from the Apocryphal *Acts* does support the kind of tradition that McGowan is proposing.

On the whole the Apocryphal *Acts* are technically too late in terms of composition to be included in this survey, as most of them date from the end of the second century and well into the third. Some elements within them, however, and the narratives that they contain, are generally recognized to go back beyond the time of composition and they may even reflect practices and events that occurred in the first century (Elliott 1993, pp. 229–30). It is for this reason that it is important to look at what they say. The other factor to bear in mind is whether it is possible to bring all these texts together and treat them as a single unit. They were collected and used by a number of Christian communities and replaced the canonical Acts of the Apostles among the Manichean community. There are also some signs of sharing and copying between the various texts and it is difficult to see which might be dependent on which. It is also generally acknowledged that in their ascetical stance, particularly in relation to sexual matters, there is a common perspective among the texts (McGowan 1999a, pp. 183–4). Having acknowledged this, however, it has to be recognized that either in their original form or through later adaptation, the various *Acts* do reflect some significant differences in theology with some elements that can clearly be identified as Gnostic, while others contain passages of a Judaizing nature. The general consensus appears to be that the *Acts* do form a common genre and clearly borrow from each other, but that they were probably composed in a number of different localities across Syria and Asia and can usually be dated to the middle of the second century.

It is clear from the texts that McGowan's identification of an ascetical milieu for these texts is correct (1999a, p. 194). It is also possible to see in a number of the texts an attitude that could justify McGowan's claim that the communities reflected in these texts reacted against the cuisine of sacrifice and particularly the sharing of meat and wine. In terms of meals, it has to be acknowledged that as a whole there are very few direct references to eating. What there is, however, is significant especially in those passages where the meal is presented in a ritual form. Looking at the texts in detail there are some relationships to the breaking of bread tradition from the writings of Luke, but I would suggest that there is less evidence for a strong 'bread and water' tradition as suggested by McGowan. In my review of the texts I will follow Elliott's suggestion for the order of composition (1993, p. 229).

In the *Acts* of Paul and Thecla, part of the larger *Acts of Paul*, the apostle is greeted at the house of Onesiphorus in Iconium with 'great joy and bowing of knees and breaking of bread and the word of God' (5; Elliott 1993, p. 365). There is also a meal of 'five loaves and vegetables and water' shared by Paul, Thecla and others at a tomb which is probably referred to as an *'agape'* although this is not clear (25; Elliott 1993, p. 369). In the longer *Acts*, Paul also heals Hermocrates by giving him bread, but with no prayers or thanksgiving, after which he and his wife are baptized (4). At Ephesus, following a miraculous release from his chains, Paul 'broke bread and brought water, gave her [Artemilla] to drink of the word, and sent her to her husband Hieronymus' (7; Elliott 1993, p. 378). This event clearly takes place at dawn of the Lord's Day. McGowan says of this last passage that 'this seems quite clearly to be a reference to water as the drink of the eucharistic meal' (1999a,

p. 185) but there is no thanksgiving here and the phrase 'gave her to drink of the word' is difficult to interpret. Finally, as Paul is about to leave for Rome we are told that 'an offering was celebrated by Paul' and after a prophecy from Myra, 'each one partook of the bread and feasted according to custom . . . amid the singing of psalms of David and of hymns' (9; Elliott 1993, p. 383). Again the reference to offering is not easy to interpret without further knowledge of the date of the text, but the emphasis on bread and on feasting, without reference to wine or water, is significant.

There are two references to eating in the *Acts of Peter* in the sixth- to seventh-century Latin text that is thought to be based on an earlier translation of the original Greek. The first reference in this text is to Paul: 'And they brought bread and water to Paul for the sacrifice that he might offer prayer and distribute it among them' (2; Elliott 1993, p. 399). This is clearly what McGowan would call a bread and water Eucharist although the reference to 'sacrifice' is unique in these documents. In a later episode Peter, following the baptism of Theon in the sea, 'took bread and gave thanks to the Lord' (5; Elliott 1993, pp. 402–3). This bread is referred to in the prayer that follows as 'your Eucharist'.

In the *Acts of John* there are three occasions where John is said to break bread (72, 85, 109–10), and there is a further reference to a 'Eucharist' at the temple of Artemis (46). In chapter 46 the Eucharist is specifically said to follow John's homily and prayer and is followed by the laying on of hands on each person assembled. Two of the references to the breaking of bread take place at tombs (72, 85) and the second also links the meal to the Eucharist (86). A passage in chapter 84, however, asks an evil soul to vanish from those who hope in the Lord, and, among other things, 'from their Eucharist, from the nourishment of their flesh, from their drink, from their dress, from their agape' and so on (84; Elliott 1993, p. 334). In the last reference, the apostle's farewell meal, the bread is specifically referred to as the Lord's 'most holy Eucharist' and John is said to give thanks, break the bread and to give a portion to all those present (109–110). There is no reference in the text, however, to any cup, whether of wine or of water.

Likewise in Gregory of Tours' *Epitome*, or summary, of the *Acts of Andrew* there are two occasions where Andrew is said to break bread with thanksgiving, once following a healing (5) and again at Andrew's farewell meal before leaving for Thessalonica (20). According to the latter text Andrew 'took bread, broke it with thanksgiving, gave it to all, saying "Receive the grace which the Lord God gives you by me his servant." He kissed everyone and commended them to the Lord' (20;

Elliott 1993, p. 279). McGowan describes this second episode, along with the farewell meal in the *Acts of John*, as a 'clear invocation of the Last Supper' (1999a, p. 190) but the meal appears long before the end of the story and is followed by a number of other episodes before Andrew's martyrdom. There is no reference in the text either to water or to any other cup.

Finally, therefore, there are the <u>*Acts of Thomas*</u>, clearly recognized as the latest of the *Acts*, probably completed towards the end of the third century, and containing much more developed structures for baptism and even for the Eucharist (49–50). There are a number of examples in this text where sharing bread (27, 49–50, 133) and on occasions herbs, oil and salt (29), and even a cup (121, 158), are mentioned. A majority of these follow baptisms or sealing (27, 49, 121, 133) and are associated with fasts. One occurs at dawn (27), and one just before the Lord's day (29). The bread, or larger meal, is clearly referred to as the 'Eucharist' (26, 27, 158) and on three occasions there is an explicit link made between the bread, in the first two instances (50, 121), and the bread and cup in the second (158), and the body and blood of Jesus: 'when they came out of the water, he took bread and a cup, blessed, and said "we eat your holy body crucified for us; and we drink your blood shed for our redemption"' (158; Elliott 1993, p. 505). McGowan suggests this might be secondary, although as he says this does not make them less interesting (1999a, p. 192).

Being a later text, with some explicit prayers associated with the blessing and distribution of the bread and the cup, there are a number of different meanings developed for the rite. The association with the 'remission of sins and everlasting transgression' (50; Elliott 1993, p. 468) clearly relates to the baptismal context of many of the rites, but the idea of a medicine for immortality, which will be seen in the work of Ignatius in the next chapter, is also present (158). As with the other *Acts* the main emphasis is on the bread, but there are some references to a cup. What is very clear, however, is an almost deliberate rejection of wine, which is associated with the ascetical context of the text as McGowan argues. The apostle is said to eat only bread and salt and to drink water (20), but more telling is the account of the preparation for a baptism, where Marcia, a nurse, is asked to 'take a loaf and bring it to me, also a very small measure of water' (120; Elliott 1993, p. 493). Marcia objects to this and offers to bring gallons of wine, but this is firmly rejected by her mistress as unnecessary.

If all this material is brought together it is clear that the evidence for what might be called a 'bread and water tradition' is quite weak. There are only two direct references to bread and water, in the *Acts of Peter* and the *Acts of Thomas*, and another possible reference in the *Acts of Paul*. The primary tradition here continues to be that of the 'breaking of bread', although the *Acts of Thomas* probably needs to be treated separately in its reference to body and blood. This does not mean that bread and water meals did not take place – the references that do exist suggest that they probably did, alongside a number of other kinds of meals – but it is difficult to define this as a 'tradition'. What none of these texts attest to is any regular weekly meal among the communities concerned. The meals almost all follow baptisms or healings, or they are associated with tombs. On a couple of occasions the time is given as dawn and there is some reference to the Lord's Day, but this is far from consistent. Finally, the continued association of 'thanksgiving' with the breaking of bread must be noted, although the reference to the bread, or the meal as a whole, as a 'Eucharist' does perhaps relate to the later date of these texts.

A reassessment

What, then, can be made of this material? Does it endorse McGowan's thesis and suggest that there was a single tradition of ascetical anti-sacrificial thought that led to a common bread and water tradition, or is it necessary to present something more in line with Lietzmann's two traditions thesis focused on the breaking of bread material? It must be noted, of course, that McGowan is not proposing one monolithic tradition. He is arguing that a number of different groups, often with significantly different theological outlooks, who were influenced by a wider cultural movement in opposition to the cuisine of sacrifice, and more specifically to meat and to wine, all tended towards the use of water in the Eucharist (1999a, pp. 251–78). This cultural stance can also be seen in more specifically Jewish forms of asceticism and in a number of Graeco-Roman philosophical positions (1999a, pp. 33–88). It is the way in which this kind of discourse is used and adapted by specific Christian groups that is the main concern of McGowan's work. Does the evidence, however, support the view that such a widespread cultural discourse led to a single tradition of Christian practice involving bread and water?

It has to be noted, first and foremost, that the *Didache* is not part of this tradition, and McGowan is happy to recognize that the 'bread and water' tradition, as he labels it, is only one of a number of possible traditions and that the bread and wine tradition continued to be strong alongside the more ascetical form. So does the *Didache* represent one example of the bread and wine tradition and the rest of the material various forms of the bread and water tradition? I do not think things are really as easy as this.

The first problem is that it is the *Didache* that stands out as an exception among the material that has been looked at. It is the one text that is explicit about the use of wine in the meal. The earlier 'breaking of bread' texts do not mention wine and nor do most of the later ones. However, it must also be noted that the few explicit references to bread and water meals in the Apocryphal *Acts* must also be seen as exceptions. Most of the 'breaking of bread' texts do not mention any kind of drink. Because bread and wine does become the norm for eucharistic practice, there is a tendency to assume that the *Didache* is normative and the rest of evidence is exceptional. If all that was available was the evidence presented in this chapter then it might appear that it is the *Didache* that is exceptional. The choice of the community underpinning the *Didache* to use wine, and to make a specific feature of the wine, probably needs some kind of explanation. One point that is made by Vööbus, but not picked up by any other scholar, is that the thanksgiving over the cup in chapter 9 is 'lackluster by comparison' with that over the bread (1968, p. 95). It is the prayer related to the bread that is elaborated with reference to the gathering in of the fragments scattered over the mountains; 'the text points emphatically to the importance of bread in the celebration' (Vööbus 1968, p. 95). This may suggest that even for *Didache* 9–10 it is the breaking of bread that is the primary focus, as with the shorter version of Luke's institution narrative, and not the balance of bread and cup.

In saying this, however, it must also be noted that, with the notable exception of the *Acts of Thomas*, none of the texts that have been explored in this chapter relate the meal back to the Last Supper, or to language of body/flesh and blood. There is no explicit link between the meal practices, of whatever form, and the Last Supper, and the Passion narratives do not appear to be the root texts for these practices. Perhaps, therefore, Lietzmann does have a point and that what has been demonstrated in these texts is a different tradition rooted in the breaking of bread. Unfortunately it is not possible to move directly from the identification of a 'breaking of bread' tradition to a clear statement that the practices reflected by this tradition must have been the giving thanks over, the breaking and the sharing of bread alone. The *Didache*, assuming that the two accounts are referring to the same event, uses 'breaking the bread' in chapter 14 while it is clear in chapter 9 that there is both bread and wine being used in the meal. 'Breaking the bread' is probably nothing more than a literary device, a title that became common, particularly in the Syrian and Palestinian communities, for the shared meal. This term found its way into the community that underpins Luke-Acts and, either from this source or independently, was also a common designation for the meal in many other communities in the region.

I think that it is perhaps possible to say what the 'breaking of bread' tradition is not, rather than specifically to say what it is. It does not appear to have any relationship back to the Last Supper, to the Passion narratives or to the idea of the body and blood of Jesus. To this extent, Lietzmann's suggestion that it refers primarily to a celebratory meal among the Christian community is certainly a possibility. The *Didache*, and perhaps Luke-Acts, suggests that such a meal was held weekly, on the first day of the week. The Apocryphal *Acts*, and other evidence, is less clear with meals held in association with baptisms, healings and death (whether at tombs or as a farewell meal). There is a definite informality about all these accounts and a close association with thanksgiving and prayer, but beyond this there is probably very little more that can be said.

6

Asia Minor

In a recent study Allen Brent (2009) has presented the journey of Ignatius of Antioch across Asia Minor as a 'martyr procession' modelled on the religious processions of the pagan culture surrounding him. He sees Ignatius as deliberately choreographing the procession to arouse certain feelings and to trigger certain associations within the wider Graeco-Roman culture. This is just the most recent, and possibly one of the most radical, of a series of more sociological studies of the writings of Ignatius of Antioch (Trevett 1992). Drawing on the language of the letters, which Brent sees as reflecting the wider Hellenistic culture, Brent argues that Ignatius is deliberately reconstructing Christianity as a mystery religion. The procession itself is seen as some kind of initiation and the idea of the god-bearer (*theophoron*, *Ephesians* 9.2) is developed to present Ignatius, or the 'bishop', as one who carries in himself the image of God (2009, p. 80). The Christian community, or church, is reconstructed as a cult association and the Eucharist as a mystery cult or pagan festival, as 'the means by which the believer finds unity with the suffering God' (2009, p. 83). The imagery of the bishop and the presbytery are developed to suggest a drama in which the bishop sat in the 'centre of a horseshoe formation with the presbyters sitting on each side of him', as a garland of apostles with the image of the Father at its centre (2009, pp. 85–6). Brent clearly has considerable knowledge of the Hellenistic culture of Asia Minor, within which he sets these letters. However, it is also clear that he is reading far more into the imagery of the text than is sustainable from the actual words, and, like so many others writing about the origins of the Eucharist, he is very deliberately taking a later practice – of the bishop sitting surrounded by his priests in the apse of a church – and reading it back into a much earlier text that does not warrant such an interpretation (2009, p. 85).

Whether the argument as presented by Brent is accepted or not, it has to be recognized that the letters Ignatius wrote on his journey across Asia Minor to his martyrdom in Rome are among the very few clear items of evidence that are available for early Christian practice in this part of the ancient world. In this chapter, therefore, I want to begin by looking at these letters in more detail and then I will move on to look at some of the other evidence from the region in much the same way that I have already done for Syria and Palestine in the previous chapter.

The letters of Ignatius

The letters attributed to Ignatius were known from a very early date within the Christian community, and a number of authors from the third and fourth centuries consider them to be canonical alongside the letters of Paul and other writings. They were rejected from the canon, because Ignatius himself was not an apostle or from the first generation of Christians. Unlike so many other texts, however, these letters were never dismissed as heretical and have remained an important source of information and theology relating to the earliest years of the Christian community throughout the centuries.

The text that was transmitted through the tradition contained 13 letters, some of which scholars began to see as later in date than others, and possibly not by Ignatius. Eusebius, writing in his *Ecclesiastical History* (*EH*), lists only six letters by Ignatius (*EH* 3.36.5–10). James Ussher, in the seventeenth century, noted that a number of English scholars only quoted from seven letters rather than the usual thirteen and that their quotations did not agree with the accepted medieval Latin version (Brent 2009, pp. 6–7). Ussher argued, therefore, that there must be another text of the letters somewhere in England that contained only seven letters and provided either a different Latin translation from the accepted version, or even an original Greek text. He found two Latin versions of this shorter document and began to reconstruct a possible Greek text from these manuscripts. Ussher published his version in 1644. Over the years other manuscripts were uncovered in Greek, Coptic and Syriac and in 1845 William Cureton published an edition of the Syriac version of the letters (Cureton 1845). These are much shorter than Ussher's Latin texts, and other Greek manuscripts, and there are only three letters. By looking at the references to the letters in early Christian authors, all of which come from the material contained in the Syriac version, Cureton argues that it is only the shorter version of the three letters presented in the Syriac manuscript that could be authentic. Speaking of the substantially shorter version of *Ephesians* he says, 'moreover, the Epistle, as it now stands, is a short, simple, earnest letter, such as we may well suppose St Ignatius to have written under the circumstances in which he was placed' (1845, p. xxvii). Subsequent scholarship has tended towards Ussher's list of seven, what is known as the 'middle recension', as opposed to the 'longer recension' of the middle ages and Cureton's 'shorter recension' (Brent 2009, p. 8). Most modern scholars accept that the seven are authentic, although it should be noted that six of these – *Ephesians, Trallians, Magnesians, Philadelphians, Smyrnaeans* and *Polycarp* – have a different manuscript tradition from the letter to the *Romans*. The generally accepted view is that Polycarp may have collected the first six together and distributed these as a bundle, while the letter to the *Romans* remained a distinct document that was transmitted through the Roman church.

In recent years there have been a number of attempts to question the authenticity of Ignatius' letters (Brent 2009, pp. 95–7; Trevett 1992, pp. 9–15). Most of these criticisms argue that the letters cannot be by Ignatius because the form of the doctrine that they are attacking is itself a product of the late second or early third century. Some also argue that the emphasis on a monarchical bishop, the single authority figure in each community, must also reflect a later stage of development as there are other texts, which clearly derive from the second and third century, that do not have such a view. In relation to the first argument, Ignatius is in fact attacking a relatively simple and unsophisticated view of Docetism, which Brent argues can also be seen in other very early Christian texts, including those of the New Testament (2009, p. 96). It would be a mistake with such early material to assume a technical use of language and a clearly worked-out understanding of, for example, the Trinity when these ideas, and the language used to talk about them, were still emerging. There is no question that in many cases Ignatius is an innovator in terms of language and image and this makes the letters both exciting to read and sometimes very difficult to interpret, but this is no reason to assign them to a later date (Schoedel 1985, p. 7). As to the second criticism, I will come back to this point below when I argue, along with most contemporary commentators, that Ignatius is probably not reflecting an actual monarchical episcopacy that existed in any of the communities he is writing to, rather he is probably trying to impose it over and against local practice. It is not surprising, therefore, that examples of such practice are only seen much later in the century.

So who was Ignatius? Eusebius mentions Ignatius as a contemporary of Polycarp, who knew the apostles, and says that he was second in the succession from Peter as Bishop of Antioch (*EH* 3.36.1–2). In the letters themselves, however, Ignatius makes no claim to have known any apostles. Peter and Paul are both mentioned (*Romans* 4.3), but there is no reference at all to John. It is Paul who is associated with the church at Ephesus and probably claimed as the founder (*Ephesians* 12.2), despite other traditions, including that of Irenaeus, which associate the church in Ephesus with John (Hengel 1989, pp. 2–5). Irenaeus claims that John lived in Ephesus until the time of Trajan, and Eusebius dates Ignatius' letters and martyrdom to the reign of Trajan (108–17 CE). It is surprising therefore to see no direct reference to John in the letters if the other accounts are to be considered as accurate. I will come back to this point later in this chapter.

According to the information that is available from Ignatius' own letters, he was condemned to be martyred in Syria and was taken under guard to be martyred in Rome (*Romans* 5.1). He travelled across Asia Minor and was met along the way by a number of representatives from different Christian communities. In Smyrna he wrote four of the letters, three to communities whose 'bishop' he had met along the journey (Ephesus, Magnesia and Tralles) and also one to Rome to anticipate his arrival there. From Smyrna he was taken to Troas where he wrote to the Philadelphians and the Smyrnaeans as well as to Polycarp before being rather suddenly taken by ship from the port in Troas to complete his journey to Rome (*Polycarp* 8.1). By this time it appears that the original dispute in Antioch had been settled (*Philadelphians* 10.1; *Polycarp* 7.1). Apart from a later account of his martyrdom, and a letter from Polycarp to the Philippians where Ignatius is mentioned (*Philippians* 8; Stevenson 1957, p. 49), nothing more is heard about him.

The letters, however, leave a number of important questions unanswered. It is impossible to know what occurred in Antioch that caused the dispute that led to Ignatius' condemnation for martyrdom. Even the fact of the condemnation is puzzling, as it has been argued that this does not follow what is known about the judicial practice of the time (Brent 2009, pp. 14–19). Prisoners were either sent to Rome for trial if they were Roman citizens, as was Paul, or they were tried and killed locally. To have been tried in Antioch and then sent to Rome to be killed appears to be a rather unusual procedure, although there could have been reasons for this in Ignatius' case. Christine Trevett, however, draws on the writings of Pliny, a contemporary of Ignatius, to suggest that the sending of prisoners to Rome to be killed was perfectly acceptable (1992, p. 5). Ignatius' role in Antioch is also unclear. He claims to have been 'the bishop of Syria' but this claim may in fact have been the reason, either directly or indirectly, for his arrest (Jefford 2005, p. 43). If, however, there was the possibility of a number of different Christian communities in Antioch, as was suggested in the previous chapter, then the possibility of a single bishop recognized by all the communities remains rather remote (Zetterholm 2003, pp. 222–4). This kind of information will probably never be known.

What is known, however, are the issues that concerned Ignatius during his travels, as these are repeated regularly in each of the letters. The overwhelming theme of all the letters is the unity of the community. This is represented in images of harmony, whether of the chorus of singers (*Ephesians* 4.2) or of a well-tuned string instrument (*Ephesians* 4.1). This unity is reflected, for Ignatius, in the leadership of the community. Each community should have just one bishop, and he names individuals in each of the Asian cities that he refers to as the 'bishop' of the community (Onesimus in *Ephesians* 1.3; Damas in *Magnesians* 2.1; Polybius in *Trallians* 1.1). It is not at all clear whether these people would have recognized the exclusiveness of the title, or what kind of leadership structures existed in the communities concerned. It is very possible that Ignatius is imposing a model that he has built up out of theological principles, rather than reflecting the reality on the ground. Ignatius presents the 'bishop' as being the image of God the Father; the deacons are the image of Jesus; and the presbyters are the image of the apostles gathered around their bishop (*Magnesians* 6.1; 13.1–2). This may have been reflected in actual practice, but the force with which he makes the point, over and over again in letter after letter, certainly gives the impression that he is aiming to impose something that is not currently happening (see *Philadelphians* 7.1–2). Why he insists on the single bishop as the focus for unity is a matter for dispute among commentators but may well have something to do with the trouble within the Christian community in Antioch that led to his arrest in the first place.

The primary cause of the disunity that Ignatius is trying to overcome in the Asian communities appears to be theological; different understandings of who Jesus was or what the community ought to be doing. Ignatius makes reference to two groups of opponents. To a lesser extent, he mentions the Judaizers of Philadelphia and Magnesia, those who wish to continue to celebrate the Sabbath and insist that the communities follow the Jewish law (*Philadelphians* 6.1; *Magnesians* 9.1, 10.3), and much more significantly he challenges the Docetists of Smyrna, those who argued that Jesus was not both spirit and flesh, but denied the flesh and probably denied that Jesus actually suffered on the cross (*Smyrnaeans* 2.1; *Trallians* 10.1; Schoedel 1985, p. 12). This latter group Ignatius finds particularly damaging, as they would appear to deny the power of the cross to save individuals. If Jesus did not suffer and die then the cross was meaningless and, by implication, the community's sharing in the suffering of Christ is also meaningless, as, of course, is Ignatius' own impending martyrdom (*Trallians* 10.1). The only way in which Ignatius can see any good in his own situation – being sent to die in the circus for his faith, as he sees it – is if he is sharing in the suffering and death of Jesus and so will share in his resurrection and his glory (*Smyrnaeans* 4.2). It is not surprising, therefore, that he is so clearly against the Docetists within the communities he is corresponding with.

The 'Eucharist' in the letters

Having looked at the texts in a more general sense it is now possible to move on to look at what they have to say specifically about the meal practices of the communities involved. In doing this it must be remembered that Ignatius may, as with the question of the leadership of the communities, be wanting to impose his own views rather than reflecting those of the communities in question. It is also important to be wary of Ignatius' own very creative use of language and imagery in his attempts to get his ideas across.

The first reference to something that could be a cultic meal comes in *Ephesians* 5.2 where Ignatius says, 'let no one deceive himself: if anyone is not within the altar, he lacks the bread of God'. There is no reason, from other references to the altar within the letters, why the image of the altar should be taken literally. Whether the bread has any more than a metaphorical meaning is more difficult to ascertain. In *Ephesians* 13.1 Ignatius writes, 'Be eager, then, to meet more often for thanksgiving and glory to God.' There is nothing here to suggest that 'thanksgiving' refers to anything more than prayers and it is only in the light of other references that it is possible to interpret this passage as anything more than a request to meet more often for worship. In *Ephesians* 20.2 the community is asked to 'come together in grace . . . breaking one bread, which is the medicine of immortality, and antidote preventing death, but leading to life in Jesus Christ for ever'. Here the breaking of bread image is taken up, but the bread is interpreted in this passage as the 'medicine of immortality'. This is the first time, in any of the 'breaking of bread' passages that have been looked at, that any kind of properties attaching to the bread itself, or to the eating of the bread, have been identified beyond the simple call to fellowship. For Ignatius, who is admittedly given to developing an image and offering new ways of looking at things, the one bread is able to offer immortality through Jesus. This has clear links, in terms of ideas if not in a literary sense, to Jesus' statement in John's Gospel that those who eat his flesh will live forever (John 6.51).

There is an interesting passage in *Trallians* 8.1 where Ignatius says, 'You, then, take up gentleness and renew yourselves in faith – which is the flesh of the Lord – and in love – which is the blood of Jesus Christ.' William Schoedel points out that the language of flesh and blood, or flesh and spirit, in relation to Jesus is used widely throughout the letters to emphasize the reality of Jesus' incarnation over again Docetic critics (Schoedel 1985, p. 149). It should not, therefore, be assumed that this passage automatically relates to the bread and cup. Schoedel also says:

> 'What our study of the linking formula ('which is') has shown is that although Ignatius uses it to bring such elements of the tradition alive by juxtaposing them in striking ways, the formula does not determine the nature of the relation between the items so joined. (1985, pp. 149–50)

He therefore rejects the possibility that this passage relates to any kind of spiritual Eucharist.

In writing to the Romans, Ignatius says:

> I take no pleasure in the food of corruption nor yet in the pleasures of this life. I want the bread of God, which is the flesh of Jesus Christ, of the seed of David; and for drink I want his blood which is incorruptible love. (6.3)

Here the reference appears to point clearly to the bread and cup of the cultic meal, understood by Ignatius as the flesh and blood of Jesus. Again, in the reference to 'incorruptible love' there may be a hint of the image of medicine of immortality, but as with other passages it may simply be that Ignatius' creative use of imagery and the juxtaposition of terms is being developed. More significant, however, is the possible relationship between this passage and John 6. There is no direct quote, but, as Hill notes, 'John 6.33 contains the only occurrence of the term αρτος θεου (bread of God) in the NT, and John 6. 51, 53, 54, 55, 56 repeatedly identify this bread with the σάρχ of Jesus' (2004, p. 433). This leads him to suggest that Ignatius must have known John's Gospel and used it to underpin this passage. If the passage is a reference to the imagery of John 6, is it also possible to state, with any kind of confidence, that this passage refers to any cultic act known to Ignatius given the possibility that John 6 can itself be interpreted in non-cultic terms?

In *Philadelphians*, Ignatius develops his central theme of the unity of the Church under the authority of a single bishop:

> Be eager, then, to celebrate one Eucharist; for one is the flesh of our Lord Jesus Christ, and one the cup for union through his blood; one ✓ the altar, just as one the bishop along with the presbytery and deacons, my fellow slaves. (4.1)

Here it is very clear that Ignatius is using 'Eucharist' to refer to the whole cultic meal, including the bread and the cup. This is more than just 'thanksgiving'; it has become a technical term. Again the use of 'flesh' as opposed to 'body' must be noted and I will come back to this later.

This idea is developed further in the letter to the *Smyrnaeans* when Ignatius says, 'Let no one do anything apart from the bishop that has to do with the church. Let that be regarded as a valid Eucharist which is held under the bishop or to whomever he entrusts it' (8.1), and later, 'It is not permissible apart from the bishop either to baptize or to celebrate the love-feast' (8.2). This is one of the first rulings concerning the role of the leader of the celebration (Rowland 1985, pp. 242–3). For Ignatius this must be a bishop, or whomever he entrusts it to. The *Didache* did say that prophets could give thanks as they saw fit (10.7), and so presumably they acted as leaders of the celebration at times, and in the Apocryphal *Acts* it was usually the apostle who took the role of celebrant. This, however, is the first formal statement that a particular officer must lead the celebration. It must also be noted that most commentators believe that Ignatius uses 'Eucharist' and 'love-feast' interchangeably, although some suggest that the love-feast is a full meal that contains the Eucharist (Schoedel 1985, p. 244). I will come back to this point below.

A little earlier in the same letter Ignatius talks of those who follow a Docetic heresy: 'they remain aloof from Eucharist and prayers because they do not confess that the Eucharist is the flesh of our saviour Jesus Christ which suffered for our sins' (*Smyrnaeans* 7.1). It is not clear at this point whether Ignatius is talking about a separate community who hold different views, or about individuals within the wider Christian community. Therefore it is difficult to say whether this is a community that does not hold a Eucharist, whether it is a community that does not see its common meals as Eucharists, or whether they are a part of the *isn't he today our belief* (handwritten note in left margin)

wider community that does not attend the Eucharists of that community. The fact that a Docetist does not understand the bread of the Eucharist to be the flesh of Jesus is entirely understandable. The possibility must also be recognized, as raised by Bradshaw, that this group simply held an older understanding of the sharing of the meal, which did not link the bread and cup with the flesh and blood of Jesus, and it is only Ignatius who suggests that these people held a fully developed Docetic Christology (Bradshaw 2004, p. 88). It is unfortunate, however, that no more concrete information can be developed from this passage.

There may be other passages where some kind of allusion to the meal is being made that I have misread. Brent, for example, in his attempt to show the importance of the mystery cult underpinning all of Ignatius' writing, tends to take any reference to 'mystery', or to 'blood' and 'flesh', or even to 'altar' and to the presbyters as 'the garland of the apostles' as in some sense a reference to the Eucharist. It is, of course, important to see how imagery reflects backwards and forwards in these texts and allows a discussion of one element, say martyrdom, to speak to another, the death of Jesus or the unity of the community, but to see references to meals in each and every text is possibly going too far. It is my view that the bulk of the references to flesh and blood, for example, relate to arguments against some form of Docetism and are not primarily related to the meal. However, in the few examples that have already been looked at, Ignatius can draw on his understanding of the bread and the cup in the meal to speak into the debate against the Docetist, but not the other way around.

If all the references that I have highlighted are brought together, there are a few things that can be said with reasonable certainty, but still a great deal that simply cannot be said. Ignatius is aware of, and uses, the 'breaking of bread' tradition, although that terminology is now competing with the term 'Eucharist' as a designation for the whole meal, and perhaps for the bread and cup within the meal. Ignatius also draws on the terminology and understanding of the bread and cup as the flesh and blood of the Lord. There is no direct reference to the Last Supper as the origin of this terminology, but the link is at least implicit, unless we see the link as being with Johannine thought processes. What is important here is the use of 'flesh' rather than 'body' for the bread. Bradshaw identifies this as a link through to the Johannine tradition where 'flesh' was used in John's Gospel in place of 'body' (2004, p. 87), the idea of the medicine of immortality may also be derived from the ideas surrounding John 6 as I have suggested. Trevett uses the same word as Bradshaw in recognizing 'affinities' with the thought and language of the fourth Gospel, but tends to claim that there are no real grounds for literary dependence (1992, p. 21). Hill, however, is keen to show that Ignatius, while not mentioning John by name, clearly draws on elements of Johannine thinking and language at various points in his letters (Hill 2004, pp. 421–43). On the other hand, Trevett, along with many other commentators, recognizes that Ignatius must have known Paul's first letter to the Corinthians as this is referenced extensively throughout the letters, which suggests that Bradshaw's comment that ✓ Ignatius 'shows no sign of knowing' Paul must be incorrect (Trevett 1992, p. 20; Bradshaw 2004, p. 87). The choices made by Ignatius that led him to use 'flesh' rather than 'body' have to be more complex than a simple statement that he preferred John's language to that of Paul or the Synoptics. I will come back to this below. For now I want to pursue another possibility, not as an alternative to the Johannine link, but possibly as being complementary to it.

I have noted above that Ignatius uses 'flesh' language quite extensively throughout the letters (Schoedel 1985, pp. 23–4, 149). In many cases Ignatius talks about the 'flesh and spirit' of Jesus, in others his reference is just to the 'flesh', and on other occasions he talks about the 'flesh and blood', or even the 'flesh, spirit and blood'. Malina (1978) argues that this language relates to the way in which Christians are seen in relation to the world. Using Douglas's ideas of natural symbols, he sees flesh/spirit language as showing that Ignatius is suggesting that the spirit works through flesh, or matter, and that the individual should be subordinate to the world (1978, p. 87). Not all this kind of language, therefore, can be assumed to sit within a eucharistic context (Morris 1971, p. 375). In all these cases, however, it is clear that Ignatius is using 'flesh' in order to counter a Docetic theology that is noted as being very influential in a number of the communities that he is writing to, although it is not entirely clear what form this Docetism might have taken (Wedderburn 2004, p. 183). By emphasizing the very material, fleshly, nature of Jesus, not just his 'body', which could after all be an illusion, Ignatius is making a very strong argument about his own Christology.✓ It has been argued that the author of the Gospel of John is doing the same thing in his Gospel through the same choice of word (Hill 2004, p. 433; Morris 1971, p. 102). It is possible, therefore, that what is demonstrated in these letters is not a direct link to John's Gospel, but rather a similar use of words in order to make a similar theological argument (Wedderburn 2004, p. 183).

Is it, however, the argument with the Docetists that leads Ignatius to draw on the flesh and blood imagery for the bread and cup in the first place? In other words is this link one that Ignatius is developing independently of a known 'eucharistic' tradition going back to either Paul or John, or both? I have already noted on a number of occasions that Ignatius is fond of imagery and the juxtaposition of different ideas to make creative links in his theological thinking, or perhaps even to shock his audience. Is the flesh and blood imagery as associated with the bread and cup one of these, created and developed by Ignatius over and against the traditions of his audience? On the whole I would argue not. This does not mean, however, that it must have been part of the regular discourses surrounding meals for the communities Ignatius is writing to. If he and his readers are familiar with Paul's writing, and perhaps with the wider context of Johannine thought, if not with his Gospel, then the link made by Ignatius cannot be said to be new, but it may be a literary dependency rather than something that is rooted in practice. If this is the case, then it is not essential to assume that some kind of 'flesh and blood' discourse was associated with the meal among those communities to whom he is writing.

Finally, therefore, do these letters provide any clues at all as to the practice of the communities concerned? Unfortunately I think the answer is 'no', despite Brent's ingenious attempt to argue for a seating plan within the imagery of the letters. There is, for example, no indication of whether Ignatius is talking of full meals, or just a sharing of bread and cup. Once again there is no direct reference to wine, just to the cup, which has been almost universal in all the texts that have been looked at so far. The brief mention of the love-feast in *Smyrnaeans* may suggest a full meal, but this single reference is very difficult to interpret. There is clearly some kind of prayer of thanksgiving associated with the meal as this has, by the time Ignatius is writing, provided the name for the meal. Clearly Ignatius would like the bishop, or one that he has appointed, to preside at the meal, but this does not say who else may be taking on that role at the time that Ignatius is writing.

There is nothing in these letters to indicate the timing or the frequency of the rite. In *Magnesians* 9.1 Ignatius talks about no longer 'keeping the Sabbath, but living in accordance with the Lord's Day'. I would not follow Brent in seeing the word 'mystery' in the following sentence as referring to the Eucharist (Brent 2009, p. 71). In Schoedel's commentary the 'mystery' clearly refers to the death and resurrection, as it is through this that faith is received (Schoedel 1985, p. 123; Bouyer 1990, p. 132). However, it is clear that for Ignatius, and probably for the communities he is writing to, the Lord's Day is an accepted term and probably reflects a tradition of meeting on that day, although whether this includes the sharing of a meal is not clear. There are also a couple of points at which Ignatius calls on the community to meet more frequently (*Ephesians* 13.1; *Polycarp* 4.2), although only in the Ephesians context is 'thanksgiving' mentioned, which could possibly be a reference to the meal. Does this mean that Ignatius wants the communities to move from a weekly to a daily celebration? It is more likely, I would suggest, that there was no fixed timing at this point for the meal or perhaps for worship in general, and that Ignatius, who may be aware of a weekly celebration in Syria, similar to that suggested by the *Didache*, wants the communities to gather more regularly for worship and perhaps to share their meals more regularly. However, on the evidence that is available, this can only ever be speculation. Very little more can be said with certainty about Ignatius' letters and so it is important to move on and to look at other evidence from the region in the same way that I did for Antioch and Syria in the previous chapter.

Pliny's letter to Trajan

Pliny was governor of Bithynia, a region in the north of Asia Minor, at about the same time that Ignatius was being taken to Rome across the south. There exists a series of correspondence between Pliny and the Emperor Trajan. In one of Pliny's letters he asks what he is supposed to do in relation to Christians (*Epp.* 10.96; Stevenson 1957, pp. 13–14). He is clearly aware that, as a Roman governor, if an individual claims to be a Christian and refuses to repent and pray to a statue of the Emperor then that person must be killed, but it appears that Pliny does not really understand what Christians are supposed to have done wrong. A number of those who come before him refuse to repent and have been killed, others either deny ever having been a Christian, or do repent under the threat of death. It is from the latter group that Pliny appears to have got some information about who the Christians are and what they do, and it is this that he includes in his letter.

We are told that the Christians meet on a fixed day before dawn to recite a form of words to Christ as a god and to commit themselves to certain oaths (Pliny, *Epp.* 10.96.7). The word that is used is *sacramentum* but it is highly unlikely that this has any kind of technical meaning for the Christian community at such an early date. What appears to be described is a simple meeting for prayer and mutual support. The text then goes on to mention the possibility of meeting again later in the day for food, although following Pliny's own ban on collective gatherings this has been abandoned. This cryptic and, in itself, largely unhelpful account has been interpreted by scholars in many different ways. Some suggest that what is demonstrated here is the abandoning of the meal element of the early Eucharist, leaving the sharing of bread and wine at a morning ritual (Bradshaw 2004, p. 65). This, however, is totally unsupported by the evidence. Others simply state that this short text indicates very little except that Christians existed and worshipped in Bithynia at the beginning of the second century.

What has to be noted is that the source that Pliny is drawing on is people who, either previous to their arrest or under the threat of torture and death, have renounced Christianity. It is not those who are currently Christians who are providing this information. If the source was current Christians then it might be assumed that if there was a sharing of bread and wine it is unlikely that they would mention it; as such people would not want to give away any more than is absolutely necessary. Would those who recant under the threat of torture have the same concerns? It may still be the case, of course, that these people, or even Pliny himself, did not think the sharing of bread and wine to be important. That, however, is unlikely. The text qualifies the reference to food with 'but ordinary and harmless food' (*Epp.* 10.96.7; Stevenson 1957, p. 14). I think that, given the context, this evidence does have to be taken at face value. What is being described is an early morning meeting, a gathering before the day's work has begun, and a tradition of regular (although the frequency is not recorded) evening meals held in common. The fact that the meal can be abandoned under threats from the authorities suggests that it did hot have an absolutely central place in the life of the community and therefore probably had no connection to the Last Supper or other kind of tradition. Very little more can be said. However, as another element of the evidence, this account adds to a growing picture of meals within the earliest Christian communities.

The New Prophecy and other later second-century evidence

It is not until sometime towards the end of the second century that other evidence begins to emerge from this region, although this is still very sketchy and not really very helpful to the overall analysis. Archaeological work within Phrygia towards the end of the twentieth century, focusing specifically on tombstones and inscriptions, has shown considerable fluidity between Christian, Jewish and Pagan communities, with many tombs containing imagery and language that would previously have been assigned to more than one community (Treblico 1991). This may reflect some kind of syncretism within the area. More probable, however, is that for many individuals these different communities were not as clearly bounded and distinct as some scholars might like to think. There is growing evidence of individual responses to a range of overlapping religious discourses that, if it existed in the contemporary world, might be described as 'postmodern' (Lieu 1996).

It is in Phrygia that the New Prophecy begins to emerge in the middle years of the century (Trevett 1996). More commonly known as Montanism, the New Prophecy began, according to orthodox Christian sources, when Montanus started to experience ecstatic utterances and to teach new doctrines based on the prophecies that he, and two women associated with him, Maximilla and Priscilla, were receiving. There is considerable debate both about the historic record of this movement and about its particular doctrines and ideas (Trevett 1996). The only sources that are available are those of the orthodox communities that were opposed to them. They clearly did make a significant impact, and over time the movement spread quite considerably. Towards the end of the century, Tertullian in North Africa was a follower and he recounts how the prophecies and ecstatic experiences had a regular part in what would otherwise be seen as a typical eucharistic rite of that time (McGowan 1999a, pp. 167–9). What kind of practices were involved in the early years of the movement and in the middle years of the century, however, is much more difficult to establish.

The only reference to food in relation to the New Prophecy is in Hippolytus' *Refutation of All Heresies* from around 220. This work claims that this group introduced 'the novelties of fast, and feasts, and meals of parched food, and repasts of radishes' (*Refutation* 8.19.2; Stevenson 1957, p. 114). McGowan translates the word ραφανοφαγια as 'cabbage eating' and adds a later association of Montanism with 'cynic mysteries' (Filastrius, *Div. Haer. Lib.* 49) – 'very probably a reference to a bread and water meal' – to conclude that Montanist meal practice appears to 'have been little more than bread and water, with some cabbage on the side' (1999a, pp. 167–8). He also recognizes that for Tertullian the abstinence from meat is only undertaken during fasts and so the bread and water meal may also have been temporary (1999a, p. 168).

Another interesting text that is loosely related to the New Prophecy is found on the tomb of Aberkios of Heiropolis, who has been linked to Avircius Marcellus, one of the figures quoted by Eusebius and others as opposing the movement (*EH* 5.16.3–5). There are two sources for this text. One is a later transcription that has come down through the hagiographical literature. The other is the significantly worn text on the tombstone itself, which was discovered in Phrygia in the later nineteenth century and is currently in the Vatican Museum. Among other statements of a rather elusive nature, there is a comment on the journeys made by Aberkios: 'Faith everywhere led the way and served food everywhere, the fish from the spring – immense, pure, which the pure virgin caught and gave to her friends to eat forever, and with good wine, giving the cup with the loaf' (Grant 2003, p. 35). This is a late second-century text and whatever may be made of the fish and the good wine, the reference to cup and loaf, without any further elaboration, certainly raises interesting questions.

McGowan, in an early paper (1995), presents an argument for the presence of a cup–bread eucharistic order across Syria and Asia Minor based in part on Luke and the *Didache*, but also on a brief reference in Papias, an early second-century Bishop of Hierapolis, as quoted by Irenaeus. The passage is an apocalyptic text in which bunches of grapes call out to each other, 'I am better, pick me, bless the Lord through me', which is followed by references to grains of wheat and fine white flour (*Adv. Haer.* 5.33.3–4). I am not sure that so much weight can be put on the order of grapes and wheat as McGowan suggests, but the reference to blessing through the grape, or through wine, has to be significant and adds to our evidence for wine in meals alongside bread and/or water.

The *Epistolorum Apostolicum* has already been mentioned in my discussion of Christian celebrations of Passover in Chapter 2. As with all documents of this kind it is very difficult to place and date. In many cases it is the reference to the Passover, and its relation to the quartodeciman controversy, that provides the main evidence for date and provenance. The text itself, however, is not referenced by any other ancient source, suggesting a limited circulation (Elliott 1993, p. 556). The second half of the second century is generally accepted as the date, and the most likely region is either Asia Minor or Egypt. It is an Ethiopian version of the text that provides the clearest reference to a Passover meal, but even this is not at all easy to interpret. Chapter 15 says:

And you celebrate the remembrance of my death, which is the Passover then one of you who stands beside me will be thrown into prison . . . and when you complete my agape and my remembrance at the crowing of the cock he will again be taken and thrown into prison. (Elliott 1993, p. 565)

The context, Jesus talking about the persecution of the community, is so intimately tied into the account of the Passover celebration that it is difficult to disinter the two strands to make any clear statement about what the *'agape'* is, apart from its timing at dawn.

The influence of Johannine literature in Asia Minor

Before concluding this chapter and providing a summary of the evidence presented, I want to go back and explore in more detail a question I have already raised in relation to Ignatius. I noted that in his letters Ignatius makes no direct reference to John, although his language in relation to the flesh and blood of Jesus and its association with the bread and the cup clearly appears to come from a Johannine milieu, or maybe a similar reaction to a form of Docetism that both John and Ignatius are combating. This raises the question of the influence of the Johannine community within Asia Minor at the end of the first century and the beginning of the second. John's name is clearly associated with Ephesus by Irenaeus and other writers at the end of the second century, with a clear statement of the succession from John, through Polycarp of Smyrna to Irenaeus (*Adv. Haer.* 3.1.1; Hengel 1989, pp. 2–5). However, the Gospel is more often associated with a Palestinian context as I outlined in Chapter 3. The three letters attributed to John do appear to be associated with Asia, as does the book of Revelation (Hengel 1989). The relationship between the Elder of the letters, the author of the Gospel and the John of Revelation does, however, appear to be a complex one and is far from settled in the literature. Only Hengel (1989) appears to put forward a clear case for the continuation of a Johannine community in Ephesus or the wider eastern edge of Asia Minor.

Charles Hill (2004) goes to some length in his book on the Johannine corpus in the early Christian communities to counter what he describes as an orthodox Johannophobia. It was fashionable, he argues, among scholars of the early Church to say that John was largely ignored in the texts that are available until the end of the second century. Various reasons have been offered for this, including the limited distribution of the material relating to a small Christian sect, to the adoption of John as the Gospel of the Gnostics (2004, pp. 62–5). Hill wishes to argue that all these theories are wrong and that John and his Gospel are known and alluded to quite widely from the end of the first century. The argument in relation to most of the specific texts appears to revolve around whether the scholar in question wanted to see an exact quotation of a Johannine text or, like Hill, whether some kind of allusion and commonality of language and imagery was enough.

We have already seen how this relates to Ignatius where there is no direct quoting of the Gospel in the text, nor is there any specific quotation from Paul or Matthew. However, there is enough commonality in the kind of anti-Docetic language of flesh and spirit, or flesh and blood, for Hill to suggest that Ignatius was at least aware of Johannine literature (2004, pp. 431–41). The question is whether Ignatius would have been familiar with that literature from his days in Syria, or whether he was introduced to it on his journey across Asia. Hill also notes that the *Epistula Apostolorum* and the *Peri Pascha* of Melito of Sardis also contain considerable allusions to Johannine literature (2004, pp. 336–74, 294–6). The same will also be seen of Justin and, from Hill's point of view, practically every other second-century Christian writer (2004, pp. 312–51). Betz even relates some of the language of the *Didache* to that of John's Gospel, which is remotely possible if it is assumed that both originated in the area around Palestine, Syria or Samaria, but is probably taking the argument a little too far (1996, p. 255).

If it is accepted that there is some knowledge and allusion to Johannine writings within a wide range of other early Christian authors, what can be said about the development of the Johannine community? Is the idea of a specifically Johannine community lasting into the early years of the second century a realistic one? Ignatius is clear that Paul has some associations with Ephesus, but there is no mention in his writings of any Johannine link. Hengel proposes that both Ignatius and Polycarp were writing so close to the date of the publication of the Gospel and letters that the influence of Paul at Ephesus was still strong and the link to John had yet to be made, although the Johannine school was already in existence and perhaps even in its dying stages (1989, pp. 14–16). It is Irenaeus, towards the end of the second century, who provides the main evidence for the link between John and Ephesus, although the letters and the book of Revelation, which are also associated with the name of John, clearly have links to the western coast of Asia Minor (Hengel 1989, pp. 2–6). Unfortunately, the evidence that is available simply not allow any further analysis in relation to a specifically Johannine community in Asia at this time, or in any real sense to the relationship between Johannine thought and that deriving from other strands within the Christian community.

Why is this important for a book on the origins of the Eucharist? Bradshaw and others have highlighted the fact that Ignatius and Justin, among others, use flesh rather than body in their references to bread and cup (2004, p. 89). Clearly this does not follow the language of Paul and the Synoptic Last Supper narratives, but does have a link with John's account of the bread of life (John 6). If this is purely coincidental, is it, as I have suggested, the consequences of similar anti-Docetic polemic, or is there possibly a direct link through from a Johannine understanding of the bread and the cup in some kind of cultic meal? In other words does Ignatius develop the idea of the flesh and blood of Jesus from John 6 or from the Synoptic accounts of the Last Supper? It may not be as simple as saying that the link is with one or the other of the earlier texts. However, if Johannine thought and texts were widely available and beginning to be influential in Asia Minor at the time that Ignatius was writing, then the possibility of a direct link to John increases.

Summary and conclusions

I have concentrated a great deal in this chapter on the language of flesh and blood. However, in order to draw the wider discussion to a conclusion I want to stand back from the use of language to ask whether any of the evidence that has been investigated in this chapter can provide any information about what kind of communal meals were being held by Christians in Asia Minor in the first half of the second century. Of course, the evidence that is available does not allow any firm conclusions to be drawn. However, if some of the questions that were raised at the end of the previous chapter are looked at again it might be possible to see what extra evidence this Asian material has to offer to the emerging picture.

The first thing to note is that the 'breaking of bread' tradition does not seem so strong within this material. Ignatius alludes to it in one of his early letters (*Ephesians* 20.2) but then drops it in favour of the use of 'Eucharist' for the meal as a whole, whatever that meal consisted of. There is some suggestion of this in the *Didache*, but there seems to be a more technical use of the word within the writings of Ignatius. 'Breaking the bread,' therefore, may not have been a term that was widely used within the communities Ignatius was writing to. This is matched by a fairly clear view from Ignatius, that the meals he refers to included both bread and cup. The bread-only focus is less clear, and there is no real evidence of bread and water meals within the communities of Asia Minor. In fact some of the evidence does not even suggest that bread was a specific part of the meal, with the letter of Pliny talking only of communal meals that have now ceased, and the *Epistula Apostolorum* picking up the word *agape*, which was also used in the *Didache* and in Jude but is not given any specific focus in terms of the content of the meal.

As there is no clear sense of what the meals consisted of there is, I would suggest, no clear evidence about how often these meals were held. Ignatius appears to ask that they be held more frequently, but in itself this indicates nothing. If he is used to a weekly meal then this request may suggest that meals in Asia were not being held on a weekly basis. However, the nature of the texts and the kind of language Ignatius uses does suggest that some kind of meal was being held on a reasonably frequent basis, probably more than annually. The emphasis on the Pascha does, of course, continue within Asia Minor as is seen in the debates around the Quartodecimans (Talley 1986, pp. 18–27). It is Asia that is holding out for a Jewish dating of the paschal celebration, and this is linked back to the apostles. Also the *Epistula Apostolorum* and the *Peri Pascha* of Melito both appear to originate in this region. The annual paschal meal, therefore, with some kind of reading, is present within the second-century material. How this relates to any more frequent meal is difficult to say. Finally, the fact that the community targeted by Pliny is able to abandon their meal so readily suggests that it probably has no specific ritual resonance for them. What strikes me very forcibly from this material, if for the moment Ignatius is set aside, is the lack of any real evidence for a regular cultic meal of any kind within the Asian communities outside of the paschal context. Certainly communal meals were held, but that is exactly what they appear to have been, communal meals, nothing more and nothing that would strike the regular second-century citizen as anything exceptional.

This, then, raises once again the question of the flesh and the blood, and the increasing evidence in the literature for an interpretation of the meal, whether this is Ignatius' 'medicine of immortality' or the development of flesh and blood language in itself. This, linked with Ignatius' own insistence that only the bishop is allowed to preside at the meal, is showing that what Ignatius is referring to was an event that he wanted to become increasingly ritualized and less like an ordinary shared meal. Whether this means that bread and wine are the only elements of the meal cannot be said. The fact that it is being surrounded by interpretation and by rules of performance is enough to say that what was beginning to emerge, at least in Ignatius' vision for the meal, was a ritual event at the heart of the community. How much of this is due to Ignatius' own vision, however, and how much reflects the wider practice of the Asian communities is something to which I will come back in the final chapter.

7

Rome

All accounts of the earliest Christian communities, whether contemporary or those written by scholars in recent centuries, appear to end in Rome. That is the way that the Acts of the Apostles is structured, and that is the model that has been used by scholars over and over again throughout the centuries. So, for example, many of the accounts of the origins of the Eucharist that were discussed in the Introduction end either with Justin Martyr's *Apologies*, written in Rome in or around 150 CE, or with the *Apostolic Tradition*, which is usually situated in Rome towards the end of the second century. Justin provides the first detailed account of what might have happened at a Christian meal that included the sharing of bread and the cup. Paul, in 1 Corinthians, does not really say what happened at the Lord's Supper, and the *Didache* provides an outline for what might be said, but the nature of the meal itself is not recounted. Justin recounts in some detail exactly what happened within his community in Rome (*Apology* I.65–7), or at least that is what he claims to be doing. Likewise the *Apostolic Tradition*, for all the difficulties that surround it in relation to authorship, dating, structure and ecclesial context (Bradshaw et al. 2002), does provide some material, like the *Didache,* of what should be said and done at a series of Christian meals, and presents elements of the Eucharist in a form that most people would clearly recognize today (Bradshaw et al. 2002). It is in Rome, therefore, that most scholars assume that the Eucharist took its final, and from that point on essentially unchanging, form.

Rome was the centre of the most powerful empire of the ancient Mediterranean world at this time and the development of the earliest Christian communities took place primarily within the context of this empire. It is natural, therefore, that many of the most significant people gravitated towards Rome and that many others look to the communities of Rome as a central and important focus. Paul eventually arrived at Rome, but felt it important to send a letter to the community in Rome even before he had visited them. Ignatius travelled the same, or rather a similar, route and again wrote to the community in Rome in advance of his arrival. Justin Martyr was born in Samaria and travelled widely, but once again was drawn towards Rome and was martyred there in 160 CE or thereabouts. Many others followed the same path. Rome was the centre of government and the most important city in the world at the time.

The centrality of Rome politically and culturally should not, however, divert from the fact that for the Christian community other cities and other communities were also very important. Jerusalem remained a central focus for activity, at least up until its sack in 72 CE. Even after that date the Christian community in Palestine clearly remained an important and influential focus. Antioch also proved to be an important centre and, over time, Alexandria came to rival Jerusalem and Antioch as the centre of Christian scholarship. Christian ideas also spread east as well as west and moved beyond the boundaries of the Roman Empire developing a very different form of Christian imagery and theology from that within the Empire. There are very few records of the early years of these eastern churches but the evidence that is available from the third century onwards indicates a unique and fascinating trajectory that is not focused on Rome, or even on Antioch or Jerusalem (Stringer 2005). There are also suggestions that Christianity moved west very early on with stories of Paul's visit to Spain and the development of the Christian community of Lyons, and the Christian communities of North Africa were to play a very important part in the development of the tradition at the end of the second century and the beginning of the third.

The other factor that must be taken into account is the level of travel that was possible between these different centres and between other sections of the Christian world (Malherbe 1983, pp. 62–70). Paul was a travelling preacher and his missionary journeys have an iconic place within our understanding of Christian origins. Others, however, joined Paul on the road or travelled through other cities and along other paths. The Apocryphal *Acts* all work on the principle that the apostles were sent out into the world and journeyed from place to place preaching and healing the sick (Lapham 2003). The itinerant preacher is a central feature of many of the earliest texts within the Christian communities. The *Didache* is interesting not least because it illustrates a community on the boundary between a travelling, peripatetic, leadership and a fixed institutional one (Niederwimmer 1998). Merchants and business people are central to the early communities of Christians. Aquila and Priscilla, for example, were tent-makers who came from Rome, met with Paul in Corinth and then moved on to other cities and communities, probably ending up back in Rome (1 Cor. 16.2–3; Rom. 16.3; Lampe 2003, pp. 11–16). It is these rootless, itinerant individuals and households that appear to have played a significant role within the earliest communities of Christians. Ignatius was a traveller, even if it was not of his own will, and Justin travelled extensively before finally settling in Rome. Others, whose names are known, such as Marcion and Tatian, who were clearly resident in Rome at some time during the second century, were not born there and went on to travel extensively in Asia Minor, Egypt or Syria (Lampe 2003). The Christian community was a very mobile one. This had its impact both on the speed with which ideas and texts could be transmitted throughout the Christian world and also on the incredible diversity and divisions that were such an obvious feature of many of the communities at this time.

In this chapter I want to sketch out what little is known about the earliest Christian communities in Rome and look specifically at Clement and his letter to the Corinthians. I then want to focus on Justin Martyr and the accounts of the Eucharist that are offered in the *Apologies*. I will look briefly at the work of Marcion, Tatian and others who were, as I have said, in Rome at the same time as Justin but who began to develop very different understandings of Christianity. This will also touch on the work of Irenaeus who, despite being based in Lyons, is one of our main sources for the activities of the Christian communities in Rome. Finally, I will look briefly at the *Apostolic Tradition*, which is technically beyond the end of the period that is of immediate interest but will offer some sense of how ideas and practices developed beyond the time that I am looking at.

Early Christian Rome

There had been a large Jewish community in Rome for some time before any Christians emerged and it is probably within this community that Christianity first took hold within the city (Brown and Meier 1983, pp. 92–7). There is evidence for between seven and eleven separate Christian congregations at the beginning of the second century and there is evidence that they each had their own organization (Stambaugh and Balch 1986, p. 162; Lampe 2003, p. 359). This is probably a consequence of the far larger population of Rome and the way in which the Jewish community was distributed throughout the city (Lampe 2003, pp. 38–40). Estimates have put the population of Jews in Rome under Augustus at around 40,000–50,000, or around 5 per cent of the population of the city (Stambaugh and Balch 1986, p. 161). Lampe uses a range of evidence to try and establish where the Christian communities of Rome may have been based (2003, pp. 19–47). These included textual traditions, burial sites, the site of Jewish communities, the distribution of the titular churches and what little archaeological evidence does exist (Jeffers 1991, p. 45). While some of this analysis has since been critiqued, the conclusions that Lampe draws are generally in line with other kinds of analysis. The community appears to have been focused in the Transtiberinum or Trastevere area of the city (Williams 2004, p. 8), with some evidence of Christians in the south and the north-east of the city itself (Sanders 1993, pp. 224–8).

There were periodic attacks on the Jewish community, most notably under Claudius, but these do not appear to have had a serious impact on the level of the population. From the evidence in the Jewish catacombs many Jews took on Latin names, but it appears that Greek was the common language and that this was in many ways a Hellenized community (Stambaugh and Balch 1986, p. 161). There is also clear evidence of very close links between the Jewish community in Rome and that in Jerusalem and Palestine (Brown and Meier 1983, pp. 95–7). The evidence suggests that the earliest Jewish communities to come to Rome were slaves brought back by Pompey and Sosius after their campaigns in Palestine in the first century BCE (Williams 2004, p. 8). One controversial feature of the Roman Jewish community, which Williams argues is related to this origin as slaves, is the practice of fasting on the Sabbath that is attested in some Roman sources (Williams 2004). Finally, it is clear that in Rome, as in many other cities, a number of proselytes were attracted to the Jewish religion, some of whom came from among the highest levels of Roman society (Stambaugh and Balch 1986, p. 161; Lampe 2003, pp. 69–79).

If Rome followed the same pattern as other cities, then the first Christians, on leaving the synagogues, would have met in the homes of wealthier members, or perhaps in public buildings, and would have worshipped in relatively small groups throughout the city. However, there is no real evidence for distinctive Christian communities until some time into the second century. It is possible to interpret a dispute within the Jewish community in the 40s that led to rioting and the crackdown by Claudius as a conflict between Christians and other Jews, although this is dependent on the interpretation of the name 'Chrestus' in the literature (Stambaugh and Balch 1986, p. 162; Lampe 2003, pp. 11–16). The position of Christians in relation to Nero's response to the burning of Rome in the 60s is perhaps even more difficult to interpret, although

legend indicates that it is in this round of persecution that both Paul
and Peter are martyred (Brown and Meier 1983, pp. 97–100; Lampe
2003, pp. 82–4).

Paul writes to a Christian community in Rome in the latter half of
the first century. Unfortunately there is little in the letter to indicate
the kind of community or communities that he is writing to (Lampe
2003, pp. 80–1). It is clear that Paul has not yet visited Rome, but he
does know something of the people and communities associated with
the city. It has been suggested that the 'theological' nature of the letter
is a response to the lack of specific knowledge and details of the kind
that are addressed, for example, in the first letter to the Corinthians.
The address is to 'all in Rome who are loved by God and called to
be saints' (1.7). This does not necessarily suggest a single community,
but it does not really indicate a range of different communities either.
There is also a long list of greetings to individuals and households in
the final chapter, which have been analysed in great detail by Lampe,
but once again they can offer very little direct evidence of the structure
of the community or communities being addressed, except to emphasize
the number of ex-slaves within the list and the predominance of names
from the East (Lampe 2003, pp. 164–83, 359).

The only section of the letter that has a direct bearing on the subject
of eating or of worship comes in chapter 14 where Paul addresses the
question of those whose faith is weak and the question of eating meat.
Paul recognizes those who eat only vegetables (14.2) and those who
eat meat. He also recognizes those who consider one day more sacred
than another and those who do not (14.5). Does this mean, therefore,
that the idea of a sacred day (the Lord's Day) was only just being established, or is it a reference to those who keep the regular feasts and
festivals, such as Passover, and others who do not? It is difficult to say
from the text. Finally towards the end of the chapter Paul says 'it is
better not to eat meat or to drink wine or to do anything else that will
cause your brother to fall' (14.21). The specific context is not the main
point of interest here, especially for the argument I have been developing through this book, but rather the wider question of whether this
could be said, or the whole discussion developed in this chapter, if there
were already a regular weekly meal among the community at Rome
which was known to have been instigated by Jesus himself. It certainly
seems unlikely given the way this particular passage is developed.

Unfortunately Ignatius' letter to the Romans in the early years of
the second century can tell us even less about the community in Rome
(Lampe 2003, pp. 88–9). However, it is clear that the dispersed nature

of the Christian communities in Rome continued for some centuries and was a distinctive feature of the middle years of the second century when many different forms of Christianity, under numerous different leaders, began to emerge (Lampe 2003, pp. 359–65). In part this reflects a very diverse city, with many different national and ethnic communities, something that is reflected in the comments that have already been made about the importance of travel to the earliest Christian communities. However, it is also clear that it is in Rome that different communities, or different community leaders, appear to develop very different, and sometimes very distinctive, understandings of what Christianity is about (Lampe 2003, pp. 381–4). Marcion had a community in Rome that had a special relationship to a limited number of Paul's letters and a version of the Gospel that is now attributed to Luke (Lampe 2003, pp. 241–52). Gnosticism in its various forms also appears to have developed in Rome during the second century although it would have grown through intellectual and physical contacts with other parts of the Empire, most notably with Egypt (Lampe 2003, p. 292). This suggests a series of very diverse, and at times bitterly opposed, communities, each of which was gathered around its own specific leader and teachers. It is in the context of this cultural and intellectual world, therefore, that the various texts that derive from the Roman communities have to be studied.

Clement

The first texts that originate in Rome are the first letter of Clement and a document known as the *Shepherd of Hermas*. The *Shepherd* is a unique text in terms of Christian literature: part apocalyptic, part pastoral handbook and part mystical journey (Brown and Meier 1983, pp. 203–4). There are some references within it to the ordering of the community and to baptism, but very little that could help to construct a sociological model of the community that produced it or its worship (Lampe 2003, pp. 90–9). There are no references to meals within the text and scholars of the Eucharist have largely ignored it. However, as with the letters of Paul that have no references to meals or to the sharing bread and cup, the silence in itself may be significant. Having said that, I would not want to make too much of the silence in relation to the *Shepherd*; the text is not aiming to comment on the practices of the community and focuses much more on the individual response to post-baptismal sin, and so it may not be too much of a surprise to find little or no reference to structures, orders or rituals within the community.

The first letter of Clement, however, is different. This letter is sent, on behalf of a group of Christian communities in Rome, to Christians living in Corinth and it deals directly with the ordering and structuring of the community. Scholars do not really know who Clement was. According to later tradition he was the third Bishop of Rome after Peter (Eusebius, *EH* 3.21). No name is mentioned in the first letter, the only one that is universally agreed to be authentically by 'Clement', and there is nothing in the letter to suggest who the author is or that the author claimed the title of bishop, unlike the writings of Ignatius. It is a reference in the *Shepherd* (*Vis.* 2.4.3), which mentions a Clement who is responsible for writing to other communities on behalf of the community in Rome, and the writings of Irenaeus (*Adv. Haer.* 3.3.3.), who mentions that the community in Rome sent a letter to the Corinthians at the 'time of Clement', which suggests that this letter can be attributed to an individual named Clement. Eusebius also quotes a letter from a later Bishop of Corinth, Dionysius, who refers to the letter sent to Corinth 'which was earlier sent to us through Clement' (*EH* 4.23.11; Brown and Meier 1983, p. 160). Clement, therefore, could perhaps be seen as some kind of secretary to the body that brought a number of different Christian communities in Rome together. He uses the first person plural throughout, and certainly speaks with authority, more specifically with the authority associated with the position of the community in the imperial capital, and that does suggest an official position, but it is not necessarily the position of one in authority within the communities themselves. The other point that can be made about Clement, from the content of the letter itself, is the emphasis that is placed on the Hebrew scriptures and the strongly Jewish feel to the argument. It has been suggested, therefore, that Clement may have come from a Jewish-Christian context, or even that this may still have represented the dominant form of Christianity in Rome at the time that Clement was writing in the early years of the second century (Sanders 1993, pp. 219–20).

The most striking feature about the letter is that the Christian community in Corinth, to whom the letter is addressed, have clearly learnt nothing from the correspondence with Paul almost 50 years previously. The complaints against the community, of factionalism and disorderliness, are very reminiscent of those of Paul in 1 Corinthians. The Corinthian community has clearly dismissed one or more elder from their office, and Clement is arguing that this goes beyond their authority. It has often been noted that *1 Clement* does not present the model of a single monarchical bishop as advocated by Ignatius, and like the Pastoral

Epistles tends to switch between the terms 'elder', or 'presbyter', and 'bishop' indiscriminately (MacDonald 1988). This suggests that at Rome there was not at this time one single bishop, but rather a community of elders/bishops, a view that is supported by some readings of the lists of bishops compiled later in the century (Brown and Meier 1983, pp. 163–4).

In this context, therefore, it is very interesting to see no direct reference to any meal. There is a reference to worship in chapter 13, but this does not provide very much practical information. It is in chapters 40–44 that modern scholars have identified possible references to the Eucharist (Bradshaw 2004, p. 86). This section deals directly with the question of order raised by the disruptions in Corinth, and the author draws on the model of the Temple priesthood to make his point. Just as there are orders within the Temple structure, of high priests, priests and Levites, so within the Christian community there are orders of apostles, elders/bishops and deacons. Both orders are ordained by God and cannot be changed by human decision (Brown and Meiers 1983, p. 170). This addresses the specific problem faced at Corinth. However, Clement appears to take this analogy between the orders of the Temple and those of the Christian community further with reference to sacrifice, and it is at this point that possibilities surrounding the eucharistic practice of the Roman community emerge.

The specific line reads, 'For it will be no small sin on our part, if we depose from the Episcopal office those who have in blameless and holy wise offered the gifts' (*1 Clement* 44.4; Stevenson 1957). The previous chapters have emphasized the role of the Temple priesthood in offering the daily sacrifices of the Temple, but it is acknowledged that these are only appropriate at the altar in Jerusalem (41.2). What, then, are 'gifts' (τά δῶρα) that are to be offered by those in episcopal office in Clement's community? In the light of eighteen hundred years of subsequent eucharistic theology it might be assumed that these gifts are bread and wine, and Hanson says 'it is obvious that τά δῶρα refers to the bread and wine in the Eucharist' (Hanson 1985, p. 88), but there is nothing in the text to support this assumption. There is similar language in other documents and texts that have been discussed. The letter to the Hebrews talks about the one sacrifice of Jesus, the high priest of the new covenant (10.10), and the first letter of Peter picks up the idea of a royal priesthood that can declare the praises of God (2.9). The *Didache* talks of the meal in terms of Malachi's pure sacrifice (14.1–3), but only in a very general sense. Ignatius uses the words bread and altar in the same sentence on a couple of occasions (*Ephesians* 5.2; *Philadelphians* 4.1). In neither case is the idea of sacrifice used of either bread or wine, and the language remains at the metaphorical level (Hanson 1985, pp. 86–7). It cannot be assumed that this is what is meant by Clement either. The language may simply be a continuation of that used of the Temple priesthood earlier in the same discussion, or the 'gifts' may have been seen as something more specific, such as the 'gifts of the Spirit' following Paul's language, or money raised for charitable acts. If the emphasis is placed on 'offering' as opposed to the gifts then Brown might be correct in saying that 'one of the roles of the episcopate is to offer sacrifices' (Brown and Meier 1983, p. 171), but these sacrifices are probably of the spiritual kind, or the offering of the whole person (Hanson 1985, p. 88). The answer cannot be known, but it is not appropriate simply to assume, with no other references to meals or to bread and cup at any other point in the letter, that Clement was referring to a eucharistic context in his use of sacrificial language.

Nodet (1998) has noted that there was a sudden flowering of the use of sacrificial language, drawn largely from the book of Leviticus and the practices of the Temple, towards the end of the first century. He argues that this cannot be entirely coincidental and asks whether there might be any connection between the various works that develop these ideas. The main texts involved (*Didache*, Hebrews, Peter, Ignatius and Clement) have already been discussed. Brown argues that as Hebrews, 1 Peter and *Clement* all originate, in his view, from Rome, this reflects 'the origins of the Roman Church in a Jerusalem Christianity loyal to the temple' (Brown and Meiers 1983, p. 171). Nodet argues for a wider distribution of the texts and this leads him to look for other possible origins. He proposes that it must be related to the destruction of the Temple and the way in which Christian communities are reacting both to this and to the contemporary Jewish attempts to reconstruct their own religious traditions out of the Pharisaic tradition. Trocmé suggests a similar process by which Christian and Jewish communities finally began to develop in different directions in the 90s as the rabbinical tradition consolidated across the Jewish Diaspora (1997, pp. 99–112).

According to this line of argument, Christian writers were beginning to reclaim and rework the Temple sacrificial tradition for themselves in reaction to their expulsion from the Jewish community, placing the role of Jesus at the heart of their tradition, but also claiming the language of priesthood, altars, sacrifice etc. for the community (Bradshaw 2004, pp. 85–7). The real question, however, if this wider analysis is correct, is whether the elements of that language referred to activity that was essentially focused on a prayer meeting (the sacrifice of praise) or whether it necessarily has to be focused on a meal, as it clearly was later in the second century. The *Didache* already uses some level of sacrificial language for the bread and cup at the meal. This, however, is not as developed in relation to Temple imagery as the other writings being explored and could be said to derive from, and perhaps develop into, a very different tradition. Ray suggests, following Nodet, that this may relate to the offering of the first fruits linked to the calendar as outlined in the *Book of Jubilees* (Ray 2004, p. 24). The real question is whether the specific reintroduction of the language of altar, priest, offering and sacrifice within the Christian tradition is associated with the development of a sacrificial understanding of a Christian meal tradition.

Of course, Hebrews, Peter and Ignatius have not necessarily led to that conclusion, and other more recent scholars have suggested that the 'parting of the ways' between Christianity and Judaism was never as easy or as complete as such an analysis suggests (Lieu 2002, pp. 11–30). Again this is an argument from silence, a lack of any clear and indisputable link between sacrifice and meals, and that is always difficult. However, if the passage in *1 Clement* is taken at face value then all that can be said is that there is no evidence for the practice of a meal, or of any rite containing the sharing of bread and cup, in Rome until the middle of the second century. No judgement can be made, therefore, as to whether there was or was not such a rite practised by one or more of the communities of the city before this date.

Justin Martyr

Justin has a special place within histories of the Eucharist (Bradshaw 2004, pp. 61–77). The accounts that he provides in the first of his two apologies of what happened at a 'Eucharist' among his own community in Rome in around 160 offers a model that is instantly recognizable by most Christians today. It begins either with a baptism or, on the regular Sunday event, with readings and a sermon, and then moves into a sharing of bread and cup preceded by thanksgiving (*Apology* 1.65–67). It is Justin's account that provides the classic fourfold shape of the Eucharist as defined by Dix, and it is his account, in the middle of the second century, that Dix (1945) takes as the end point of the transition that he identifies from the sevenfold shape of the Last Supper to the classic fourfold shape of all subsequent Eucharists. As authors such as McGowan (1999a) have explored other possibilities in terms of bread and water, or even bread only eucharistic meals, Justin's account may have slipped from its iconic status, but it is presented so clearly within the *Apology*, it looks so like what contemporary commentators think of as a Eucharist, and in many ways it comes so surprisingly fully formed out of nothing, that it has to be engaged with and exactly what might be going on has to be understood.

Justin was born in Flavia Neapolis in Samaria (*Apology* 1.1; Buchanan 2007, 4). He was not a Jew, but he was a Roman citizen. He clearly came from a moderately wealthy family as he was able to be educated and to pursue his own particular passion for philosophy and the search for the ultimate answers. All the information that is available for his life, however, comes from his own writings and that must always suggest some cause to be suspicious (Lampe 2003, pp. 260–1). His first explorations led him to become a student of a Stoic and then of a Platonist, with brief encounters with a peripatetic and a Pythagorian in between (*Dialogue* 2.3, 2.6). For some time he appears to have been satisfied with the explanations these Greek philosophical schools offered. At some point, however, his Platonist teacher became a Christian and Justin found in Christianity at least some of the answers that he was looking for. Justin continued to live what at the time would have been considered a typical philosophical life (*Apology* 2.2). He wore the distinctive philosopher's mantle and gathered around him a group of disciples. He debated with anybody who would come and challenge him, and he travelled around teaching, writing and developing his own philosophical position.

One of the problems associated with Justin is that his writings are among the first within the Christian corpus to offer a specifically philosophical take on Christianity, and to offer an apologetic against the general thinking of the day (Lampe 2003, p. 273). Paul and Ignatius, among others, had written letters that in part contained hints of wider philosophical thinking. The *Didache* is a series of different kinds of text, some pastoral, some clearly forming an early church order, some apocalyptic. The letter to the Hebrews, the *Shepherd of Hermas* and other texts provide meditative reflections, generally from within a Jewish thought world, on aspects of Christianity. The Gospels and Acts (both canonical and apocryphal) provided narrative accounts with some incidental philosophical reflection. We have some references in Eusebius to apologies from Quadratus and Aristides presented to the Emperor Hadrian in Athens in 125 (*EH* 4.3.1–3; Stevenson 1957, p. 55). The text of Quadratus' apology is lost while that of Aristides can be reconstructed in part from later texts (Stevenson 1957, pp. 56–8). Justin, however, set out to provide a much more systematic association of philosophy and Christian thinking. His aim, in all his writings, is to defend Christianity against those, both Jews and Gentiles, who were attacking it. It is this apologetic stance that defines the way Justin develops both his philosophical thinking and his choice of Christian ideas and practices (Lampe 2003, pp. 283–4). He is not, so far as is known, part of a school in the way that this developed most clearly in Alexandria towards the end of the second century, although he did establish his own school in Rome and did have followers, both in the literal sense (Lampe 2003, pp. 276–9) and in terms of the style and genre of writing, the most important of whom was probably Irenaeus of Lyon. Justin's works, therefore, represent something new within Christian writing and probably within Christian thinking, and that makes the interpretation of the texts very difficult.

According to Eusebius, Justin produced a number of works (*EH* 4.18.1–6), but only three have survived, the *Dialogue with Trypho* and two *Apologies*. The *Dialogue* is aimed at countering Jewish opposition to Christianity and is constructed as a fictional debate between Justin and Trypho. Because of its polemic and apologetic nature, Trypho does not get much to say, apart from asking the right questions, and so much of the text is taken up with long philosophical answers (Lampe 2003, p. 270). In this text there are some references to the Eucharist and to sacrifice, picking up a number of the themes that have already been looked at in the previous section (Buchanan 2007, pp. 43–7). In one passage in particular, quoting Isaiah 33, Justin says:

> It is plain therefore that in this prophecy there is reference to the bread, which our Christ gave us to eat in remembrance of his being made flesh for the sake of those who believe in him . . . and to the cup which he gave us to drink with thanksgiving in remembrance of his blood. (*Dialogue* 70.15; Buchanan 2007, p. 45)

He thereby links the language of flesh and blood, ideas of the incarnation and allusions to the Last Supper, which will also be seen in the *Apology*. Eusebius sets the *Dialogue* in Ephesus in the 130s (*EH* 4.18.6), but it is clear that Justin completed the text in Rome after the two *Apologies* (Buchanan 2007, pp. 2–3).

Assuming that the fictional context of the *Dialogue* does relate to some period of Justin's own life, this places him fairly close to the geographical setting for Ignatius' letters, although Justin was probably in western Asia Minor some 30 years later than Ignatius. Whether Justin mixed with the same Christian communities in the city as Ignatius may have written to, or what relationship either of them had to notional Johannine communities in the city, is very difficult to determine (Hill 2004, pp. 342–4). Justin does recount the view that Revelation was written by the apostle John (*Dialogue* 81.4). For our purposes, however, it is clear that Justin through his travels, and probably by the time he was resident in Ephesus, had come to accept without further question that the sharing of bread and cup was a common Christian activity, that it was closely associated with the flesh and blood of Jesus and that 'Eucharist' was an appropriate title for the meal and for the bread and cup. Interestingly, following on from the discussion in the previous chapter, Justin also uses the language of flesh rather than body in his discussion of the Eucharist and the incarnation in the *Dialogue* (70.15). Does this therefore reflect the generally accepted terminology within Asia Minor, which has already been noted in Ignatius and the Johannine tradition, or is it a direct reference to John 6? Hill presents a strong argument that Justin knew and used the Gospel of John in his writings, but he has nothing to say about the use of 'flesh' as opposed to 'body' (2004, pp. 312–51). Unfortunately, therefore, it is probably difficult to say anything more at this stage.

Justin's *Apology*

Justin addressed two *Apologies* to the Emperor Antoninus Pius and to his co-regents Marcus Aurelius and Lucius Versus (1.1, 2.15.5). It is usually assumed that these were written in Rome (Buchanan 2007, p. 5). It is difficult to assess exactly why he did this and whether he really did expect the Emperor to read them, or whether this, like the dialogue in the previous text, was itself part of the fiction. Either way these texts are clearly aimed at those who were outside the Christian community and address issues that Justin believes non-Christians might want to know. Much of the early part of the first *Apology* consists of a plea to stop persecution on the basis that the accusations offered against Christians are simply wrong. Among these is an accusation of cannibalism and of debauchery following Christian banquets (Lampe 2003, p. 302). There is a tendency in a range of literature of the time to accuse any group that is not in favour of cannibalism and improper sex, and Christians begin to do it themselves in the following century, accusing Jewish and heretical groups that they wish to condemn. It is difficult to assume, therefore, that accusations of cannibalism relate to the presumed widespread talk of eating the flesh and blood of Jesus in Christian communities. The accusations are not specific enough for this link to be significant, but they do assume that banquets or other kinds of meal are a common feature of Christian communities, common enough to be noted by outsiders and commented on.

It is towards the end of the first *Apology*, however, that Justin turns from philosophical issues to the practice of the community of which he is a member and probably a leader. Almost as an afterthought he presents an account of two meetings for worship. The first consists of a baptism followed by the sharing of bread and the cup (*Apology* 1.65) and the second of readings and a sermon followed by the sharing of bread and the cup (*Apology* 1.67). These are presented in a very matter-of-fact way with very little fuss or subsequent explanation. Their role within the *Apology* itself has been questioned, as has the possibility that Justin may have toned down the accounts for external consumption. The accounts themselves, therefore, may be fictional. It is difficult to see, however, when reading them at face value, what it is that Justin might have removed (apart from any detail in terms of the actual prayers used), or added, and why they could not represent the practice of his own community at this time (Bradshaw 2004, p. 63).

The first question, therefore, is what can be said about Justin's own community? In the *Apology* Justin says, 'and on the day called "of the Sun" an assembly is held in one place of all living in town and country' (*Apology* 1.67.3; Bradshaw 2004, p. 62). This cannot be referring directly to Rome as it is unlikely that any space owned by Christian groups would have been big enough to hold all the Christians of the city, and, as I have already noted, there were considerable ethnic and doctrinal differences between the many different communities in the city. In the account of the martyrdom of Justin, which is one of the earliest such texts and probably based on older records, Rufinus the prefect asks Justin where the community assembles, and Justin is noted as replying that he lives above the baths of Myrtinus (although the texts of the various versions of the martyrdom do vary slightly on this (Snyder 2007, p. 350)). Snyder provides an interesting analysis of the kind of space an apartment above a public baths might have been in Rome at the time of Justin and why it might have been a suitable space for a meeting called by a foreign philosopher (2007, pp. 337–49). Snyder goes on to suggest that the unknown baths of Myrtinus might be the baths of Mamertinus close to the intersection of the Via Appia and the Via Latina (2007, pp. 353–6). This was a very diverse community at the time with evidence for a Jewish community and also for possible Valentinian inscriptions not very far away (2007, pp. 360–1). If this was the case, then the community that gathered at Justin's residence may well have been a community of Syrian or Palestinian Christians (Justin's disciple Tatian also originated in this region and returned to it following Justin's death). If it did meet in the apartment itself then it may have been quite small, but there is no real evidence to provide a judgement on this either way. Justin's own term 'president' for the leader of the event also adds very little, except to note that it is not one of the standard terms for Christian leadership such as presbyter or bishop (Buchanan 2007, pp. 13–15).

The second question goes back to the comment from the *Apology* that has already been quoted. The community met on the day called 'of the Sun' (*Apology* 1.67.3). This is the first reference within the Christian literature to the Roman naming of the days, but otherwise this is the same tradition as the *Didache* and the meal at Troas in the Acts of the Apostles that sets the meal on the first day of the week. There has been considerable discussion in the literature about whether this meal was to be celebrated in the morning or the evening, with some suggesting that Justin provides evidence of a move from evening to morning (Bradshaw 2004, pp. 68–9). The text itself makes no mention of the time of day at which the meal takes place and the assumptions about timing are made entirely on the content of the event as described by Justin. It is assumed that the normal service with readings and sermon would have followed the synagogue practice and therefore would have taken place in the morning, and that the meal would have been attached to that event (Bradshaw 2004, p. 69). However, as no mention of time is made then we cannot know the exact timing.

What Justin provides is two accounts of the structure of the meal. The Sunday event begins with the reading of memoirs of the apostles and the writings of the prophets for as long as time allows (*Apology* 1.67.3). This order has led some commentators to suggest that Gospel readings came before those from the Hebrew scriptures, but the informality inherent in the whole account probably makes it more likely that the readings came from a variety of sources in no particular order. The term 'the memoirs of the apostles' has been a cause for investigation and it is not at all clear whether Justin is referring to the Gospels as we know them, some unpublished version of the gospel stories, or a text that brings the various Gospels together in a harmony, such as his disciple Tatian's *Diatessaron* (Hill 2004, pp. 337–42). What is missing is any reference to letters, but it is not clear how significant this is. The readings are followed by an admonition and exhortation by the president. The community stands for prayers (*Apology* 1.67.4), which assumes that they sat or reclined for the readings and sermon.

The meal following baptism has a greeting with a kiss at this point (*Apology* 1.65.2), but it is disputed as to whether this is part of the initiation process, that is, the end of the baptism, or the beginning of the sharing of bread and wine (Bradshaw 2004, pp. 74–5; Phillips 1996). The second account misses out this detail. The bread and the cup are brought in and the president sends up prayers and thanksgivings according to his ability (*Apology* 1.67.5). Those who are interested in the history of the Eucharistic Prayer may ask how many prayers are said and whether they are said over the bread and cup separately or together, but Justin does not provide this kind of detail (Bradshaw 2004, pp. 75–6). The peoples assent to the prayers with an 'Amen', a point that Justin makes with a significant comment in both accounts of the meal (*Apology* 1.65.4, 1.67.5). The bread and cup are shared and they are also sent out to those who are not present. The Sunday meal ends with the taking of a collection for the needy (*Apology* 1.67.6).

This is the first time that there is a clear association of readings, sermon and prayers with the sharing of bread and cup, but as no other text really provides a detailed account of the structure of the meal they discuss, it is not possible to say how much of an innovation this might be. The traditional view has been that this indicates the joining of the bread and cup rite, shorn of the meal, with the traditional synagogue morning service (Dix 1945, pp. 36–7). Recent scholarship, however, has indicated that very little is known about synagogue worship at this time and that the most likely practice would not have been formal liturgical worship at all, but rather a time of reading and teaching and discussion around the scriptures (Falk 1995). Bradshaw, among others, suggests that the readings and other elements of Justin's account probably developed within a Christian context (Bradshaw 2004, pp. 69–72). It seems highly probable that some kind of readings and prayers would have accompanied a weekly sharing of bread and cup, and the only real point to note here is that these precede the meal rather than following as might be assumed if the symposium were the model for the event (Smith 2003). This is roughly the same order as the event at Troas, although there the teaching continued after the meal and on into the night (Acts 20.7–11), and the same order is suggested in the Emmaus story (Luke 24.13–35). What relation this might have to the worship time discussed by Paul in the first letter to the Corinthians (1 Cor. 14.26) is difficult to determine. There is also no specific reference to any food other than bread and cup, and so Dix and others have assumed that by this time the 'meal' as such had become separated (Dix 1945, pp. 96–102; Bradshaw 2004, pp. 64–8). However, if the 'meal' never really consisted of more than bread and drink, perhaps with salt and herbs or other flavouring, then this idea of separation begins to make very little sense. We do not know from Justin just how much bread and drink were consumed at the event or were subsequently distributed by the deacons to those who were not present (*Apology* 1.65.5, 1.67.5).

One of the significant areas of ambiguity, and therefore of controversy, in Justin's text, relates to the place of the cup, and what the cup contained. In the baptismal rite the text talks about the cup containing water, which is qualified by the phrase, 'and wine-mixed-with-water' (κραμα) (*Apology* 1.65.3). In the second rite the people bring 'bread and wine and water' to the president (*Apology* 1.67.5). It was normal practice throughout the ancient world to drink wine diluted by water, sometimes with significant amounts of water, but the ambiguity of Justin's text has raised questions about exactly what drink is being used within the rite. McGowan argues that Justin may be a significant piece of evidence for his own understanding of bread and water Eucharists (1999, p. 153). This is based on the possibility, first raised by von Harnack's suggestion in the late nineteenth century, that the reference to wine in the text is probably a later scribal addition to bring the text into line with current practice in other parts of the church (Harnack 1891). The clumsiness and ambiguity of the text in the baptismal rite certainly needs some kind of explanation and the possibility that the original reading was of water alone would certainly clear up the problems. The same argument could be made for the second rite, although the need to find a solution here is not nearly so great.

It is not only within the texts of the rites, however, that water is suggested as the drink at the meal. Following the account of the first rite Justin adds a comment that the Eucharist is demonically prefigured in the rites of Mithras, where specific mention is made of bread and water (*Apology* 1.66.4). As Daly-Denton makes clear, Justin is more than aware of the Dionysiac rites where bread and wine play a prominent part and could easily have chosen these as his example (2007, p. 363). Why, therefore, does he choose the Mithraic example, unless the similarity of bread and water is important (Bouyer 1990, p. 133)? Daly-Denton offers a very detailed analysis of the use of wine and water imagery throughout Justin's writings to demonstrate that he is, in her terms, following John in emphasizing the living water as a drink, and the imagery of manna and the rock as the source of water in the desert (2007, pp. 364–7). Clearly there is ambiguity and uncertainty in the way in which water imagery is used in some of the early Christian texts, and Daly-Denton suggests that it may not be until the writing of

Cyprian in the mid third century that the automatic association of water with baptism becomes normative (2007, pp. 367–9).

✓   Unfortunately, there is no clear way of settling the argument. It is perfectly feasible that Justin knew of a bread and water rite; the evidence is not clear but it would certainly be a plausible reading of the text that deals with a number of the difficulties presented. It is also possible that the text has not been corrected and that wine is assumed. Mazza makes a strong case for two cups in the baptismal rite, one of water and one of water mixed with wine, while in the second rite it is assumed that the water and wine will be mixed (1999, p. 107). Like so many other arguments this is based primarily on references to later practice where more than one cup is used in baptismal rites, but it does provide a sensible reading of the text. The answer will never be known, but I think that the question is important, if only to suggest that what the rite that Justin is describing might have looked like, if the eucharistic lens through which the rite is usually seen is removed, cannot be taken for granted.

The final element that needs to be discussed in relation to this particular text is the references to flesh and blood and the Last Supper in the chapter that divides the two accounts of the meals. Justin makes a number of points in quick succession and it is very easy to take each one and make a great deal out of it in the light of subsequent eucharistic theology. However, as a series of statements, brought together in close association with the accounts of the meals themselves, it is difficult to make too much of the finer points of theological debate. Justin says that 'this food is called "thanksgiving"' and that no person can eat of the food unless they have been baptized (*Apology* 1.65.1). Verse 2 begins with the statement that the food is not common bread and drink, and then refers to the fact that Jesus took both flesh and blood, so Justin has been taught that the 'the food over which thanks has been given through a word of prayer which is from him' (*Apology* 1.65.2) is the flesh and blood of Jesus that feeds our own flesh and blood. The next statement relates this to the memoirs of the apostles, called Gospels, and the tradition of what was commended to them in the account of the Last Supper. The passage finishes with the reference to the Mithraic rites that I have already mentioned.

Once again the language here is that of 'flesh and blood', and despite the reference to the Last Supper appears to pick up the concerns of John and Ignatius to emphasize the real flesh and blood of Jesus, although for Justin the focus is on the bread and cup not on the incarnation for its own sake (Bradshaw 2004, p. 89). The strange wording of verse 2, which relates to the food over which thanks has been given, is very difficult to interpret without reference to later theological thinking. The question is what 'the word of prayer which is from him' consists of and Bradshaw comes to the conclusion that we will never know (2004, pp. 91–3; Buchanan 2007, pp. 24–5). The specific version of the account of the Last Supper used by Justin does not follow any of the four found in the New Testament, so whether he is recalling this from memory or has a different text in front of him is, once again, difficult to determine (Bradshaw 2004, pp. 15–16). What we do see here, however, is some attempt being made to provide a meaning for the sharing of the bread and cup which clearly brings together the idea of flesh and blood, the Last Supper narrative and an understanding of the incarnation (Heintz 2003). It cannot be assumed that these had any part in the words of the prayers, which are said in an extemporary fashion by the president; but they are clearly linked in Justin's own theological imagination, although they are in this text far from fixed in any kind of liturgical formula.

Johnson notes that in baptismal terms Justin must be counted with the Syrian material because of his origins, not with contemporary Roman practice (Johnson 1999, pp. 37–8). Is the idea of a weekly meal and the loose association with the flesh and blood of Jesus, even with the Last Supper, also of Syrian origin and out of place in the Rome of the middle of the second century? Justin provides the first direct account of a meal within the capital and he clearly belongs to a community that is not at the centre of the Christian society of the city. While I think the question, and the possibility, is an interesting one, there is nothing in Justin's own work to suggest that he is doing anything unusual, and the references in the *Dialogue,* and earlier in the *Apology,* that assume knowledge of the bread and cup as the flesh and blood of Jesus do assume a wider understanding of this imagery at the time. There is nothing here, however, that can really be called a 'rite' or a 'ritual', in the sense that is assumed by Dix and other later commentators on the meal. It still has the feel of a common meal, preceded by some readings and some teachings, and shared among all those present and others who do not happen to be there that week. Ignatius' attempts to formalize the event under the control of the bishop have clearly had no impact on Justin and his community.

Other Christians in Rome

As I have already indicated there were numerous communities in Rome in the middle of the second century who would have called themselves

Christians or would claim to follow the teachings of Jesus (Lampe 2003, pp. 359–65). The evidence that is available comes primarily from those who opposed the teachings of the various groups, most notably Irenaeus' and Hippolytus' refutation of 'heresies'. As this material focuses on teachings, those who are identified are primarily the teachers, and the groups that follow them are presented as disciples of the different teachers and, in general, are named for their teacher. Whether this is a fair representation of the organization of these communities is difficult to determine, but as Justin is also presented as a teacher with a group of disciples who gather at his apartment then it might have some element of truth. It is also unclear what kind of relationship the various communities had with each other. Justin mentions that Marcion was teaching in Rome at the same time as himself and clearly objected to the nature of Marcion's teaching (*Apology* 1.26). Tertullian later mentions that Valentinus walked out of a particular community because he was not chosen to take over as its leader, and this led him to develop a very different body of teaching (*Against the Valentinians* 4). Again, the veracity of these accounts may be difficult to assess, but the idea of a group of different teachers, each gathering their own disciples around them and developing their own teachings, often in opposition to other teachers, does not sound to be an implausible scenario. A detailed analysis of the nature of the Christian communities in Rome is, however, beyond the scope of this work (see Lampe 2003).

Unfortunately there are no significant texts from the various non-mainstream communities themselves, and so there are no direct accounts of meals or other ritual practices from among them. There are later accounts of the rites of various 'Gnostic' groups associated with the teachings of Valentinus or Basileides, but it is difficult to date these back to the early days of the groups in Rome. Irenaeus provides an account of a ritual undertaken by Marcosians, a group associated with Valentinian teachings (*Adv. Haer.* 1.13.2). He presents this rite in derogatory terms as a form of magic trick involving the changing of the colour of the wine and appearing to produce more than originally started with through pouring from cup to cup. What can be gleaned from the account, however, is that only drink is mentioned in a series of cups which, without being specific, are assumed to contain wine mixed with water; that women play an important role in the rite, and that thanksgiving is made over the cups by the women and by others within the rite. There is no way of telling whether this is anything like an accurate account of a real meal. Lampe also mentions a series of inscriptions on the Via Latina, which he takes to be Valentinian and dating from the end of the second century (2003, pp. 298–313). Two of these are funeral inscriptions, but one is a general statement that probably hung on the wall of a villa used by a Valentinian group and that mentions baths and banquets (Lampe 2003, p. 298).

Tertullian, at the beginning of the third century, provides an account of a baptism carried out by Marcion (*Adv. Mar.* 1.14.3). This is part of his wider critique of Marcion's ideas and is related to Marcion's rejection of the creator and Tertullian's accusation that to use created elements in worship is hypocritical. The list is a relatively standard one for the date: water, oil, milk, honey and bread, but there is no mention of wine. It is, of course, possible to argue that Tertullian was not aware of Marcion's own practice in the middle of the previous century, or that this is merely an oversight, but McGowan draws on other evidence of Marcion's own ascetical stance to suggest that this text might hint at a bread and water Eucharist among Marcion's followers (1999a, pp. 164–7).✓ However, as with a number of other references to bread and water Eucharists identified by McGowan, the original text only mentions the bread; neither wine nor water is mentioned as part of the ritual meal.

Others, such as Tatian, who was a disciple of Justin up to his death and then moved back to Syria, are clearly associated by early writers with forms of asceticism including the abstinence from wine (McGowan 1999a, pp. 155–60). This leads McGowan to associate him with a bread and water tradition of the Eucharist, which he suggests was common in Syria, but this would only be legitimate if there was evidence for any kind of regular communal meal practice, of whatever kind (1999a, p. 158). McGowan simply assumes that some kind of bread and cup rite, such as that recounted by Justin, must have been part of the practice of Tatian's community and that if he rejected wine then the cup must have contained water. There is no contemporary evidence to suggest this, although both Epiphanius (*Pan.* 46.1–4) and Theodoret (*Haer. Fab.* 1.20) in the fourth and fifth centuries include references to the use of water in the Eucharist as part of their accounts of Tatian's heresy (McGowan 1999a, p. 156).

The *Apostolic Tradition* and beyond

If the discussion is taken up to the end of the second century then there are two other texts that need to be mentioned. Irenaeus was a very prolific writer who provides some interesting insights into the nature of the Christian communities of Rome despite being born in Asia Minor and acting as bishop in Lyons. His writing against the heresies and other works provides some fascinating information on the history, structure and organization of the Roman community. Unfortunately it does not include any account of a standard Christian meal. The Eucharist as a concept is clearly present and in a long discussion linking ideas of sacrifice, offering and incarnation, and resonating with many of the authors that have already been looked at in the last three chapters, Irenaeus makes it clear that he understands the bread and cup in the Eucharist as the body (not flesh) and blood of Christ (*Adv. Haer.* 4.17–18, 5.2.2–3). In other texts he also assumes that the bishop will preside at the Eucharist and that elements of the Eucharist will be sent to other communities in Rome (*EH* 5.24.14–15). I will return to some of these theological themes in the final chapter, but it is clear that Irenaeus can offer little that is new to an understanding of Roman practice in relation to meals.

The other text that scholars in the mid to late twentieth century would have had to mention when talking about the development of Christian meal traditions in Rome in the second century is the *Apostolic Tradition*. Both Mazza and Daly-Denton, from different starting points, talk about a continuing *agape* tradition that is seen to be firmed up in the *Apostolic Tradition* and beyond, into the writings of Tertullian and Clement of Alexandria (Mazza 1996, p. 285; Daly-Denton 2007). The *Apostolic Tradition* is a church order that was 'discovered' and disinterred from other church orders at the beginning of the twentieth century (Bradshaw et al. 2002, pp. 1–6). The resulting text was linked to an entry on a list of books, supposedly by Hippolytus, a bishop associated with the Roman church at the end of second century, and gained the title *Apostolic Tradition*. The most significant part of the text for scholars of the mid twentieth century was that it contained a complete Eucharistic Prayer (*Ap. Trad.* 4; Bradshaw et al. 2002, pp. 38–41), which, if it was by Hippolytus, and written at the beginning of the third century, would have been the earliest known example of such a prayer (assuming that the *Didache* texts were not really a Eucharistic Prayer in the modern sense of the word).

It was the prayer, however, among other things that caused scholars at the end of the century, beginning with Metzger (1988), to ask more searching questions of the text and to come to the conclusion that it is probably a combination of texts, drawn together perhaps as late as the fourth century and probably originating in many different communities (Bradshaw et al. 2002, pp. 13–15). As a witness to the practice of the Roman communities at the end of the second century, therefore, it would have very little value. Despite this, it is worth noting some of what the text does contain as it does not provide as clear a picture as some earlier commentators may have suggested.

Bradshaw et al., in their reconstruction and commentary on the text, identify three bodies of material that may represent the earliest strata (2002, p. 15). These are elements of the work on ministries, a section on initiation, and a series of statements on community meals and prayer. In the first section, following the order for the ordination of a bishop, there is a very brief account, not dissimilar to Justin, of a meal involving the thanksgiving over bread and a cup (*Ap. Trad.* 4). It is here that the Eucharistic Prayer has been placed, and Bradshaw et al. do not consider this to be part of the earliest strand. Prayers for the offering of oil, cheese and olives follow, but again these are not considered early. In the initiatory material there is a meal following baptism, as has been seen in many different texts throughout this book, and this consists of bread, wine and a cup containing milk and honey (*Ap. Trad.* 21.27–8). This is presented as a development, based on the symbolic associations of milk and honey with heaven.

It is the series of comments on eating and fasting in the third body of material that is perhaps most interesting. Chapters 23–30 deal primarily with the etiquette of eating at private and communal meals, the need for blessings and the need for everything to be in order. There follows a short section on the blessing of fruits (but not vegetables (*Ap. Trad* 31–32)) by the bishop and some comments on times for prayer. This material raises the possibility of a more longstanding tradition of offering a wide range of goods including fruit, oil, wheat etc. However, as there has been no other direct allusion to this kind of tradition in any other text, and as it is not possible to offer a clear date or even place for the kind of material that eventually got included in the *Apostolic Tradition*, it is probably fair to say that this is a line of enquiry that cannot be developed at this stage.

Summary

In Chapter 2 I looked at the material surrounding the celebration of a possible Christian Passover and I noted that there is a suggestion in a letter from Irenaeus to Victor, preserved by Eusebius, that the Pascha in Rome does not claim to have apostolic roots. Irenaeus claims that Anicetus, in a dialogue with Polycarp, appealed to the custom of the elders for the practice of the Pascha at Rome (*EH* 5.24.16). Irenaeus traces this

Roman custom to the time of Soter, and perhaps to Sixtus in the first years of the second century (*EH* 5.24.14). Talley dated the origins of the Sunday Pascha to Jerusalem in 135CE (1986, pp. 20–7). Given the close associations between the Christian communities of Palestine and Rome, it is possible that the practice may have arrived in Rome in the later 130s. Whatever date is chosen, the limited evidence that is available does suggest that the celebration of the Pascha at Rome does not go back much beyond the beginning of the second century. If this is the case then the kind of meal that is recounted by Paul in 1 Corinthians, linked as I have suggested to some kind of Christian celebration of the Passover, may never have been a regular part of the tradition at Rome for most, if not all, of the different Christian communities in the city.

The question that is raised by this chapter, however, is whether there is any real evidence for the celebration of a regular cultic meal of any kind within the context of the Roman communities before Justin. If not, then it is necessary to ask whether Justin is developing a practice that had, by the middle years of the second century, actually arrived in Rome, or was he bringing something that he knew from his travels in Samaria and Ephesus? That is a question that I need to address in my conclusion.

8

Conclusions

I noted in the Introduction that the most recent trend in works on the origins of the Eucharist is to turn to sociological or anthropological models. Malina argues that the way in which anthropology is to be used by biblical critics, and by implication others writing on the early Christian communities, is to develop models that can be tested against the data (2001, pp. 1–25). Clearly this is a relatively narrow understanding of anthropology or sociology and their possible uses within this field (Elliott 1995; Esler 1994; Fuglseth 2005). However, it does describe the process for two of the most influential books on the origins of the Eucharist from the last ten years or so. Smith (2003) developed the model of the symposium and related it to all meal practices, including the Eucharist, and McGowan (1999a) developed a model of the cuisine of sacrifice and the ascetical reaction to it.

In this conclusion I want to begin by engaging more fully with those two sociological models to see how they fare against the evidence I have presented so far. In doing this I will look at the relationship between literature and practice and try to demonstrate that both these previous models are probably literary, rather than strictly sociological, in that they identify patterns in the literature rather than inform us of practices on the ground. I will then develop an alternative model, equally sociological, although not of meal practices in the ancient world. I will develop a model of the relationship between literature and practice, with a specific emphasis on textual and oral literatures. From this perspective I will then be able to provide my own outline of how I think the evidence can be brought together to construct a plausible narrative of how the Eucharist developed within early Christian communities during the first 150 years of their existence.

Smith and the symposium

While it is possible to see Smith's work (2003) as an almost ideal application of the principles underlying sociological models, his actual development and use of the model is much more subtle than is usually presented in subsequent discussions. It is Alikin (2009), and others who have followed Smith's lead, who have developed a more unthinking approach based on the model. In principle, however, Smith is doing what Malina says the anthropological critic should do: he is identifying a specific pattern or model within the known data that can be compared with contemporary activity to suggest ways in which other, less explicit, aspects of the data can be understood (Malina 2001, pp. 17–24). The model that Smith chooses is that of the banquet and the symposium. This derives from a specific literary tradition of Greek meal practices that are primarily associated with elite dining practices and the meals associated with the *collegia*. In each case the evidence suggests a clear structure to the meal (with some minor alterations over time and between Greece and Rome). This consists of a gathering, a specific layout of the room, a seating, or reclining, plan based on rank, a meal with libations and certain limitation on menu, a break perhaps with specific drinking, and a time of conversation or entertainment with a wider and more liberal use of strong drink (Smith 2003, pp. 20–38). This is the banquet and the symposium. It can be clearly constructed as a model, with a simple diagrammatic outline, which can then be applied to many other situations.

That this model existed for the ancient world is not in doubt, it is referred to in the literature, even identified by contemporary authors, and is used to provide the basis for the description of other meals such as Philo's account of the Therapeutae (Smith 2003, pp. 158–9). This is not, therefore, a contemporary sociological model that is imposed on the data; it is a model that is derived inductively from the data of the period. It therefore seems appropriate to apply it to other contexts where the texts themselves do not make specific reference to the symposium. This is what Smith does in a more sophisticated fashion for New Testament and other literature, and what Alikin appears to do indiscriminately for all early Christian meals (Smith 2003; Alikin 2009).

It is important to ask, however, what kind of model the symposium is. It was derived primarily from textual accounts of meals, and more specifically from literary accounts, that is, accounts where the meal plays a subsidiary role to the literary elements of the text rather than accounts that set out to describe specific meals or to control their practice. This is clearly recognized by Smith (2003, pp. 18–20, 49). There is a practice that is clear from other kinds of evidence, that associated with the *collegia* for example, which shows that the model was followed in some fairly structured meal situations, and it is clear that there is a relationship of sorts between the literary tradition and the shared meals of some of the *collegia*. In part this links to ideas of status, elite dining, and the attempt, even in relatively low-class *collegia*, to mimic the practices of the elite. The symposium, as Smith shows, is clearly related to a series of values that are inculcated within the practice of the meal itself, and explored beyond the meal as a basis for wider social values within the literary symposia tradition (2003, pp. 47–65). It is a complex area, and it is clear that this is understood by Smith and developed with some sophistication within his work. As such, however, can this tradition, or model, be applied as indiscriminately as Smith and some of his followers suggest?

If, for example, we were to look at contemporary British society we may want to suggest that there is still an ideal 'model' for a meal based on three courses, a seating arrangement round a table, specific foods (roast meat and two vegetables perhaps, but that is becoming far less common) and even containing within itself some element of values that can be applied much more widely within society. The model is seen in its most ideal form in the elite restaurant meals (and the television celebration of this tradition); perhaps it is still sought after within the dinner party; and it is celebrated most clearly in festal meals, particularly those associated with Christmas. The Sunday Carvery at pubs throughout the country enables a less elite version of the same structure, and the model, along with its values, can be clearly identified in a number of different contexts (even in the way Indian and Chinese meal traditions have adapted to the British context). To suggest, however, that this is the only meal structure, or even the most common model of eating within Britain today, is plainly nonsense. The nostalgic call for families to eat together and the condemnation of fast food both attest to this. This does not mean that the 'dinner' model is not important; its relationship with practice and values is just far more complex and needs to be explored in each and every situation before any kind of generalization can be made.

There are some contexts, therefore, where the symposium model does work when brought into dialogue with early Christian texts. As a literary model it does help us to understand the way in which meal stories are recounted in Luke-Acts and can, therefore, bring some insights into these accounts (Smith 2003, pp. 253–72). That the values inherent in the symposium tradition may also underpin some of Paul's thinking within 1 Corinthians is also plausible and well argued by Smith in his book (2003, pp. 173–217). To argue, however, that all meals must follow this model, and that all collective eating must be of the symposium type, is to take the argument too far. What is abundantly clear from the evidence that I have explored is that there is not one single example in the early Christian accounts of collective meals, such as they are, that unambiguously follows the symposium model. In fact, I would probably go further and suggest that the structures for the meals that are presented, with a good number beginning with teaching or having no element of discussion, entertainment or teaching associated with them, mean that the symposium model is actually of little or no relevance in trying to determine the structure and form of early Christian meals. It is important, therefore, to focus on the evidence and not on some model, however interesting that might be, to determine meal practices among the earliest Christian communities.

McGowan and the 'cuisine of sacrifice'

At first sight McGowan (1999a) is constructing a very similar kind of model in his own work, although he is clearly doing something very different with it. The cuisine of sacrifice that McGowan constructs as his starting point is clearly related to, and rooted in, the symposium tradition as developed by Smith (1990, pp. 45–66). The majority of meals covered by the symposium model are sacrificial meals, and it is common place in the literature on early Christian meals to be told that the distinction between sacred and profane meals in the ancient world does not exist, or that all eating of meat is by necessity a sharing in sacrificial practices, whether Jewish or Pagan (Gooch 1993). It is not, however, the cuisine of sacrifice that is the primary concern of McGowan's work. Having identified the sacrificial traditions underpinning the symposium model, McGowan postulates an oppositional tradition that rejects both the content and the values of the cuisine of sacrifice and develops an alternative model of the ascetic meal (1999a, pp. 67–88).

McGowan has no real interest in the structure or form of the meals that he is discussing; it is not the shape of the ascetic meal that is of interest to him. What concerns McGowan is the content of the meal, the foodstuffs that are enjoyed, and the values that are associated with the meals. With Smith he recognizes that the symposium model has clear associations with elite eating, with *collegia*, and most specifically with ideas of hierarchy and excess that are associated with both these contexts. What is significant about McGowan's presentation is that the ascetic tradition that concerns him is not seen simply as an alternative model, with different values, but as an oppositional model, one that is specifically constructed in opposition to the sacrificial symposium model and its values (1999a, pp. 67–9). It is because meat and wine play such a central part in the cuisine of sacrifice that they are rejected in the ascetic tradition. This is an important position and helps us to understand asceticism, not as an end itself, but as always in opposition to a wider set of values associated with eating and consumption in its widest sense: 'the issue of asceticism raises ideas and practices which are distinguished by their *resistance* to cultural norms' (1999a, p. 67, italics in original).

To this extent the 'bread and water' tradition of the Eucharist, which is the primary focus of McGowan's work, has a direct, and oppositional, relationship to the 'meat and wine' focus of the cuisine of sacrifice. It is this overemphasis on the structural opposition, I would suggest, that causes McGowan to miss the fact that much of the evidence does not support a widespread bread and water tradition, any more than it supports a symposium/*collegia* model. McGowan, like Smith, does recognize that the cuisine of sacrifice, like the symposium, is a literary construction; in fact, in literary terms they are essentially identical. This is important for McGowan's own construction, as it is this literary tradition, and the values it contains, that allows for and enables an oppositional tradition of ascetic resistance. What is not so clear is that this oppositional tradition is itself, whether in Cynic writing, Jewish texts, or even early Christian narratives, also a literary tradition (1999a, pp. 69–86). This is not to say that there is no relationship to practice. Clearly some individuals and communities tried to live according to the values of the ascetic literature, although it is easier to see how they could have achieved this in their eating habits than they could in terms of sexual abstinence. This does not detract, however, from the fact that the model or tradition that McGowan is developing is primarily a literary one, and the evidence of actual practice, such as it is, may not support the strict structural opposition between meat-and-wine and bread-and-water that McGowan wants to develop.

Pre-textual and post-textual orality

What should be clear from both these models, which I originally described as 'sociological', is that they are essentially 'literary' in form. This should not be surprising as the vast majority of the evidence that is available, and that has been looked at within this work, is textual and literary in nature. In both cases, however, the assumption is made, and some evidence of another kind is provided to support the assumption, that the literary tradition had some impact on, and relationship to, actual practice. In both cases it is also assumed that the literary tradition has a dominant role in society such that the values, and perhaps the practice, associated with the tradition is noted and understood beyond the literary forms that have remained. To this extent both the symposium tradition (along with the cuisine of sacrifice associated with it) and the ascetic tradition can be described as 'discourses' in the way I constructed that term in my previous book on the *Sociological History of Christian Worship* (2005, pp. 6–23). In other words, there are a series of associated ideas, terms, practices and values that are combined in the thinking of society and can be identified clearly within the texts that are available. While great diversity and creativity can be expressed within a specific discourse, it also has clear boundaries so that speakers, or writers, are aware when they are functioning within the discourse and when they have moved beyond it. Also, to follow Baumann (1996), it is probably fair to say that the discourse of the symposium is the dominant discourse within ancient Graeco-Roman society relating to dining practices, while the discourse of asceticism is clearly demotic, or oppositional. However, as McGowan shows, the demotic discourse of asceticism is entirely dependent on the dominant discourse of the cuisine of sacrifice for its structure and shape (1999a, pp. 67–9).

If the symposium and the ascetic tradition are discourses within wider Graeco-Roman society then they may not be quite as 'literary' as I have suggested in the previous sections. They may simply have survived in literary forms. It is also clear, however, that while the symposium may be the dominant discourse on meals, even in non-literary contexts, this does not suggest that all meals actually followed the shape and structure of the symposium, and the vast majority clearly would not. This kind of discourse, as both Smith and McGowan make clear, with reference to the work of Douglas, has far more to say about values than it does about actual practice (Smith 2003; McGowan 1999a; Douglas 1972).

There is, however, another kind of model, which could be called 'sociological', that I feel is probably more relevant to this discussion than that associated with discourses relating to meals. The emphasis on literary forms and their relationship to wider discourses begins to show the kind of direction this model might take. In most biblical criticism since the middle of the nineteenth century there has been a clear assumption that the elements of the texts of the New Testament had an earlier life as oral literature, and part of the role of the biblical critic was to try and trace the oral history of the text before it became part of the known

New Testament texts. The model here is of a form of orality that allowed for the transmission of texts from generation to generation in a more or less accurate form until they were finally written down by the evangelist, or perhaps by a proto-evangelist who provided the source for the final text. Some of the discussion of the Last Supper in work on the origins of the Eucharist clearly takes this form (for example, Léon-Dufour 1987).

This model of orality is relatively simple and unsophisticated. It assumes a more or less fluid oral transmission from person to person that ends in the fixed form of the written text. In reality, of course, this model is far from adequate as a description of the practice as it occurs. In recent years a whole series of other ideas has been developed to add a greater level of sophistication to the model (Ong 1982). Walter Ong's concept of 'secondary orality', for example, has been picked up by a number of biblical scholars and used to try and understand the complexities of biblical transmission where texts and the oral tradition interact in a more complex fashion (Lapham 2003). As Ong developed the term, however, 'secondary orality' is an aspect of contemporary society where the predominance of electronic media means that most people receive a text orally through radio or television, even when it originates in a written form. Secondary orality is 'essentially a more deliberate and self-conscious orality based permanently on the use of writing' (Ong 1982, p. 136). As such, it is difficult to see how the concept can be applied to the early Christian communities where the use of writing was still very sporadic. That there was some kind of orality that followed on from the writing of the texts, as well as preceding it, is clear, but it is not really secondary orality as outlined by Ong. Kelber, one the first biblical scholars to use and develop Ong's term, proposed a threefold classification using primary orality for the original oral tradition, secondary orality for the way in which the Christian community developed the literary tradition in an oral form, and then tertiary orality for what Ong defines as secondary orality in the contemporary world (1997, p. 226). Such a process, however, does not really help the analysis. Clearly some form of secondary orality, in Ong's terms, did occur even in Graeco-Roman society, when texts were read out in public arenas. This is not really what interests me for this analysis, and so I probably need to look elsewhere for the terms that I wish to use.

I want to propose a distinction between what I would call 'pre-textual orality', the kind of oral tradition that predated the writing of a text and is probably encapsulated in the text itself, and 'post-textual orality'. Post-textual orality is based on the principle that the vast majority of the society, and even the early Christian community, was illiterate. The text, therefore, the written form of the tradition, may not have been as decisive and as influential as earlier scholars have assumed. One thing that is clear from the writings of the early Christian community is that where references to what were to become New Testament texts do occur, these seldom follow the received texts exactly (Hill 2004). This may be because a number of different versions of the text were in circulation, but the fact that most of the references are in fact allusions to the text and not even alternative readings probably makes this less likely. One obvious solution is that the relevant authors were quoting from memory. At this time the Gospels and the writings of Paul may have been circulating in different formats among different communities, but they were not understood to be scripture in the same way as the Hebrew Bible, and they may only be more widely known through public readings within the community. As Nodet and Taylor suggest, the texts were not 'published' in the sense of being made widely and publicly available in a written form (1998, pp. 3–14). The authors are unlikely to have had the text in front of them as they wrote their own work. It is even possible, given that many texts were dictated to scribes, that some of the relevant authors could not read themselves and so the only form of the text that they had available to them was one that was memorized.

If this principle is widened out, then the fact that some stories and sayings were written down does not mean that the fluidity of the oral stage of the process comes to a halt. Post-textual orality occurs when a written text is read in the context of an illiterate community and the content of that text begins to circulate within that community in an oral form, perhaps undergoing changes and shifts in content and meaning as it passes between the individuals within the community freed from its original textual mediation. Many early Christian texts must have been subject to this process, and the range of different ways in which the oral element of this transmission could have taken place must also be recognized. Some texts would have maintained a common form and content (with perhaps slight changes in detail) as would be expected from scholarly analysis of oral literature. The Passion narrative, for example, if that was proclaimed at a regular event associated with Passover, may have fallen into this category. Other stories and sayings, if passed from individual to individual within the community, or from community to community by travelling preachers, may have been transformed quite extensively as the sayings and stories were adapted to different situations and contexts to express different messages and values.

It is possible to ask, at this point, whether this kind of analysis can really be called 'sociological'. The concept of post-textual orality does not, in itself, provide us with a model, or even a discourse, about the nature of meals within the Graeco-Roman world. Following this line, it is not the nature, or even the content, of the meal itself that is the subject of sociological analysis. Rather, post-textual orality is based on a sociology of the text, a theory about the way in which texts function within society, especially within societies where the majority of the population is illiterate. As the primary source of evidence for the development of Christian meals is textual, then it is important not just to look at the relationship between the texts, what might be called inter-texuality, how one text encompasses or refers to another; rather, if pre- and post-textual orality are important parts of the process, then the texts will also be interacting with actual practice, and with methods of oral transmission within the community, far more than they are interacting with other texts. It is important, therefore, not only to understand the limited and perhaps marginal nature of the texts that are available for this period, but also the limited and marginal role that these texts may have played within the development of the meal itself.

When it comes to meals within the Christian community, it may be necessary to deal with a complex interrelation between the texts that we have and the reality on the ground. The chances of a straightforward line from the Last Supper through to a ritual meal on a weekly basis involving bread and wine and some kind of association with the body and blood of Christ is highly unlikely, and is a view that has been rejected since the beginning of the twentieth century. The exact nature of the relationship between any possible meals and the various texts is, however, much more difficult to determine, although it is essential that some attempt is made to do so. In my own reconstruction of the possible history of the origins of the Eucharist it is this interrelationship between text and practice that will form the basis for the reconstruction.

Bradshaw's dots

In my Introduction I suggested that Bradshaw's presentation of the origins of the Eucharist (2004), while extremely influential, was not really as sociological as those of Smith and McGowan. Bradshaw, however, does begin to recognize the complexity of the relationship between text and practice and sees the texts within their social context within his work. The starting point, however, has to be Bradshaw's comment, in his *Search for the Origins of Christian Worship*, that what is available to the scholar of this period is little more than a series of dots scattered across a blank sheet of paper, and the question he asks is whether, and in what way, these dots could be connected (1992, p. 56). Intertextuality would assume that there were clear black lines between the dots, with one having a direct impact on the next. Post-textual orality may lead to the assumption that most of those lines are, in fact, faint, or even dotted, with only hints of, or allusions to, other texts within each bit of the evidence that is available.

Bradshaw is perhaps among the most extreme of the recent theorists in that he almost appears to assume that the lines between the dots cannot be identified at all, and that liturgical scholars must work on the assumption that each text only provides information about the time and place of its own creation, leaving large tracts of blank space on the page about which nothing can be said. In practice, however, Bradshaw does begin to draw, or at least to suggest, some dotted lines. The links between the Johannine literature, the writing of Ignatius and the writing of Justin is questioned around the use of the word 'flesh' (2004, pp. 87–91). It is Bradshaw's attempt, and ultimate failure, to convince himself that there is a direct textual link between these usages that leads to a rather non-committed conclusion that suggests that we cannot say anything at all about the link.

The idea of the dots on the page, however, has one major flaw. The general image of the printed page is still of something that is static and relatively fixed. Ideas associated with quantum mechanics and the uncertainty principle do exist to a certain extent in textual criticism, and postmodernism has led to a view that theories, narratives and texts are not as fixed or as final as was previously thought. However, the page of dots as described by Bradshaw is not static in any sense, and this is probably one of the reasons why the image was dropped in the second edition of the book (2002). In reality there is not only a large blank sheet of paper with a few tiny dots, but those dots, in themselves, are not fixed and may even appear and disappear depending on who is undertaking the analysis. The vast majority of the texts that have been looked at in this book are uncertain in terms of date and provenance. There is so much that is not known about the origins and pre-history of the texts themselves that any attempt to fix them firmly on the page is impossible. The first job of the liturgical scholar, therefore, is to a greater or lesser extent to fix the dots, to pin them down in and of themselves before the process of trying to join them together can be started.

One good example of the dramatic effect this fixing process can have can be seen in Mazza's works on the origin of the Eucharist (1995,

1999). Mazza differs from practically all other recent scholars in the field in that he sets specific, and somewhat different, dates to important texts, particularly the *Didache*, and he is clear in drawing distinct and fairly solid textual lines between the texts. In a couple of books, the first of which deals specifically with the development of the Eucharistic prayer, rather than actual practice (1995), and the second of which expands this into a wider theory, but with a specific focus on interpretation (1999), Mazza focuses on intertextuality. For Mazza, the earliest Christian text is the *Didache*, which he dates before 48–49 CE and situates in a Judaeo-Christian context (1995, pp. 40–1). This text is itself, according to Mazza, based on earlier Jewish prayer models, which can be seen in later literary forms. In offering such an early date for the *Didache*, Mazza is able to propose a direct, textual, influence of the *Didache* on 1 Corinthians (1995, pp. 90–4), and subsequently on all the other texts that he goes on to look at. Such a radical redating of the texts, and the pushing of the data to fit the intertextual theory, demands a wide-scale repositioning of the dots. Most scholars, as I have shown, are not nearly as radical as this.

There must be a middle course between Bradshaw's position in which no lines, or perhaps only very few and very faint lines, can confidently be drawn between the dots, and Mazza's attempt to reposition the dots in order to draw large clear intertextual lines between them. This, I would suggest, is where pre-textual and post-textual orality may provide a way forward. I have been very careful throughout this book both to suggest some of the readings that I would want to place on texts, but also to insist on the provisional nature of those readings. It is, I would propose, only when the various readings are brought together and mapped onto the page of dots to provide a potential narrative, or series of narratives, that link the dots with lines of pre- and post-textual orality, that the solidity of the lines themselves begins to become apparent and the plausibility of the narratives can be tested. The next and final stage of this conclusion has to be a process of reconstruction, a retelling of the narratives, from my own particular perspective, of the origins of the Eucharist in the earliest Christian communities.

The Last Supper, the Passion and pre-textual oral traditions

I begin with the very earliest Christian communities, meeting in Jerusalem, or perhaps in Galilee and other parts of Palestine, in the first few years after the death and resurrection of Jesus. These communities found themselves reflecting on the death and the resurrection of Jesus particularly at the time of the Jewish Passover, that is, on the anniversary of the death itself. The community was not really interested in celebrating a Passover as such; the death of Jesus had already superseded that, and much of the ritual of the Jewish Passover, whatever that might have been at this period, was probably abandoned, particularly the sacrifice of the lamb. They did, however, begin to tell the story of the Passion, beginning with an account of the meal and ending with the empty tomb. Without the practical focus on the details of the Passover meal the various elements of that meal were irrelevant to the narrative, but two elements were significant, the eschatological sayings – 'I will not drink again of the fruit of the vine until that day when I drink it anew in the kingdom of God' (Mark 14.25) – and the link that Jesus made between the bread and cup of the meal and his own body and blood.

This developed very clearly as a pre-textual oral tradition, probably at a very early date. From the existing textual versions that have survived it is possible that an outline structure emerged quite early to be fleshed out in the telling within the different local communities. It is not my place in this book to speculate on the pre-textual oral history of the Passion narrative itself. The pre-textual oral history of the meal element of that narrative, however, does probably deserve more elaboration. I stressed in Chapter 2 that this must always be seen as an integral part of the wider Passion narrative rather than as a distinct and separate item in itself. However, the two elements of the eschatological sayings and the references to body and blood do still need some explanation.

There are three relatively recent attempts to provide this pre-textual oral history. Léon-Dufour is perhaps the more traditional of the three in that he traces two different tendencies, the Antiochene and the Markan (1987, pp. 96–7), but also two different traditions within the text, the eschatological vine statements and the reference to the bread as the body of Christ (1987, pp. 82–95). The context for the development of these tendencies and traditions, according to Léon–Dufour, is catechetical, the pre-textual oral environment in which new Christians are taught about what is happening within the weekly sharing of bread and wine. It is from this oral context that the various versions of the textual narrative are constructed. This is a careful and detailed piece of work, and as a plausible attempt to get behind the text of the Last Supper narrative it certainly has some merits. Where I would disagree is in the catechetical context of the meal. If the Last Supper narrative is part of the wider Passion narrative then it is to the pre-textual oral traditions of the Passion, and its use within an annual celebration, that scholars need to look, not to the development of the weekly meal tradition.

Chilton (1994) provides a different kind of engagement with pre-textual orality in his attempt to trace the meanings of the institution narrative through a series of phases only some of which are apparent in the texts of the Gospels and in Paul. The methodology here is closer to the kind of textual archaeology that can be seen in the work of Lietzmann for example (1979), although Chilton is attempting to push much further back than Lietzmann's own work. Chilton develops a series of stages beginning with the focus on purity within Jesus' wider ministry and the meals he shared with the disciples, the emphasis on sacrificial surrogates in Jesus' own final meal, Peter's emphasis on covenant, James' introduction of Passover themes, Paul's introduction of the symposium context, and finally Paul and John's emphasis on miraculous food. Many of the themes and issues that have been raised within this work can be seen in Chilton's analysis, although he condenses them all into a period of pre-textual orality while I would want to put the development of many of them into the post-textual oral stage that I will outline below. Chilton's willingness, however, to see the meal as encapsulating a variety of different, and perhaps even contradictory, meanings for different groups and communities is a position that I am very keen to endorse.

Nodet and Taylor (1998) develop a much more sophisticated history based on both textual and oral traditions. They also represent a line in contemporary biblical and early Christian studies that sees the understanding of the Essene and other non-Pharisaical forms of Jewish thought in the Second Temple period as central to the development of Christianity. For Nodet and Taylor the primary issues are calendrical and cultic. It is very difficult to summarize a very complex argument in a few sentences, but in relation to the Christian meal they argue that the Last Supper as it appears in the Passion narratives represents a combination of two traditions. In this they follow the same distinction as Léon-Dufour in separating the eschatological and the body and blood sayings. Nodet and Taylor presume a regular meal tradition within early Christianity, probably originating with Jesus but clearly linked to the daily blessing of bread and wine as noted in Essene practices (Josephus, *Jewish War* 2.129–32) and linked conceptually to the Pentecost themes of the first fruits (1QS 6.6). This tradition accounts for the thanksgiving over bread and wine and the association of these with the offering of the body of Jesus (Nodet and Taylor 1998, pp. 120–1). This is then linked to a Passover tradition that brings in the eschatological material.

As the death of Jesus took place at about the time of the Passover then, according to Nodet and Taylor, this forms the narrative structure for the Last Supper, although the content is provided by the Essene/Pentecost tradition of bread and wine (1998, pp. 122–3).

All three of these analyses recognize the point made by Bradshaw and others, that the Last Supper narrative may not, in the form that it finally took in the textual traditions, have ever reflected actual practice (2004, p. 13), but they all recognize that the textual form of the narrative has serious problems. In many ways Nodet and Taylor's solution is the most complete, in that it does make an attempt to address all the anomalies, contradictions and uncertainties in the texts, but like those of Chilton, and particularly Léon-Dufour, it still presupposes a weekly, or even daily, meal practice within the community as the primary context for the pre-textual oral traditions. A wide range of authors note Baumstark's (1958) original observation that ritual practice is always more conservative than the justifications surrounding it and use this to assert a continuity of weekly meal practices around which the various pre-textual oral traditions develop before they are fixed within the Last Supper narrative itself. There is still no real evidence, however, that the Last Supper story, contained within the longer Passion narrative, was ever linked to a weekly practice, or that a weekly practice has been contained within the narrative. It remains my view that the solution to the issues raised by the Passion narrative has to be found within the pre-textual oral history of that narrative, and not in the context of another kind of practice or tradition. That task, however, remains beyond the scope of this particular text.

The development of the annual meal

As the number of communities increased and the followers of Jesus were driven out of Jerusalem, moved out along trade routes, or otherwise spread to other cities and towns of the region, this practice of remembering the death and resurrection of Jesus at or around the time of the Jewish Passover would have continued with a shared meal and a retelling of the narrative as an oral tradition, which would have maintained a common shape but probably varied in terms of its details. Paul was probably introduced to this at Antioch and clearly advocated it as a practice in the various communities that he founded in Asia Minor and beyond. Whether it ever reached as far as the emerging Christian communities in Rome is difficult to assess, although what evidence we have suggests to me that it probably did not. It is this meal at the time of the Jewish Passover, but shared within a largely non-Jewish community in Corinth, that caused Paul to write what he wrote in the letter and to refer to the 'tradition' that he had learnt at Antioch, the relevant part of the longer Passion narrative. The letter clearly has other Passover allusions and Paul weaves this into his text with specific reference to bread and the cup. He also refers a second time to the tradition of the Passion narrative as something that was 'received' and 'passed on' in his discussion of resurrection in chapter 15 (1 Cor. 15.3–7).

For Paul the Passion narrative probably remained a pre-textual oral tradition and therefore the form of words that are given in 11.23–26 are likely to be Paul's own, although adapted from a known oral text. It is also probably Paul, therefore, who adds the command to 'do this in remembrance of me' as that serves his own purposes of referring to a meal that 'proclaims the Lord's death until he comes'. This phrase is not found in the version used by Mark and Matthew and I would argue *whoa* that it only comes into Luke through a direct textual referent when later editors felt that the original version, with a preliminary cup followed by the bread, was no longer adequate. The focus on remembrance would have been taken for granted in the context of a meal to celebrate the death and resurrection of Jesus, but before Paul's attempt to use the text to comment on the mishandling of that meal, the remembrance would always have focused on the wider events. It is Paul who is asking the Corinthians to remember Jesus in the actions of the Last Supper meal. At no point, however, does Paul say, or suggest, that the actions of the Last Supper should be repeated in the Lord's Supper and it is my contention that neither he, nor the Corinthians, would have considered this necessary.

A similar practice is seen, much less clearly, in the Gospel of John. Here the author is aware of an annual meal associated with the Passover at which the reference to eating Jesus' flesh and blood is made. The compiler of the Gospel, however, chooses to remove this element from his own Passion narrative, probably because he did not want to confuse his own received chronology by emphasizing the Paschal nature of the meal. He then uses the idea of eating and drinking the flesh and blood of Jesus to develop a separate argument against an emerging series of ideas that wanted to deny that Jesus was a real human person consisting of real human flesh. By linking the eating and drinking to the feeding of the five thousand, which is also linked textually to the time of the Passover, and by emphasizing the word 'flesh' rather than 'body', the compiler of the Gospel is able to make a much stronger point about the necessity of eating the flesh of Jesus and drinking his blood, and therefore about the continuing reality of his fleshly existence. There is no suggestion in the Gospel that this is associated with any specific ritual meal – it is a narrative elaboration on the first section of the Passion narrative, cut loose and elaborated for polemic reasons – but it does suggest that a continuing celebration of the Passion at the time of the Jewish Passover continued in the community that compiled the Gospel.

An annual celebration, with a shared meal, held on the date of the Jewish Passover, clearly continued within many Christian communities in Asia Minor, although there is little evidence for the continuation of this practice elsewhere. The evidence for the practice is seen in the Quartodeciman controversy of the second half of the second century and the claim for apostolic authority from the bishops of Asia Minor. Where the Sunday tradition of Easter originated, whether in Jerusalem or elsewhere, is a very different question and probably shows that in some parts of the Christian community the original practice had died out. It could well have been Paul's own insistence on using the Passion, and the celebration at the time of Passover, as one basis for his own teaching that reinforced the practice in Asia Minor, but this is impossible to determine.

The breaking of bread

Christian communities would clearly have shared other meals at times other than the Passover and, despite the fact that this caused some difficulties among the very earliest groups where Jews and non-Jews came together, that particular issue appears to have been settled relatively quickly. What is very clear, however, is that in most communities, including that of Antioch in the early days of the movement, these meals had no real significance for the community and may have been held on an irregular basis, as appropriate within the community for fellowship purposes. What forms these meals took and how they related to the telling of stories about Jesus, the passing on of his teachings, or other more extended forms of teaching and discussion is difficult to assess, but the story of the event at Troas in Acts provides a very good example of the kind of event that was probably beginning to emerge (Acts 20.7–12). Here the meal is simply a part, and a relatively incidental part, of an all-night preaching and teaching event. No specific importance appears to have been placed on the meal itself.

The term 'the breaking of bread' clearly became associated with these meals and began to be quite widespread as a title for the meal especially throughout Palestine and Syria. The question that has to be asked in relation to this title, however, is whether it was a standard title that was taken over by Luke in his writing, or whether the term derives from the writings themselves and is, in that sense, an invention of the author of the Acts of the Apostles. In other words, is the breaking of bread part of the pre- or post-textual oral tradition? Given that the term also appears in the *Didache* (14.1) which, even if it did not predate the writing of the Gospel of Luke and Acts, is clearly not influenced by it in any way, then it is most probable that the term was widely used within the communities of northern Palestine and southern Syria when Luke picked it up. It is therefore a pre-textual oral tradition. Its appearance in the Apocryphal *Acts* of the Apostles, however, is not so easy to characterize as this could easily be derived either directly from the Lucan writings, or indirectly through a subsequent post-textual oral tradition associated with Acts. The other important point about the title is that it carries no specific meaning in itself, although stories such as that associated with Emmaus (Luke 24.13–35) may have provided the post-textual use of the term with a sense of the presence of Jesus in the breaking of the bread.

In terms of frequency there is some evidence, again in Acts and the *Didache*, that the breaking of bread was a normal part of the celebration of the first day of the week (Acts 20.7; *Didache* 14.1), probably held in the morning. Thanksgivings would have been said over the bread, undoubtedly following current Jewish models, especially in Syria and Palestine. The bread may also have been accompanied by other foodstuffs – salt, olives, herbs etc. – and almost certainly by a cup, whether of wine or water. Again following contemporary Jewish models, this would have attracted its own thanksgiving, picking up themes of unity and eschatology from these sources and from wider Christian reflections on Hebrew scriptures. The actual practice of the meal and the kind of drink that accompanied it would probably vary from community to community depending on the local norms and what was available. This, then, is the model that is seen in the *Didache* and suggested in other texts from the same region. There is no evidence that this ever becomes as formal as the Essene meals for example (1QS 6), although, at least in the community that produced the *Didache*, there are clear indications that presence at the meal is restricted to those who have been baptized.

It is fairly clear that these regular weekly 'breaking of bread' meals were not well established at the time that Paul was in Antioch and he did not introduce them to his own communities in Asia Minor and

187

Greece. Some of the Anatolian communities may have begun to pick up similar practices over time, as might other communities in other parts of the empire, but there is no real evidence of this, especially in Rome, and the evidence of Pliny suggests a much less frequent and much less elaborated meal tradition among the ex-Christians he interrogated (*Epp.* 10.96). The breaking of bread tradition, therefore, is essentially a localized tradition, focused on the area around Antioch and continued, and to some extent regularized, among those communities who maintained relatively close links with local Jewish communities. It is from here that texts such as the Pseudo-Clementine literature and other Jewish Christian texts derive their use of the term.

What is seen in the first fifty to a hundred years of Christian development, therefore, are two distinct traditions for Christian meals. One of these, the breaking of bread tradition, is in part the kind of tradition that Lietzmann (1979) highlighted in his development of the two meals theory. I do not think that it was anywhere near as formal as Lietzmann suggests. The emphasis is on bread, and only incidently and locally on bread and wine or bread and water. Nor do I want to associate any specific meaning to this meal, although it would clearly have reminded some of the meals Jesus took part in, or stories associated with the post-resurrection meals, and so on. These stories would still have existed in an equally informal pre-textual oral tradition at this time and so the association of meal with story would itself have been very loose and dependent on local interpretation. The second tradition, however, the annual meal at the time of the Jewish Passover, is nothing like Lietzmann's second strand, although it is seen most specifically in the writings of Paul. It is clearly not an invention of Paul and never, because of its annual nature, had the kind of impact that Lietzmann proposes for his own second tradition. It was, however, important and had a significant post-textual impact, as I will show, on the development of the weekly meal in the first half of the second century.

Ignatius and the combination of post-textual oral traditions

With the letters of Ignatius, in the early years of the second century, three distinct changes and developments can be observed. I am not suggesting that Ignatius was the instigator of these changes, although his writings probably helped to establish them more widely. However, the fact that he was moving from Antioch, through Asia Minor, towards Rome does follow what I believe to be the direction of travel of all these developments. What is also clear from the writings of Ignatius is a move from pre-textual orality to post-textual orality. It is often assumed that the compilers of letters and other texts in the ancient world must have been able to read as well as write. However, if, as is generally acknowledged, letters and other texts were, in fact, dictated to scribes (Rom. 16.22) then it is fair to assume that the authors themselves may not have been able to write. If they could not write then it may also be the case that they could not read as well and that they derived all their knowledge of previous texts from hearing the texts being read aloud in a public setting. I assume that Paul, who was trained as a Pharisee in a tradition of scriptural scholarship, and Justin, who trained under a number of philosopher-teachers, could both read a range of texts that were available to them. Ignatius, however, does not appear to have the same level of education and the way he alludes to ideas and images from other texts suggests that he certainly did not have texts in front of him. It is highly likely that he only heard them read and relied on memory rather than a detailed knowledge of the texts themselves when dictating his own letters. Ignatius, therefore, is relying on post-textual orality. This will become important when I look at how he combined a number of post-textual oral traditions in his discussions of Christian meals.

The first change and development in the discourse surrounding the meal seen in the letters of Ignatius is a gradual move from the title of 'the breaking of bread' to that of 'the Eucharist'. This is very natural. Thanksgiving over the bread, and where relevant over the cup as well, is an important part of the meal that is often mentioned in association with the title 'the breaking of bread' in earlier texts, and the two terms were clearly interchangeable for many decades. The title of 'the Eucharist', however, probably never took on a highly technical sense until much later, at least well into the second century. Ignatius certainly uses the two titles interchangeably although it is interesting to note that it is only in an earlier letter that the breaking of bread is used (*Ephesians* 20.2), and in later letters (for example *Philadelphians* 4.1) that 'Eucharist' appears to become a technical term. It is also important to note the reference to '*agape*' in *Smyrnaeans* 8.2, although it is difficult to know the derivation of this title, as there are so few references in the remaining literature.

The second change is to a greater sense of formality associated with the meal. It is not entirely clear why Ignatius got into trouble with the authorities in Antioch, but disputes within the Christian community relating to matters of authority may have had some part in it. Ignatius is very clear in his understanding of the role of the bishop within the community and he sets out in all his letters to stress the importance and centrality of that role. It is very likely that he was a bit of a lone voice at this time, trying to impose something over and against the pattern that he found in the communities that he travelled through. He may also have been used to a weekly meal within the Antioch communities along the lines of the breaking of bread meals already mentioned. For Ignatius, in Antioch, there was clearly an emphasis on the necessity of baptism as a prerequisite for participation in the meal, but how much further formality was associated with the meal is difficult to judge. Part of what he is trying to convince his readers of, therefore, is a more frequent celebration of their own meals, an emphasis on thanksgiving, that is, on the prayers said within the meal, and the importance, for him at least, of the role of the bishop as the celebrant of the meal. This suggests that a weekly meal, of the kind Ignatius was used to in Antioch, was not a regular or fixed part of the lives of the Christian communities of Asia Minor, any more than a single bishop was a fixed part of their organization. How much impact Ignatius had at his own time is difficult to say, but it is clearly the case that the subsequent publishing and distribution of his letters led others to pick up the idea of the single bishop with almost complete authority over his community and to enforce it at a later date drawing on the post-textual oral traditions that derived from the letters, as part of their own justification.

Finally, Ignatius begins to link the bread and cup at the meal with the flesh and blood of Jesus. I am not suggesting that Ignatius is the first, or the only person, to do this, and the reasons why he does it still remain very speculative. Flesh and blood language is introduced into Ignatius' letters for much the same reasons as John introduces it into an earlier part of his Gospel, to counter those who claimed that Jesus was not present in real human flesh. Like John, or perhaps following John, it then seems natural to Ignatius to apply the same language to the bread and the cup. This does not inform any kind of theology or meaning for the bread and cup themselves, and certainly does not initiate a textual link through to the Last Supper, but within the wider play of ideas the association appears to be a fruitful one. The meal itself becomes the 'medicine of immortality' (*Ephesians* 20.2), which again is probably little more than an association of ideas at the moment of writing, although the link to John 6 and the promise of eternal life (6.54) is evocative. Ignatius is not quoting John in any sense. There is not a direct textual link between the Gospel of John and the letters of Ignatius. However, the language and imagery inherent in John 6 has clearly become part of the post-textual oral environment inhabited by Ignatius, perhaps at Antioch, perhaps during his travels in Asia Minor.

It is through recalling, probably at an unconscious level, this language, and the imagery associated with it, that Ignatius is able to draw on the same kinds of imagery, and through his own creative imagination to link the language of John to the meal that he is trying to impose more fully within the communities he is writing to.

What I think can be observed in the writings of Ignatius, therefore, is a glimpse of the process by which the regular weekly meal, celebrated within many of the Palestinian and Syrian communities, slowly begins to move West along with travelling preachers, teachers, prisoners and merchants. Some, like Ignatius, have more celebrity status or more authority within the local Christian communities. Others simply spread practices and ideas by word of mouth, recalling previous texts that they have heard and associating them with new practices and ideas. I am not saying that Ignatius himself is the sole cause, or even the sole example, of this gradual process, but his writings do highlight the process and may even have accelerated it as the letters were read within other communities and become themselves part of the growing post-textual oral traditions of those communities. There is no attempt at this stage to collect together the writings of Paul or the emerging Gospels, no *Not* sense that these writings are being published, to use Nodet and Taylor's term (1998, p. 3). However, there is clearly an emerging engagement with the texts, either in the forms that are known today or in earlier versions. It is the writing down of the ideas into letters and stories that slowly gives them solidity and greater influence on others, and then the transmission of these through further oral traditions that spreads them wider into the community. For Ignatius, as for John, it is useful to link bread and cup with flesh and blood, and having done so, for primarily doctrinal reasons, the imagery becomes associated with the meal where bread plays a prominent role and where cups, whether of wine or water, or some mixture of the two, are probably an inevitable part. It takes time for the weekly celebration of the meal to become normative and there is no evidence of any attempt to link the weekly meal to the annual meal at the time of the Passover. Both traditions begin to mature slowly and steadily within Asia Minor through the first 50 years or so of the second century.

Arrival at Rome and the celebration of the Eucharist

So, when did a weekly meal arrive in Rome, and who brought it there? The answer to that question can never be known. My guess, from the evidence that I have surveyed in this book, is that it was probably quite late, well into the first few decades of the second century. Clement shows no knowledge of a regular weekly meal within the communities that he is associated with and nor does the *Shepherd of Hermas*. Justin is used to a weekly meal and takes it entirely for granted as part of his own community in the middle of the second century, but he came from the East and probably celebrated within a community of Syrian, Palestinian and Samaritan Christians. There is no direct evidence to suggest that his practice was common to all the Christian communities of Rome, even those that were later to be described as 'catholic', let alone those that were developing new and creative interpretations of the Christian story. By the end of the second century the weekly meal of bread and wine was probably normative among the vast majority of Roman communities, as it was within the vast majority of Christian communities across the ancient world, and it was possible to distinguish the rite with bread and wine from other less formal meals, those that were being given the label of '*agape*'. Writings from Irenaeus in Lyon, Tertullian in North Africa and Clement in Alexandria, among others, make this very clear. The fixing of the date and form for the celebration of the Pascha had been disputed openly and vocally between bishops in Rome and those in Asia Minor, but the gradual fixing of the meal around readings, sermon, prayers, the thanksgiving and the sharing of bread and wine had gone on quietly and without dispute.

Justin also shows another step along the way in terms of the association of the bread and the cup with the flesh and blood of Jesus. The link is already unquestioned in his *Dialogue with Trypho*; it does not need to be explained either to Trypho, the fictional audience within the text, or the real audience of those listening in on the dialogue. In the *Apology* the link is also made explicitly back to the Last Supper narratives (*Apology* 1.65.3), even though it is clear that this is not seen as a warrant for the rite itself. As with Ignatius the use of the word 'flesh' assumes a familiarity with the post-textual oral traditions surrounding the Gospel of John, but Justin takes this thinking, and the associations underpinning it, further by linking the idea of bread and wine as flesh and blood right back to the Last Supper narrative itself. Once again, however, Justin does not quote from any of the known texts, rather he draws either on his memory of the text or on some other more widespread form of post-textual orality. With Justin, however, the binding of the form of the meal with the narrative of the Last Supper is far from complete and it will take another century and a half, and probably even longer in the Eastern communities where the weekly meal originated, before that process has been completed.

What I am proposing, therefore, is that the Eucharist as the churches understand it today – a weekly sharing in bread and wine linked conceptually to the Last Supper narrative's association of bread and wine with the body and blood of Jesus – is a product of a long series of gradual changes that did not fully materialize until the beginning of the second century at the earliest. There is no direct line from the supper held by Jesus on the night that he was betrayed to a ritual act performed by all his followers in identical fashion, and for much of the first 100 years of the Christian community's existence there was probably not even a regular weekly meal outside of Syria and Palestine. It was as the practice of the weekly meal spread from the communities around Antioch, and as thinkers attempted to link the bread and cup of that meal to understandings from the post-textual oral traditions of John, in the first instance, and eventually of the Last Supper itself, that the Eucharist as it is understood today gradually emerged and became a central part of the life of the Church.

Bibliography

Alexander, L., 'IPSE DIXIT: Citation of Authority in Paul and in the Jewish and Hellenistic Schools', in T. Endberg-Pedersen (ed.), *Paul Beyond the Judaism/ Hellenism Divide*, Louisville: Westminster John Knox Press, 2001.

Alikin, V. A., *The Earliest History of the Christian Gathering: Origin, Development and Content of the Christian Gathering in the First to Third Centuries*, Leiden: Brill, 2009.

Ashton, J., *Understanding the Fourth Gospel*, Oxford: Oxford University Press, 1991.

Barclay, J. M. G., *Jews in the Mediterranean Diaspora: From Alexander to Trajan (323 BCE – 117 CE)*, Edinburgh: T. & T. Clark, 1996.

Barclay, J. M. G., 'Diaspora Judaism', in D. Cohn-Sherbok and J. M. Court (eds), *Religious Diversity in the Graeco-Roman World: A Survey of Recent Scholarship*, Sheffield: Sheffield Academic Press, 2001, pp. 47–64.

Barrett, C. K., *The Gospel of John and Judaism*, London: SPCK, 1975.

Barrett, C. K., *The Gospel According to John: An Introduction with Commentary and Notes on the Greek Text*, London: SPCK, 1978.

Barrett, C. K., *Acts: A Shorter Commentary*, London: T. & T. Clark, 2002.

Barton, S. C., 'Mark as Narrative: The Story of the Anointing Woman (Mark 14: 3–9)', *Expository Times* 102 (1991), pp. 230–4.

Barton, S. C., *Life Together: Family, Sexuality and Community in the New Testament and Today*, Edinburgh: T. & T. Clark, 2001.

Barton, S. C. and Horsley, G. H. R., 'A Hellenistic Cult Group and the New Testament Churches', *Jahrbuch fur Antike und Christentum* 24 (1986), pp. 7–41.

Bauer, W., *Orthodoxy and Heresy in Earliest Christianity*, Philadelphia: Fortress Press, 1971.

Baumann, G., *Contesting Culture: Discourses of Identity in Multi-Ethnic London*, Cambridge: Cambridge University Press, 1996.

Baumstark, A., *Comparative Liturgy*, London: Mowbray, 1958.

Best, E., 'Mark's Readers: A Profile', in F. Van Segbroeck et al. (eds), *The Four Gospels 1992: Festschrift Frans Neirynck*, Leuven: Leuven University Press, 1992, II, pp. 839–58.

Betz, J., 'The Eucharist in the Didache', in J. A. Draper (ed.), *The Didache in Modern Research*, Leiden: Brill, 1996, pp. 244–75.

Black, M., *An Aramaic Approach to the Gospels and Acts*, Oxford: Oxford University Press, 1969.

Borgen, P., *Early Christianity and Hellenistic Judaism*, Edinburgh: T. & T. Clark, 1996.

Bornkamm, G., *Early Christian Experience*, London: SCM Press, 1966.

Bouyer, L., *The Christian Mystery: From Pagan Myth to Christian Mysticism*, Edinburgh: T. & T. Clark, 1990.

Bradshaw, P., *The Search for the Origins of Christian Worship: Sources and Methods for the Study of Early Liturgy*, London: SPCK, 1992.

Bradshaw, P., *The Search for the Origins of Christian Worship: Sources and Methods for the Study of Early Liturgy* (revised and enlarged edition), London: SPCK, 2002.

Bradshaw, P., 'Parallels between Early Jewish and Christian Prayers: Some Methodological Issues', in A. Gerhards, A. Doeker and P. Ebenbauer (eds), *Identität durch Gebet: Zur gemeinschaftsbildenden Funktion institutionalisierten Betens in Judentum und Christentum*, Paderborn: Schöningh, 2003, pp. 21–36.

Bradshaw, P., *Eucharistic Origins*, London: SPCK, 2004.

Bradshaw, P. Johnson, M. E. and Phillips, L. E., *The Apostolic Tradition: A Commentary*, Minneapolis: Fortress Press, 2002.

Brent, A., *Ignatius of Antioch: A Martyr Bishop and the Origin of Episcopacy*, London: T. & T. Clark, 2009.

Brown, R. E., *The Community of the Beloved Disciple: The Life, Loves and Hates of an Individual Church in New Testament Times*, London: Geoffrey Chapman, 1979.

Brown, R. E. and Meier, J. P., *Antioch and Rome: New Testament Cradles of Catholic Christianity*, London: Geoffrey Chapman, 1983.

Bruce, F. F., *New Century Bible Commentary: I and II Corinthians*, London: Marshall, Morgan & Scott, 1971.

Buchanan, C., *Justin Martyr on Baptism and Eucharist: Texts in Translation with Introduction and Commentary*, Joint Liturgical Studies 64 (2007).

Bultmann, R., *The Gospel of John: A Commentary*, Oxford: Blackwell, 1971.

Burns, S., Slee, N. and Jagessar, M. N. (eds), *The Edge of God: New Liturgical Texts and Contexts in Conversation*, Peterborough: Epworth Press, 2008.

Carrington, P., *The Primitive Christian Calendar: A Study in the Making of the Markan Gospel, Volume I, Introduction and Text*, Cambridge: Cambridge University Press, 1952.

Chilton, B., *A Feast of Meanings: Eucharistic Theologies from Jesus through Johannine Circles*, Leiden: Brill, 1994.

Chow, J. K., *Patronage and Power: A Study of Social Networks in Corinth*, Sheffield: JSOT Press, 1992.

Cirlot, F. L., *The Early Eucharist*, London: SPCK, 1939.

Cohick, L. H., *The Peri Pascha Attributed to Melito of Sardis: Setting, Purpose and Sources*, Providence: Brown Judaic Studies, 2000.

Conzelmann, H., *A Commentary on the First Epistle to the Corinthians*, Philadelphia: Fortress Press, 1975.

Conzelmann, H., *A Commentary on the Acts of the Apostles*, Philadelphia: Fortress Press, 1987.

Cross, F. L., *1 Peter: A Paschal Liturgy*, London: Mowbray, 1954.

Crossley, J. G., *The Date of Mark's Gospel: Insight from the Law in Earliest Christianity*, London: T. & T. Clark, 2004.

Cullmann, O., *Early Christian Worship*, London: SCM Press, 1953.

Cullmann, O., 'The Meaning of the Lord's Supper in Primitive Christianity', in O. Cullmann and J. Leenhardt, *Essays on the Lord's Supper*, London: Lutterworth Press, 1958.

Cullmann, O., *The Johannine Circle*, London: SCM Press, 1976.

Cureton, W., *The Ancient Syriac Version of the Epistles of St Ignatius to St Polycarp: The Ephesians and the Romans*, London: Rivingtons, 1845.

Daly-Denton, M. M., 'Water in the Eucharistic Cup: A Feature of the Eucharist in Johannine Trajectories through Early Christianity', *Irish Theological Quarterly*, 72 (2007), pp. 356–70.

de Boer, M. C., 'The Composition of 1 Corinthians', *New Testament Studies* 40 (1994), pp. 229–45.

Deissman, G. A., *Paul: A Study in Social and Religious History*, New York: Harper & Row, 1957.

Dix, G., *The Shape of the Liturgy*, London: Adam & Charles Black, 1945.

Donfried, K. P., *Paul, Thessalonica, and Early Christianity*, Grand Rapids: Eerdmans, 2002.

Douglas, M., *Purity and Danger: An Analysis of Pollution and Taboo*, London: Routledge & Kegan Paul, 1966.

Douglas, M., *Natural Symbols: Explorations in Cosmology*, London: Barrie Rockcliffe, 1970.

Douglas, M., 'Deciphering a Meal', *Daedalus* 101 (1972), pp. 61–81.

Duchesne, L., *Christian Worship: Its Origin and Evolution*, London: SPCK, 1904.

Dugmore, C. W., 'The Study of the Origins of the Eucharist: Retrospect and Revaluation', in G. J. Cuming (ed.), *Studies in Church History, Volume II, Papers Read at the Second Winter and Summer Meetings of the Ecclesiastical History Society*, London: Nelson, 1965, pp. 1–18.

Dunn, J. D. G., 'The Incident at Antioch (Gal 2:11–18)', *Journal for the Study of the New Testament* 18 (1983), pp. 3–75.

Dunn, J. D. G., *1 Corinthians*, Sheffield: Sheffield Academic Press, 1995.

Elliott, J. K., *The Apocryphal New Testament: A Collection of Apocryphal Christian Literature in an English Translation*, Oxford: Oxford University Press, 1993.

Elliott, J., *Social-Scientific Criticism of the New Testament: An Introduction*, London: SPCK, 1995.

Ellis, E. E., 'Traditions in 1 Corinthians', *New Testament Studies* 32 (1986), pp. 481–502.

Esler, P. F., *Community and Gospel in Luke-Acts: The Social and Political Motivations for Lucan Theology*, Cambridge: Cambridge University Press, 1987.

Esler, P. F., *The First Christians in their Social Worlds: Social-Scientific Approaches to New Testament Interpretation*, London: Routledge, 1994.

Esler, P. F., 'Making and Breaking an Agreement Mediterranean Style: A New Reading of Galatians 2:1–14', *Biblical Interpretation* 3.3 (1995), pp. 285–314.

Falk, D. K., 'Jewish Prayer Literature and the Jerusalem Church in Acts', in R. Bauckham (ed.), *The Book of Acts in its Palestinian Setting*, Carlisle: Paternoster Press, 1995, pp. 267–301.

Fee, G. D., *The First Epistle to the Corinthians*, Grand Rapids: Eerdmans, 1987.

Feely-Harnik, G., *The Lord's Table: The Meaning of Food in Early Judaism and Christianity*, Washington: Smithsonian Books, 1994.

Fiorenza, E. S., *In Memory of Her: A Feminist Theological Reconstruction of Christian Origins*, London: SCM Press, 1983.

Fuglseth, K. S., *Johannine Sectarianism in Perspective: A Sociological, Historical and Comparative Analysis of Temple and Social Relationships in the Gospel of John, Philo and Qumran*, Leiden: Brill, 2005.

Furnish, V. P., *The Theology of the First Letter to the Corinthians*, Cambridge: Cambridge University Press, 1999.

Garrow, A. J. P., *The Gospel of Matthew's Dependence on the Didache*, London: T. & T. Clark, 2004.

Gärtner, B., *John 6 and the Jewish Passover*, Lund: C. W. K. Gleerup, 1959.

Gooch, P. D., *Dangerous Food: 1 Corinthians 8—10 in its Context*, Waterloo: Wilfred Laurier University Press, 1993.

Goulder, M. D., *Paul and the Competing Mission in Corinth*, Peabody: Hendrickson, 2001.

Grant, R. M., *Second-Century Christianity: A Collection of Fragments*, Louisville: Westminster John Knox Press, 2003.

Guilding, A., *The Fourth Gospel and Jewish Worship: A Study of the Relation of S. John's Gospel to the Ancient Jewish Lectionary System*, Oxford: Clarendon Press, 1960.

Hagner, D. A., 'An Analysis of Recent "Historical Jesus" Studies', in D. Cohn-Sherbok and J. M. Court (eds), *Religious Diversity in the Graeco-Roman World: A Survey of Recent Scholarship*, Sheffield: Sheffield Academic Press, 2001, pp. 81–106.

Hall, D. R., *The Unity of the Corinthian Correspondence*, London: T. & T. Clark, 2003.

Hanson, R., *Studies in Christian Antiquity*, Edinburgh: T. & T. Clark, 1985.

Harland, P. A., *Associations, Synagogues and Congregations: Claiming a Place in Ancient Mediterranean Society*, Minneapolis: Fortress Press, 2003.

Harnack, A. von, 'Brot und Wasser: Die Eucharistischen Elemente bei Justin', in *Über das Gnostiche Buch Pistis-Sophia: Brot und Wasser: Die Eucharistischen Elemente bei Justin, Zwei Untersuchungen*, Leipzig: J. C. Hinrichs, 1891, pp. 115–44.

Heil, J. P., *The Meal Scenes in Luke Acts: An Audience-Orientated Approach*, Atlanta: Society of Biblical Literature, 1999.

Heintz, M., 'δι ευχης λογου παρ αυτου (Justin, *Apology* 1.66.2): Cuming and Gelston Revisited', *Studia Liturgica* 33 (2003), pp. 33–6.

Hempel, C., 'The Essenes', in D. Cohn-Sherbok and J. M. Court (eds), *Religious Diversity in the Graeco-Roman World: A Survey of Recent Scholarship*, Sheffield: Sheffield Academic Press, 2001, pp. 65–80.

Hengel, M., *The Johannine Question*, London: SCM Press, 1989.

Hiers, R. H. and Kennedy, C. A., 'The Bread and Fish Eucharist in the Gospels and Early Christian Art', *Perspectives in Religious Studies* 3 (1976), pp. 20–47.

Higgins, A. J. B., *The Lord's Supper in the New Testament*, London: SCM Press, 1952.

Hill, C. E., *The Johanine Corpus in the Early Church*, Oxford: Oxford University Press, 2004.

Horsley, G. H. R., 'A Fishing Cartel in First-Century Ephesos', in G. H. R. Horsley (ed.), *New Documents Illustrating Early Christianity*, vol. 5, Sydney: Macquarrie University Ancient History Documentary Research Centre, 1989.

Hurd, J. C., *The Origin of 1 Corinthians*, London: SPCK, 1965.

Jaubert, A., *La Date de la Cène, Calendrier Biblique et Liturgie Chrétienne*, Paris: Gabalda, 1957.

Jeffers, J. S., *Conflict at Rome: Social Order and Hierarchy in Early Christianity*, Minneapolis: Fortress Press, 1991.

Jefford, C. N., 'The Milieu of Matthew, the Didache, and Ignatius of Antioch: Agreements and Differences', in H. van de Sandt (ed.), *Matthew and the Didache: Two Documents from the Same Jewish-Christian Milieu*, Assen: Royal Van Gorcum, 2005, pp. 35–48.

Jeremias, J., *The Eucharistic Words of Jesus*, Oxford: Basil Blackwell, 1955.

Johnson, M. E., *The Rites of Christian Initiation: Their Evolution and Interpretation*, Collegeville: The Liturgical Press, 1999.

Johnson, M. E., 'Tertullian's *"Diem Baptismo Sollemniorem"* Revisited: A Tentative Hypothesis on Baptism and Pentecost', in M. E. Johnson and L. E. Phillips (eds), *Studia Liturgica Diversa: Essays in Honor of Paul F. Bradshaw*, Portland: Pastoral Press, 2004, pp. 31–43.

Johnson, S. E., *The Gospel According to St Mark*, London: Adam & Charles Black, 1960.

Kee, H. C., *Community of the New Age: Studies in Mark's Gospel*, London: SCM Press, 1977.

Kelber, W. H., *The Oral and the Written Gospel: The Hermeneutics of Speaking and Writing in the Synoptic Tradition, Mark, Paul and Q*, Bloomington IN: Indiana University Press, 1997.

Kilpatrick, G. D., *The Origins of the Gospel According to Matthew*, Oxford: Clarendon Press, 1946.

Kilpatrick, G. D., *The Eucharist in Bible and Liturgy: The Moorhouse Lectures 1975*, Cambridge: Cambridge University Press, 1983.

Klauck, H.-J., *Apocryphal Gospels: An Introduction*, London: T. & T. Clark, 2003.

Klein, G., 'Die Gebete in der Didache', *Zeitschrift für die Neutestamentliche Wissenschaft* 9 (1908), pp. 132–46.

Klinghardt, M., *Gemeinschaftsmahl und Mahlgemeinschaft: Soziologie und Liturgie frühchristlicher Mahlfeiern*. Tübingen: A. Francke, 1996.

Lampe, P., *From Paul to Valentinus: Christians at Rome in the First Two Centuries*, London: T. & T. Clark, 2003.

Lampe, P., 'The Eucharist: Identifying Christ on the Cross', *Interpretation* 48 (1994), pp. 36–40.

Lapham, F., *An Introduction to the New Testament Apocrypha*, London: T. & T. Clark, 2003.

La Verdiere, E., *The Eucharist in the New Testament and the Church*, Collegeville: The Liturgical Press, 1996.

Leach, E. R., *Genesis as Myth and Other Essays*, London: Jonathan Cape, 1969.

Léon-Dufour, X., *Sharing the Eucharistic Bread: The Witness of the New Testament*, New York: Paulist Press, 1987.

Leonhard, C., 'Blessings over Wine and Bread in Judaism and Christian Eucharistic Prayers: Two Independent Traditions', in A. Gerhards and C. Leonhard (eds), *Jewish and Christian Liturgy and Worship: New Insights into its History and Interaction*, Leiden: Brill, 2007, pp. 309–26.

Lietzmann, H., *Mass and Lord's Supper: A Study in the History of the Liturgy*, Leiden: Brill, 1979.

Lieu, J. M., *Image and Reality: Jews and Christians in the Second Century*, Edinburgh: T. & T. Clark, 1996.

Lieu, J. M., *Neither Jew Nor Greek? Constructing Early Christianity*, London: T. & T. Clark, 2002.

Lunny, W. J., *The Sociology of the Resurrection*, London: SCM Press, 1989.

MacDonald, M. Y., *The Pauline Churches: A Socio-Historical Study of Institutionalization in the Pauline and Deutero-Pauline Writings*, Cambridge: Cambridge University Press, 1988.

Malherbe, A. J., *Social Aspects of Early Christianity*, Philadelphia: Fortress Press, 1983.

Malina, B. J., 'The Social World Implied in the Letters of the Christian Bishop-Martyr (named Ignatius of Antioch)', in P. J. Achtemeier (ed.), *SBL Seminar Papers 1978*, Missoula: Scholar's Press, 1978, pp. 71–119.

Malina, B. J., *The New Testament World: Insights from Cultural Anthropology*, Louisville: Westminster John Knox Press, 2001.

Martimort, A. J., Dalmais, I. H. and Jounel, P., *The Liturgy and Time*, Collegeville: The Liturgical Press, 1983.

Martin, R. P., *Worship in the Early Church*, Grand Rapids: Eerdmans, 1974.

Martyn, J. L., *The Gospel of John in Christian History*, New York: Paulist Press, 1979.

Mazza, E., *The Origins of the Eucharistic Prayer*, Collegeville: The Liturgical Press, 1995.

Mazza, E., 'Didache 9–10: Elements of a Eucharistic Interpretation', in J. A. Draper (ed.), *The Didache in Modern Research*, Leiden: Brill, 1996, pp. 276–99.

Mazza, E., *The Celebration of the Eucharist: The Origin of the Rite and the Development of its Interpretation*, Collegeville: The Liturgical Press, 1999.

McDonald, J. I. H., *The Crucible of Christian Morality*, London: Routledge, 1998.

McGowan, A., 'First Regarding the Cup . . .: Papias and the Diversity of Early Eucharistic Practice', *Journal of Theological Studies* 46:2 (1995), pp. 551–5.

McGowan, A., *Ascetic Eucharists: Food and Drink in Early Christian Ritual Meals*, Oxford: Oxford University Press, 1999a.

McGowan, A., 'Is there a Liturgical Text in this Gospel? The Institution Narratives and their Early Interpretive Communities', *Journal of Biblical Literature* 118 (1999b), pp. 73–87.

McGowan, A., 'The Meals of Jesus and the Meals of the Church: Eucharistic Origins and the Admission to Communion', in M. E. Johnson and L. E.

Phillips (eds), *Studia Liturgica Diversa: Essays in Honor of Paul F. Bradshaw*, Portland: Pastoral Press, 2004, pp. 101–15.

Meeks, W. A., 'The Man from Heaven in Johannine Sectarianism', *Journal of Biblical Literature* 91 (1972), pp. 44–72.

Meeks, W. A., *The First Urban Christians: The Social World of the Apostle Paul*, New Haven: Yale University Press, 1983.

Meeks, W. A., 'Corinthian Christians as Artificial Aliens', in T. Endberg-Pedersen (ed.), *Paul Beyond the Judaism/Hellenism Divide*, Louisville: Westminster John Knox Press, 2001.

Metzger, M., 'Nouvelles Perspectives pour le Prétendue *Tradition Apostolique*', *Ecclesia Orans* 5 (1988), pp. 241–59.

Milavec, A., 'When, Why and for Whom was the Didache Created? Insights into the Social and Historical Setting of the Didache Communities', in H. van de Sandt (ed.), *Matthew and the Didache: Two Documents from the Same Jewish-Christian Milieu?*, Assen: Royal Van Gorcum, 2005, pp. 63–84.

Miller, S., *Women in Mark's Gospel*, London: T. & T. Clark, 2004.

Mitchell, M. M., *Paul and the Rhetoric of Reconciliation: An Exegetical Investigation of the Language and Composition of 1 Corinthians*, Louisville: Westminster John Knox Press, 1992.

Morris, L., *Revelation: An Introduction and Commentary*, London: Tyndale Press, 1969.

Morris, L., *The Gospel According to John: The English Text with Introduction, Exposition and Notes*, Grand Rapids: Eerdmans, 1971.

Munro, W., 'Women Disciples in Mark?', *Catholic Biblical Quarterly* 44 (1982), pp. 225–41.

Niederwimmer, K., *The Didache: A Commentary*, Minneapolis: Fortress Press, 1998.

Nodet, É. And Taylor, J., *The Origins of Christianity: An Exploration*, Collegeville: The Liturgical Press, 1998.

Oesterley, W. O. E., *The Jewish Background of the Christian Liturgy*, Oxford: Clarendon Press, 1925.

Ong, W. J., *Orality and Literacy: The Technologizing of the Word*, New York: Methuen, 1982.

Perrin, N., *Rediscovering the Teaching of Jesus*, London: SCM Press, 1967.

Peterson, D., *Engaging with God: A Biblical Theology of Worship*, Downers Grove: IVP Academic, 1992.

Peterson, D. N., *The Origins of Mark: The Markan Community in Current Debate*, Leiden: Brill, 2000.

Phillips, L. E., 'The Proof is in the Eating: Dionysius of Alexandria and the Rebaptism Controversy', in M. E. Johnson and L. E. Phillips (eds), *Studia Liturgica Diversa: Essays in Honor of Paul F. Bradshaw*, Portland: Pastoral Press, 2004, pp. 53–63.

Phillips, L. E., *The Ritual Kiss in Early Christian Worship*, Bramcote: Grove Books, 1996.

Pietersen, L. K., *The Polemic of the Pastorals: A Sociological Examination of the Development of Pauline Christianity*, London: T. & T. Clark, 2004.

Ray, W. D., 'Towards a Narrative-Critical Approach to the Study of Early Liturgy', in M. E. Johnson and L. E. Phillips (eds), *Studia Liturgica Diversa: Essays in Honor of Paul F. Bradshaw*, Portland: Pastoral Press, 2004, pp. 3–30.

Richardson, R. D., 'A Further Enquiry into Eucharistic Origins with Special Reference to New Testament Problems', in Lietzmann, H., *Mass and Lord's Supper: A Study in the History of the Liturgy*, Leiden: Brill, 1979, pp. 217–699.

Rivkin, E., *What Crucified Jesus?*, London: SCM Press, 1986.

Rordorf, W., *Sunday: The History of the Day of Rest and Worship in the Earliest Centuries of the Christian Church*, London: SCM Press, 1968.

Rordorf, W., 'The Didache', in W. Rordorf et al. (eds), *The Eucharist of the Early Christians*, New York: Pueblo Publishing Company, 1978.

Rouwhorst, G., 'The Quatrodeciman Passover and the Jewish Pesach', *Questions Liturgiques* 77 (1996), pp. 152–73.

Rouwhorst, G., 'Didache 9–10: A Litmus Test for the Research on Early Christian Liturgy Eucharist', in H. van de Sandt (ed.), *Matthew and the Didache: Two Documents from the Same Jewish-Christian Milieu?*, Assen: Royal Van Gorcum, 2005, pp. 143–56.

Rouwhorst, G., 'The Roots of the Early Christian Eucharist: Jewish Blessing or Hellenistic Symposia?', in A. Gerhards and C. Leonhard (eds), *Jewish and Christian Liturgy and Worship: New Insights into its History and Interaction*, Leiden: Brill, 2007, pp. 295–308.

Rowland, C., *Christian Origins: An Account of the Setting and Character of the Most Important Messianic Sect of Judaism*, London: SPCK, 1985.

Runesson, A., *The Origins of the Synagogue: A Socio-Historical Study*, Stockholm: Almquist & Wiksell International, 2001.

Rutgers, L., *The Jews of Late Ancient Rome*, Leiden: Brill, 1995.

Sanders, E. P., 'Jewish Associations with Gentiles and Galatians 2:11–14', in R. T. Fortna and B. R. Gaventa (eds), *The Conversation Continues: Studies in Paul and John in Honour of J. Lois Martyn*, Nashville: Abingdon Press, 1990.

Sanders, E. P., *Judaism, Practice and Belief, 63BCE–66CE*, London: SCM Press, 1992.

Sanders, J. T., *Schismatics, Sectarians, Dissidents, Deviants: The First One Hundred Years of Jewish–Christian Relations*, London: SCM Press, 1993.

Schilling, F. A., 'The Liturgy of St John', *The Living Church* 128 (Nov. 1953), pp. 1–31.

Schoedel, W. R., 'Are the Letters of Ignatius of Antioch Authentic?', *Religious Studies Review* 6 (1980), pp. 196–201.

Schoedel, W. R., *A Commentary on the Letters of Ignatius of Antioch*, Philadelphia: Fortress Press, 1985.

Schütz, J. H., 'Introduction', in G. Theissen, *The Social Setting of Pauline Christianity: Essays on Corinth*, Philadelphia: Fortress Press, 1982, pp. 1–23.

Schweitzer, A., *The Quest for the Historical Jesus*, London: SCM Press, 2000.

Segal, P., 'Early Christian and Rabinic Liturgical Affinities: Exploring Liturgical Acculturation', *New Testament Studies* 30 (1984), pp. 63–90.

Shepherd, M., *The Paschal Liturgy and the Apocalypse*, London: Lutterworth Press, 1960.

Shiner, W., *Proclaiming the Gospel: First-Century Performance of Mark*, Harrisburg: Trinity Press International, 2003.

Sim, D. C., *The Gospel of Matthew and Christian Judaism: The History and Social Setting of the Matthean Community*, Edinburgh: T. & T. Clark, 1998.

Smalley, S., *John: Evangelist and Interpreter*, Exeter: Paternoster Press, 1978.

Smith, D. E. and Taussig, H. E., *Many Tables: The Eucharist in the New Testament and Liturgy Today*, London: SCM Press, 1990.

Smith, D. E., *From Symposium to Eucharist: The Banquet in the Early Christian World*, Minneapolis: Fortress Press, 2003.

Snyder, H. G., '"Above the Bath of Myrtinus": Justin Martyr's "School" in the City of Rome', *Harvard Theological Review* 100:3 (2007), pp. 335–62.

Stambaugh, J. and Balch, D., *The Social World of the First Christians*, London: SPCK, 1986.

Stevenson, J., *A New Eusebius: Documents Illustrative of the History of the Church to AD 337*, London: SPCK, 1957.

Stringer, M. D., *On the Perception of Worship: The Ethnography of Worship in Four Christian Congregations in Manchester*, Birmingham: Birmingham University Press, 1999.

Stringer, M. D., *A Sociological History of Christian Worship*, Cambridge: Cambridge University Press, 2005.

Stringer, M. D., 'Rethinking the Origins of the Eucharist: A Socio-Historical Approach', *Jaarboek voor Liturgieonderzoek* 25 (2009), pp. 19–34.

Talley, T. J., 'From Berakah to Eucharistia', *Worship* 50 (1976), pp. 115–37.

Talley, T. J., *The Origins of the Liturgical Year*, New York: Pueblo, 1986.

Theissen, G., *The Social Setting of Pauline Christianity: Essays on Corinth*, Philadelphia: Fortress Press, 1982.

Theissen, G., *The Gospels in Context: Social and Political History in the Synoptic Tradition*, Edinburgh: T. & T. Clark, 1992.

Thistelton, A. C., *The First Epistle to the Corinthians: A Commentary on the Greek Text*, Carlisle: Paternoster Press, 2000.

Treblico, P., *Jewish Communities in Asia Minor*, Cambridge: Cambridge University Press, 1991.

Trevett, C., *A Study of Ignatius of Antioch in Syria and Asia*, Lewiston: Edward Mellen Press, 1992.

Trevett, C., *Montanism: Gender, Authority and the New Prophecy*, Cambridge: Cambridge University Press, 1996.

Trocmé, E., *The Formation of the Gospel According to Mark*, London: SPCK, 1975.

Trocmé, E., *The Passion as Liturgy: A Study of the Passion Narratives in the Four Gospels*, London: SCM Press, 1983.

Trocmé, E., *The Childhood of Christianity*, London: SCM Press, 1997.

Vokes, F. E., *The Riddle of the Didache: Fact or Fiction, Heresy or Catholicism?*, London: SPCK, 1938.

Vööbus, A., *Liturgical Traditions in the Didache*, Stockholm: Estonian Theological Society in Exile, 1968.

Ward, P., *Selling Worship: How What We Sing has Changed the Church*, Milton Keynes: Paternoster Press, 2005.

Wedderburn, A. J. M., *A History of the First Christians*, London: T. & T. Clark, 2004.

Weeden, T. J., *Mark: Traditions in Conflict*, Philadelphia: Fortress Press, 1971.

Weiss, J., *Earliest Christianity: A History of the Period* AD *30–150*, New York: Harper Row, 1959.

Wengst, K., *Bedrängte Gemeinde und Verherrlichter Christus: Der Historische Ort des Johannesevangeliums als Schlüssel zu seiner Interpretation*, Neukirchen-Vluyn: Neukirchener Verlag, 1981.

Wengst, K., *Didache (Apostellehre), Barnabasbrief, Zweiter Klemensbrief, Schrift an Diognet, Eingeleitet, Herausgegeben, Übertragen und Erläutert*, Munich: Kösel, 1984.

White, L. M., *The Social Origins of Christian Architecture, Volume 1, Building God's House in the Roman World: Architectural Adaptations among Pagans, Jews and Christians*, Valley Forge: Trinity Press International, 1990.

Wilkens, W., *Die Entstehungsgeschichte des Vierten Evangeliums*, Zollikon: Evangelischer Verlag, 1958.

Williams, M., 'Being a Jew in Rome: Sabbath Fasting as an Expression of Romano-Jewish Identity', in J. M. G. Barclay (ed.), *Negotiating Diaspora: Jewish Strategies in the Roman Empire*, London: T. & T. Clark, 2004, pp. 8–18.

Wilson, S. G., *Luke and the Law*, Cambridge: Cambridge University Press, 1983.

Winter, B. W., *After Paul Left Corinth: The Influence of Secular Ethics and Social Change*, Grand Rapids: Eerdmans, 2001.

Yarnold, E., *The Awe-Inspiring Rites of Initiation: The Origins of the RCIA*, Edinburgh: T. & T. Clark, 1994.

Zetterholm, M., *The Formation of Christianity in Antioch: A Social-Scientific Approach to the Separation Between Judaism and Christianity*, London: Routledge, 2003.

Index of Biblical and Primary Sources

Index